D1194401

Second Edition

Cases in Corporate Financial Reporting

PAUL A. GRIFFIN

PRENTICE HALL, Englewood Cliffs, New Jersey 07632

Library of Congress Cataloging-in-Publication Data

Griffin, Paul A.
    Cases in corporate financial reporting / Paul A. Griffin. -- 2nd
ed.
        p.   cm.
    ISBN 0-13-116716-2
    1. Financial statements--Case studies. 2. Corporations--Finance-
-Case studies.   I. Title.
HF5681.B2G788 1991
657'.3--dc20   90-38914
                                                              CIP

Cover design: John Gilligan
Manufacturing buyer: Trudy Pisciotti/Bob Anderson

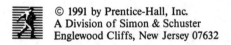 © 1991 by Prentice-Hall, Inc.
A Division of Simon & Schuster
Englewood Cliffs, New Jersey 07632

All rights reserved. No part of this book may be
reproduced, in any form or by any means,
without permission in writing from the publisher.

Printed in the United States of America
10 9 8 7 6 5 4 3 2 1

ISBN 0-13-116716-2 01

Prentice-Hall International (UK) Limited, *London*
Prentice-Hall of Australia Pty. Limited, *Sydney*
Prentice-Hall Canada Inc., *Toronto*
Prentice-Hall Hispanoamericana, S.A., *Mexico*
Prentice-Hall of India Private Limited, *New Delhi*
Prentice-Hall of Japan, Inc., *Tokyo*
Simon & Schuster Asia Pte. Ltd., *Singapore*
Editora Prentice-Hall do Brasil, Ltda., *Rio de Janeiro*

CONTENTS

PREFACE

Textbooks that introduce students to the concepts, methods, and uses of financial accounting and reporting often provide little exposure to actual financial statements. Questions, problem sets, and other assignment material tend to be hypothetical, simplistic, and devoid of the contextual richness of the corporate reporting milieu. One consequence of such assignment material is that students who have completed the typical introductory course in financial accounting are sometimes bewildered and overwhelmed when confronted with real world accounting issues. Real world accounting issues form a part of the changing and complex environment of business. That environment is all-too-often characterized by a lack of defined structure, an overabundance of irrelevant data, and an absence of a clear right or wrong answer.

This casebook attempts to bring theory and practice closer together. The book stems from a conviction that the learning process is incomplete unless the student understands the applications of the concepts and methods of accounting in the real world. Accordingly, the materials explore and analyze the fundamentals of financial accounting and reporting in the context of actual annual reports—the primary means of communication by business enterprises to investors, creditors, governments, and other users. The overriding thrust of each case is to instill in students a critical ability to *identify* a particular accounting issue or concern and *evaluate* its potential alternative treatments. Many of the cases go further. They provide a situation that requires an analysis of certain financial and economic *consequences* of accounting and reporting treatments and an evaluation or conjecture as to what *motivates* managers and preparers of accounting statements to choose and report on the basis of particular accounting methods. Thus, the book places accounting and reporting squarely in the context of management behavior and business decision making.

This book is best used as a supplement to one of the standard textbooks in financial accounting. However, it could also be used by itself or accompanied by readings to study topical and often controversial aspects of accounting and reporting. The cases are mostly aimed at students with some prior exposure to the concepts and methods of accounting. At the undergraduate level, such students could be those who are at the intermediate accounting level or above. Graduate Masters of Accounting, M.B.A. students, and business executives, on the other hand, should find the material appropriate at several levels. The book presents cases that cover not only the basics of double-entry record-keeping but also several more advanced and current topics. For instance, a number of cases are directed at specific standards and rulings of the Financial Accounting Standards Board. Other cases deal with issues of judgment about how much information a company should disclose and the likely economic consequences of such disclosure.

One last aspect of the casebook should be emphasized. A general theme throughout the book is the perspective that accounting statements are the product of managerial decisions about the measurement and disclosure of financial information where those decisions have implications for managers, investors, creditors, and others. Many cases, therefore, can be used to spotlight the interaction between accounting measurements, financial and managerial policy, and market valuation, and thus they are potentially applicable to *all* persons who wish to understand the importance of the role of accounting information in business decision making. In addition, accounting researchers have studied most comprehensively the role of accounting information in a variety of contexts in recent years. Many cases provide an excellent opportunity to introduce relevant research results and other new accounting knowledge into the classroom. A small number of cases even allow the instructor to discuss common accounting research approaches, such as whether accounting numbers and disclosures affect stock market prices.

Since the publication of the first edition of this book, an increasing number of textbooks have included problems and assignments based on information extracted from actual company financial statements. I have also observed the introduction of several financial accounting casebooks into the marketplace. This trend is most encouraging. Not only does the case approach make accounting and business students more knowledgeable about accounting and reporting issues per se but it also allows a broader discussion of the implications of such issues. As such, it helps change students' and professionals' *perceptions* of accounting— from that of a number-crunching, technical operation to that of an information-producing activity that has a direct and critical bearing on the interests of managers and investors—and ultimately the company's market value. Accounting and reporting policy issues such as those illustrated and diagnosed in this book are often considered and resolved at the very highest levels of the corporation.

The contents of this book are listed by topic. Apart from the cases in Section I—on fundamental accounting relations—the sequencing of the material is best left to the instructor. The topics cover most issues that would be relevant to a first course in financial accounting and reporting. Topics that normally would be included in an intermediate or advanced course in accounting are included also. As well, a number of cases are appropriate for an undergraduate or graduate courses in accounting theory (and policy) and financial statement analysis.

This second edition contains 53 new cases not in the first edition. The new cases examine recent standards or proposals from the Financial Accounting Standards Board (e.g., pensions, statement of cash flow, post-retirement health benefits, real estate, and plant abandonments). In addition, all cases from the first edition have been revised and updated, though a few of the cases that cover what might be coined as classic situations remain basically in their original form. Most, including revisions of the earlier cases, use data from the mid-1980s or later, though such data have been expressed neutrally in terms of 19X1, 19X2, and so forth, unless the chronological dates are relevant.

Instructors with beginning students should carefully review each case before it is assigned to ensure adequate coverage of the accounting or reporting issues.

Also, some cases use basic concepts and notions from financial economics that beginning students may not have encountered in their accounting or business curriculum (e.g., present value, compound growth).

A solutions manual containing detailed numerical solutions as well as teaching suggestions is available to instructors. As is evident from the solutions manual, financial spreadsheets have been used often as a means of analyzing the accounting issues. Their use by students should thus be encouraged. An appendix to this casebook lists check figures.

In assembling the material for this second edition, M.B.A. candidate Kevin Tam of the Davis Graduate School of Management provided competent research and technical assistance. I am very grateful for his efforts in reviewing company financial statements and in thoroughly checking each case and case solution. Also, I wish to thank master's candidate David L. Bauer and John Grant Rhode, University of San Francisco, who worked on many of the cases that I have carried over from the first edition, and the students at the Davis Graduate School of Management, who helped in class testing the many additional cases in this second edition. Cases developed from materials or suggestions provided by Professors George Foster, Robert K. Jaedicke, James M. Patell, and Mark A. Wolfson of Stanford's Graduate School of Business are also included.

The reviewers of this text merit special recognition. These included Wayne R. Landsman, University of California, Los Angeles; Michael F. van Breda, Southern Methodist University; and Mark E. Zmijewski, University of Chicago—all of whom did an outstanding job. I am particularly indebted to Wayne Landsman, who class tested many of the cases in this second edition and offered innumerable valuable comments and insights. Others involved in the development and production of this book who deserve mention are Josephine Chu, University of California, Davis, who typed and formatted the manuscript; Joseph S. Heider, Executive Editor, Prentice Hall, who very competently managed the entire project; and Linda Albelli, Editorial Assistant, Nancy DeWolfe, Production Editor, Esther Koehn, Production Supervisor, and the many other editorial staff persons at Prentice Hall, all of whom gave their full support and professional dedication to the publication process. Of course, all remaining errors are my own. I would appreciate comments and suggestions from instructors and students, as well as from the management of those companies whose statements have been analyzed.

Paul A. Griffin
Graduate School of Management
University of California, Davis

1

Fundamentals

1.1 UAL CORPORATION

*Accounting identities
and terminology*

UAL Corporation (formerly United Airlines) is one of the world's largest air transportation companies, with domestic routes throughout the United States and international routes mostly in Asia and the Pacific. Listed on the New York Stock Exchange (Ticker = UAL).

The following data were extracted from the company's financial statements for the fiscal year ended December 31, 19X2.

ACCOUNT TITLE (OR GROUPING OF ACCOUNT TITLES) (listed in alphabetical order)	DOLLARS IN MILLIONS
Accounts payable	$ 520
Accounts receivable, gross	756
Accrued expenses payable	729
Accumulated amortization on flight equipment acquired as capital leases	223
Accumulated depreciation on property and flight equipment	3,618
Accumulated retained earnings on common shares retired during year	994
Advance ticket sales (paid in advance of customers' travel)	600
Aircraft fuel, spare parts, and supplies	175
Allowance for doubtful accounts	14
Cash and cash equivalents	1,086
Common stock held in Treasury, 1,730,400 shares	123
Common stock, authorized and issued, 23,333,154 shares	146
Deferred pension other noncurrent liabilities	543
Dividends declared and paid on preferred shares	1
Flight equipment, acquired as capital leases, at cost	522
Gain on sale of discontinued operation, net of income tax	524
Income tax expense on continuing operations	388
Intangible and other assets, net of accumulated amortization	588
Long-term debt and capital leases, due within one year	84
Long-term debt, due beyond one year	1,649
Long-term obligations under capital leases, due beyond one year	411
Non-operating revenues	324
Operating expenses	8,317
Operating revenues	8,981
Other current liabilities	490
Prepaid expenses	167
Property and flight equipment, owned, at cost	7,261
Redeemable cumulative 5-1/2 % preferred stock, $100 par value	3
Retained earnings at beginning of fiscal 19X2	1,073
Short-term borrowings	446

Based on the account title descriptions and amounts, assemble this information so as to demonstrate that the following fundamental accounting equations hold for fiscal year 19X2. If an account title (or account grouping) does not exist, enter zero for that amount in the appropriate equation.

1. Assets = Liabilities + Stockholders' equity: at end of 19X2

2. Revenues - Expenses + Gains - Losses = Net income: for 19X2

3. Stockholders' equity = Contributed capital + Retained earnings + Other stockholders' equity: at end of 19X2

4. Retained earnings at beginning of 19X2 + Net income for 19X2 - Dividends declared during 19X2 = Retained earnings at end of 19X2

5. Working capital = Current assets - Current liabilities: at end of 19X2

1.2 FEDERAL EXPRESS CORPORATION

Double-entry equations for income statement, retained earnings, and balance sheet

Federal Express Corporation specializes in an overnight, door-to-door delivery service for small packages and documents throughout the United States and to many foreign countries. Listed on the New York Stock Exchange (Ticker = FDX).

Use the data below from the company's May 31, 19X5 annual financial statements to find the unknowns, A, B, C, etc. Show computations to support your answers. It is not necessary to derive the unknowns in strict alphabetical order.

ACCOUNT TITLE (OR GROUPING OF ACCOUNT TITLES)	DOLLARS IN MILLIONS
Total assets, beginning of 19X5	$ 2,276
Total assets, end of 19X5	A
Current assets, beginning of 19X5	613
Current assets, end of 19X5	507
Current liabilities, beginning of 19X5	432
Current liabilities, end of 19X5	504
Other liabilities, beginning of 19X5	751
Other liabilities, end of 19X5	916
Total stockholders' equity, beginning of 19X5	H
Total stockholders' equity, end of 19X5	1,079
Retained earnings, beginning of 19X5	B
Retained earnings, end of 19X5	536
Revenue	3,178
Operating expenses and operating gains and losses (excluding provision for taxes on income (loss) from continuing operations)	G
Provision for taxes on income (loss) from continuing operations	144
Net income (loss) from continuing operations	C
Loss on discontinued operations for 19X5 (net of income tax benefits of $182)	232
Net income (loss)	(65)
Dividends declared and paid	1
Prior-period adjustment (added directly to retained earnings) in 19X5	5
Capital contributions by stockholders in 19X5	47
Contributed capital, beginning of 19X5	D
Contributed capital, end of 19X5	E
Increase (decrease) in working capital in 19X5	F

GOODYEAR TIRE & RUBBER COMPANY I

Fundamental balance sheet equations

Goodyear's principal business is the development, manufacture, distribution, and sale of tires throughout the world. In addition to being one of the world's largest producer of tires, Goodyear is a diversified company which manufactures a broad spectrum of rubber, chemical, and plastic products. The company also has oil and gas drilling operations in California and Louisiana. Listed on the New York Stock Exchange (Ticker symbol = GT).

Actual data from its December 31, 19X3 financial statements include:

ACCOUNT TITLE (OR GROUPING OF ACCOUNT TITLES)	DOLLARS IN MILLIONS
Assets, beginning of period	$ 6,954
Assets, end of period	E
Current assets, beginning of period	2,558
Current assets, end of period	F
Current liabilities, beginning of period	1,607
Current liabilities, end of period	2,143
Liabilities, beginning of period	A
Liabilities, end of period	5,607
Contributed capital, beginning of period	749
Contributed capital, end of period	D
Retained earnings, beginning of period	2,758
Retained earnings, end of period	C
Net change in working capital for 19X3	(54)
Revenues for 19X3	9,225
Cost of goods sold and expenses for 19X3	B
Income tax expense for 19X3	138
Net income before taxes for 19X3	262
Cash dividends declared and paid for 19X3	174
Treasury stock purchases in 19X3 (contributed capital)	548

Find the unknowns, A, B, C, etc. (in millions), showing computations to support your answers.

1.4 CAMPBELL SOUP COMPANY I

*Analyze fundamental transactions
and derive account balances*

The Campbell Soup Company is a diversified grower, producer, and processor of consumer food products. Well known for its soups, Campbell's activities also include Pepperidge Farm, Pietro's Corp., Godiva chocolates, and Vlasic Foods (pickles). Listed on the New York Stock Exchange (Ticker = CPB).

Study the Campbell Soup's August 3, 19X1, Balance Sheet and the company's August 3, 19X2 Statement of Earnings. Other information and key assumptions are supplied below. Numbers in millions of dollars.

1. All sales made on credit; cash received from customers, $4,450.5.

2. The cost of producing sold and unsold inventories except for depreciation on plant assets and all expenses except interest (see Part 5 below) were credited to various current liability accounts. Include all current liabilities items in a single account, current liabilities.

3. Prepaid expenses for interest only. Cash payments for interest during the year, $33.4.

4. Temporary investments purchased for cash, $29.3.

5. Cost of producing inventories, except for the cost of depreciating the plant assets, $3,061.6. Depreciation on the plant assets, $132.0, was wholly absorbed into the cost of production *sold*. Cash payments made to reduce the current liability accounts, $3,995.3.

6. Plant assets purchased for cash, $312.9.

7. Other assets purchased for cash, $50.6.

8. Cash generated by increased long-term debt and other liabilities, $17.4.

9. Transactions involving deferred taxes during the year netted out to zero.

10. Paid cash dividend of $54.7.

11. Other than the dividend in Part 10, stockholders' equity transactions involved only $1.6 cash sales of Treasury stock (reissued at cost).

Using the financial reports and the information above, compute the following account balances as of year end, August 3, 19X2.

a. Temporary investments
b. Accounts receivable
c. Inventories
d. Prepaid expenses
e. Plant assets, net
f. Other assets
g. Cash
h. Current liabilities
i. Long-term debt and other liabilities (one number)
j. Deferred income taxes
k. Capital stock issued, at par
l. Capital surplus
m. Earnings retained
n. Capital stock in Treasury

CAMPBELL SOUP COMPANY
STATEMENT OF EARNINGS
for the year ended August 3, 19X2

	DOLLARS IN MILLIONS
NET SALES	$ 4,490.4
COSTS AND EXPENSES	
Cost of production sold	3,180.5
Marketing and sales expenses	626.2
Administrative expenses	198.8
Research and development expenses	44.8
Interest expense	22.2
Total expenses other than taxes	4,072.5
EARNINGS BEFORE TAXES	417.9
Taxes on earnings	170.6
NET EARNINGS	$ 247.3

CAMPBELL SOUP COMPANY
BALANCE SHEET
as of August 3, 19X1

	DOLLARS IN MILLIONS
CURRENT ASSETS	
Cash	$ 35.9
Temporary investments	357.9
Accounts receivable	299.0
Inventories	610.5
Prepaid expenses	31.5
Total current assets	1,334.8
PLANT ASSETS, net of accumulated depreciation	1,168.1
OTHER ASSETS	259.9
TOTAL ASSETS	$ 2,762.8
CURRENT LIABILITIES	
Notes payable	$ 88.9
Payable to suppliers and others	321.7
Accrued liabilities	186.0
Accrued income taxes	49.6
Total current liabilities	646.2
LONG-TERM DEBT AND OTHER LIABILITIES	378.6
DEFERRED INCOME TAXES	199.1
TOTAL LIABILITIES	1,223.9
STOCKHOLDERS' EQUITY	
Capital stock issued, at par	20.3
Capital surplus (in excess of par)	38.1
Earnings retained in the business	1,528.9
Capital stock in treasury, at cost	(48.4)
Total stockholders' equity	1,538.9
TOTAL EQUITIES	$ 2,762.8

THE FIRESTONE TIRE & RUBBER COMPANY I

*Analyze fundamental transactions
and derive account balances*

The Firestone Tire & Rubber Company is one of the largest tire manufacturers in the world and is a major supplier of automotive maintenance and repair services in the United States, with approximately 1,500 company-operated tire and automotive service centers and thousands of independent dealer locations. Firestone was acquired by Bridgestone Tires in 1987 and is thus no longer a publicly traded company.

Study Firestone's 19X3 Statement of Income and 19X2 Balance Sheet. Assume that the following information has been gathered from the company ledgers and that no other transactions have occurred. Use a single account for all current liability items. Numbers in millions of dollars.

1. All sales were on credit; cash received from customers amounted to $3,790.
2. All costs of producing inventory except plant depreciation (see 8 below) were credited to various current liability accounts. Production costs exceeded the cost of products sold by $14 during the year due to slower sales in the automobile industry.
3. Selling, administrative, and general expenses, except office depreciation and pension expenses (see 8 and 13 below), were also charged to current liability accounts.
4. The company accrued estimated restructuring expenses to a current liability account.
5. Due to a general weakening of the U.S. dollar, cash held in foreign currencies and converted to dollars produced gains of $39 during the year.
6. Prepaid expenses were for interest expense only. Cash payments during the year for interest expense amounted to $87.
7. Interest income was received in cash. Net other income, also received in cash, included $3 loss on sales of short-term investments (cost, $8); and $9 deferred income from certain sale and lease-back transactions was realized.
8. The company acquired plant assets for $306 and sold a discontinued plant for $100 in a tax-free transaction. Total depreciation during 19X3 consisted of plant depreciation, $154, and general office depreciation, $18.
9. The deferred portion of income tax expense was $27 and extraordinary tax credits of $22 were charged against the deferred income tax liability.

10. The company acquired Treasury stock at $147 and resold a portion of it for $10 (cost $15). Also, a $45 cash dividend was declared, $35 of which was paid by Firestone before the end of the year.

11. Long-term investments were sold for zero gain or loss (cost $9); and other assets were acquired for $122.

12. Cash payments for current liabilities as a whole amounted to $3,261. The current portion of long-term debt becoming payable in the next 12 months amounted to $36.

13. Pension expenses of $23 were charged to pension liabilities.

14. Net income for the year was transferred to Retained Earnings.

Using the financial statements and the information above, compute the following account balances as of October 31, 19X3.

    a. Cash and cash-related items
    b. Short-term investments
    c. Accounts and notes receivable, net
    d. Inventories
    e. Prepaid expenses
    f. Properties, plants, and equipment, net
    g. Investments, at cost
    h. Other assets
    i. Total current liabilities (one number)
    j. Long-term debt and capital leases
    k. Pension liabilities
    l. Deferred income from sale and leaseback
    m. Deferred income taxes
    n. Common stock, without par value
    o. Additional paid-in capital
    p. Retained earnings
    q. Treasury stock

Firestone Tire & Rubber Company
Statement of Income

Dollars in millions (October 31)	19X3
Net sales	$ 3,867
Costs and expenses	
Cost of sales	2,979
Selling, administrative, and general expenses	690
Provisions for restructuring	18
Foreign currency (gains) losses	(39)
Interest expense	43
Interest income	(21)
Other income, net	(6)
Total costs and expenses	3,664
Income (loss) from continuing operations before income taxes	203
Income taxes	100
Income (loss) from continuing operations	103
Discontinued operations: gain on sale of plant	20
Income (loss) before extraordinary tax credits and cumulative effect of accounting change	123
Extraordinary tax credits	22
Net income	$ 145

FIRESTONE TIRE & RUBBER COMPANY
Balance Sheet

Dollars in millions (October 31)	19X2

Assets

CURRENT ASSETS

Cash and cash-related items	$ 163
Short-term investments	12
Accounts and notes receivable, net of allowances	582
Inventories	468
Prepaid expenses	71
TOTAL CURRENT ASSETS	1,296

Properties, plants and equipment, net of accumulated depreciation	1,119
Investments, at cost	35
Other assets	143
TOTAL ASSETS	$ 2,593

Liabilities and shareholders' equity

CURRENT LIABILITIES

Short-term loans	13
Accounts payable	336
Accrued compensation	202
Domestic and foreign taxes	106
Long-term debt due within one year	15
Other accrued current liabilities	172
TOTAL CURRENT LIABILITIES	844

Long-term debt and capital leases	285
Pension liabilities	182
Deferred income from sale and leaseback transactions	66
Deferred income taxes	49

Shareholders' equity

Common stock, without par value, 120,000,000 shares authorized, 60,090,127 shares issued in 19X3	63
Additional paid in capital	180
Retained earnings	1,290
Treasury stock, at cost	(366)
TOTAL SHAREHOLDERS' EQUITY	$ 1,167

1.6 WRATHER CORPORATION

*Journal entries and construction
of financial statements*

Wrather Corporation is a diversified company operating principally in the hotel, oil and gas, and motion picture industries. Wrather operates the Queen Mary and Spruce Goose in Long Beach, California, and produced the film *Legend of the Lone Ranger*. Listed prior to 1989 on the American Stock Exchange (Ticker = WCO).

Study the 19X1 Consolidated Balance Sheet and the 19X0–19X2 Consolidated Statements of Income. Other information is provided below. All expenses other than depreciation and amortization and interest should be treated as general expenses. All numbers in thousands.

1. All 19X1 prepaid expenses were used in 19X2. Prepaid expenses purchased for cash in 19X2 amounted to $1,988.
2. Interest expense was paid in cash.
3. Depreciation on property, plant, and equipment amounted to $3,173; depletion and amortization on oil and gas properties amounted to $3,251.
4. All expenses other than prepaid expenses, depreciation, taxes on income, and interest were charged to various liability accounts. Film distribution costs incurred in 19X2 amounted to $5,000; costs incurred associated with accrued liabilities amounted to $5,000; the remaining expenses on account were charged to accounts payable. Cash payments in 19X2 for film distribution costs, accrued liabilities, and accounts payable were $4,956, $2,110, and $37,760, respectively.
5. The credit for income taxes ($1,860) comprised current taxes payable of $3, which was credited to the account Other Liabilities, a loss carry forward of $1,157, and a reduction in deferred taxes of $706. Cash payments for Other Liabilities amounted to $88.
6. All sales were on credit. Cash received from customers, $60,977.
7. Property, plant, and equipment purchased for cash, $8,145; oil and gas properties purchased for cash, $6,173; cash investments in *Lone Ranger* motion picture, $6,642.
8. Certain other assets were sold at their book value for $60.
9. Common stock issued for cash amounted to $192.
10. A dividend was paid in cash.
11. Long-term debt repayments of $2,186 were made, and $1,156 of long-term debt became payable in 19X3. Cash received from issuance of bank notes and mortgages amounted to $20,964.
12. Other current assets were purchased for cash, $699.

WRATHER CORPORATION AND SUBSIDIARIES
Consolidated Balance Sheet

December 31	19X1
ASSETS	
Current assets:	
Cash	$ 336,000
Accounts and notes receivable	4,770,000
Prepaid expenses	1,813,000
Other current assets	1,463,000
Net operating loss carryforward	
Total current assets	8,382,000
Teleprompter Corporation common stock, at cost	10,023,000
Property, plant, and equipment, at cost	72,936,000
Less accumulated depreciation and amortization	16,728,000
Property—net	56,208,000
Oil and gas properties (under full cost method)—net	11,127,000
Investment in *Lone Ranger* feature joint venture	450,000
Land and other assets	5,545,000
Total	$ 91,735,000
LIABILITIES AND STOCKHOLDERS' EQUITY	
Current Liabilities:	
Current portion of long-term debt	$ 2,186,000
Accounts payable	1,948,000
Accrued film distribution costs	810,000
Accrued liabilities	3,515,000
Total current liabilities	8,459,000
Long-term debt	66,203,000
Deferred income taxes	2,205,000
Other liabilities	874,000
Commitments and contingent liabilities	
Stockholders' equity:	
Preferred stock, $1 par value—authorized 1,000,000 shares; issued, none	-
Common stock, no par value—authorized 10,000,000 shares; issued and outstanding shares; 19X2, 2,328,180; 19X1, 2,271,030	7,552,000
Retained earnings	6,442,000
Stockholders' equity	13,994,000
Total	$ 91,735,000

WRATHER CORPORATION AND SUBSIDIARIES
Consolidated Statements of Income

For the years ended December 31	19X2	19X1	19X0
Revenues:			
Hotel room revenues	$ 27,500,000	$ 23,923,000	$ 19,245,000
Food and beverage	22,528,000	18,412,000	18,233,000
Other	12,457,000	10,075,000	5,937,000
	62,485,000	52,410,000	43,415,000
Expenses:			
Operating expenses	29,080,000	23,833,000	18,651,000
Cost of sales	7,926,000	6,506,000	5,209,000
Selling, general and administrative expenses	14,603,000	10,752,000	9,767,000
Depreciation, depletion and amortization	6,424,000	4,441,000	4,162,000
Interest expense	10,888,000	8,026,000	4,673,000
	68,921,000	53,558,000	42,462,000
Income (loss) before income taxes and extraordinary item	(6,436,000)	(1,148,000)	953,000
Income taxes (credit)	(1,860,000)	(314,000)	(48,000)
Income (loss) before extraordinary item	(4,576,000)	(834,000)	1,001,000
Extraordinary item		(191,000)	(118,000)
Net income (loss)	$ (4,576,000)	$ (1,025,000)	$ 883,000
Per common share:			
Income (loss) before extraordinary item	$ (1.98)	$ (.37)	$.43
Extraordinary item		(.09)	(.05)
Net income (loss)	$ (1.98)	$ (.46)	$.38

WRATHER CORPORATION AND SUBSIDIARIES
Consolidated Statements of Retained Earnings

For the years ended December 31	19X2	19X1	19X0
Retained earnings–beginning of year	$ 6,442,000	$ 7,581,000	$ 6,810,000
Net income (loss)	(4,576,000)	(1,025,000)	883,000
Cash dividend ($.05 Per Share)	(116,000)	(114,000)	(112,000)
Retained earnings–end of year	$ 1,750,000	$ 6,442,000	$ 7,581,000

1. Prepare general journal entries for all transactions in 19X2. Use only the accounts indicated in the 19X1 and 19X2 statements. Assume all general journal and adjusting entries are made at the end of each year.

2. Prepare a Consolidated Balance Sheet as of December 31, 19X2.

1.7 WHAT SHOULD MISS ANNIE DO?

Derive accounting-based measures of performance, basic concepts, and ratio analysis

J. P. and Ronnie Richards are in competition to take over the Richards Oil Company. J. P. told Ronnie, "This oil company ain't big enough for both of us."

The Richards boys have run out of money and, with a glut of oil, there isn't much of a market left for their oil. However, they can trade produced crude oil to purchase oil-drilling equipment and other goods and services. In Jack's (the recently deceased father of J. P. and Ronnie) will, J. P. and Ronnie were each left 12,000 barrels of produced crude oil and some land. J. P.'s parcel of land (15 acres) is smaller than Ronnie's (20 acres) because Ronnie was Jack's favorite.

According to the will, Miss Annie must hand over the controlling rights to the son who does better. Neither of the boys have enough oil to purchase drilling equipment outright, but arrangements can be made for payment after the wells produce. The boys have exactly one year to start the wells and produce crude for comparison of their performance.

One year later, J. P.'s wells have produced 82,500 barrels of crude oil. During the year, he had made arrangements to buy 10,000 barrels' worth of drilling equipment. The equipment is now capable of producing 247,500 additional barrels of oil. Of the original 12,000 barrels given to J. P. by Jack, he used 8,000 barrels for drilling expenses.

At the end of the year, Ronnie had an inventory of 115,000 barrels of oil. At the beginning of the year, he had made arrangements to purchase 15,000 barrels' worth of equipment, but after a fire he found that he only had 5,000 barrels' worth of equipment left. The equipment had not been insured. What remains of the equipment has 180,000 barrels of production capability left. Ronnie used up all of his original 12,000 barrels for drilling expenses.

During the year, however, Ronnie, having a soft heart for Miss Annie, sent 5,000 barrels of produced oil to Miss Annie so that she could go to summer camp. Upon hearing what Ronnie did, J. P. sent Miss Annie a brand new automobile just before the end of the year. The car was acquired for 12,000 barrels of produced oil. Miss Annie was charmed by both of her son's gifts.

Now Miss Annie must determine which son did better so that, in accordance with Jack's will, she can hand over to him full control of Richards Oil.

2

Cash Flow

2.1 DOW JONES & COMPANY, INC. I

Statement of cash flows

Dow Jones & Company, Inc. is a leading publisher of business news and information and community newspapers. The *Wall Street Journal*, the company's best known publication, is the largest daily newspaper in the United States, with a daily circulation of nearly two million copies. Listed on the New York Stock Exchange (Ticker = DJ).

Review the company's Consolidated Statement of Cash Flows for the year ended December 31, 19X3. Based on that statement and the information below, answer the following questions.

1. Provide the "original" aggregate journal entries for the following noncurrent asset or noncurrent liability items that the company reports as Adjustments to reconcile net income to net cash provided by operating activities. The "original" entry is what the company would have entered, in aggregate, for the item during the year. A portion of each entry should involve a noncurrent asset or noncurrent liability account. Use appropriate account titles.

   For example, the original entry for the Depreciation adjustment would have been: DR: Depreciation (expense/income statement) $117,314,000; CR: Accumulated depreciation (contra noncurrent asset) $117,314,000.

   a. Amortization of excess of cost over net assets of businesses acquired.
   b. Gain on disposition of plant and property (ignore tax effects).
   c. Gain on disposition of businesses (ignore tax effects).
   d. Equity in losses of associated companies, net of distributions.
   e. Minority interest in earnings, net of dividends paid.

2. State *net working capital* provided by operating activities. Assume all the accounts listed, except for Deferred taxes of $1,393,000, under the subheading Changes in assets and liabilities represent changes in current asset or current liability accounts related to operating activities.

3. The balances in the Minority interest account were $129,176,000 on January 1, 19X3 and $116,706,000 on December 31, 19X3, respectively, and the minority interest share of net income for the year ended December 31, 19X3 was $38,887,000. During fiscal 19X3, the company increased its ownership interest in the Telerate, Inc. subsidiary from 45 to 56 percent. Assuming no other changes, calculate the change in Minority interest account during 19X3 as a result of the company's increased ownership interest in the Telerate subsidiary. Also, state cash dividends paid to minority interest shareholders during the year. What percentage of the subsidiary's assets and liabilities would be reflected in Dow Jones' balance sheet as of December 31, 19X3?

4. The Retained earnings balance as of January 1, 19X3 was $779,081,000. State the Retained earnings balance as of December 31, 19X3.

5. Interpret the line item "Effect of exchange rate changes on cash ($2,130,000)." Comment on what the wording suggests about the way in which the company recognizes in the Statement of cash flows changes in assets and liabilities due to exchange rate changes.

DOW JONES & COMPANY, INC.
CONSOLIDATED STATEMENT OF CASH FLOWS
For the year ended December 31, 19X3

(In thousands)

OPERATING ACTIVITIES	
Net income	$ 228,178
Adjustments to reconcile net income to net cash provided by operating activities	
Depreciation	117,314
Amortization of excess of cost over net assets of businesses acquired	22,895
Gain on disposition of businesses	(106,495)
Gain on disposition of plant and property	(4,171)
Equity in losses of associated companies, net of distributions	8,350
Minority interest in earnings, net of dividends paid	26,374
Changes in assets and liabilities	
Accounts receivable—trade	1,313
Unexpired subscriptions	(9,489)
Inventories	(4,404)
Other current assets	(14,429)
Accounts payable and accrued liabilities	15,736
Federal and state income taxes	24,679
Deferred taxes	1,393
Other, principally provision for noncurrent liabilities	1,678
Net cash provided by operating activities	$ 308,922
INVESTING ACTIVITIES	
Additions to plant and property	(183,501)
Disposition of plant and property	17,664
Businesses acquired, net of cash received	(34,704)
Businesses sold, net of cash given	124,520
Other investments	(20,467)
Disposition of investments	6,527
Other, net	(1,841)
Net cash provided by (used in) investing activities	$ (91,802)
FINANCING ACTIVITIES	
Cash dividends	(66,270)
Increase in long-term debt	15,356
Reduction in long-term debt	(169,399)
Proceeds from sale under stock purchase plans	4,555
Purchase of treasury stock	(2,367)
Stock issued by consolidated subsidiary	1,006
Net cash provided by (used in) financing activities	$ (217,119)
EFFECT OF EXCHANGE RATE CHANGES ON CASH	(2,130)
INCREASE (DECREASE) IN CASH AND CASH EQUIVALENTS	$ (2,129)
Cash and cash equivalents at beginning of year	62,920
Cash and cash equivalents at end of year	60,791

2.2 GOODYEAR TIRE & RUBBER COMPANY II

Statement of cash flows

Goodyear's principal business is the development, manufacture, distribution, and sale of tires throughout the world. In addition to being one of the world's largest producer of tires, Goodyear is a diversified company which manufactures a broad spectrum of rubber, chemical, and plastic products. The company also has oil and gas drilling operations in California and Louisiana. Listed on the New York Stock Exchange (Ticker symbol = GT). This case should be viewed independently of the Goodyear Tire & Rubber Company I Case.

Based on the end of 19X2 and 19X1 balances from consolidated balance sheets of the Goodyear Tire & Rubber Company and the following information, prepare a worksheet that would be the basis for the preparation of a statement of cash flow under the "indirect" method. In accordance with FASB Statement No. 95, classify the cash flows in the worksheet into four categories: (a) cash from operations, (b) cash applied to (from) financing activities, (c) cash applied to (from) investment activities, (d) other. All numbers are in millions of dollars.

Additional information, notes, and assumptions

1. Net income for 19X2, $412.4; cash dividends declared and paid, $171.3.

2. Income from discontinued operations (included in net income of $412.4) of $111.1 included a gain on disposition of $103.0 net of taxes of $32.9. The discontinued operations were disposed during 19X2 for cash of $443.5. Report proceeds from dispositions of discontinued operations as cash from investing activities.

3. Depreciation and depletion on properties and plants included in net income, $300.5. Properties and plants purchased, $1,667.6, included capitalized interest of $40. Assume all other changes in properties and plants related to dispositions were made at their net book value (i.e., no gain or loss on disposition).

4. Define cash in terms of cash plus short-term securities.

5. Cash flow provided by operations should include all changes in current assets and current liabilities resulting from accrual accounting entries that affect operating activities (including deferred taxes—current liability portion).

6. As simplifying assumptions, include the following items in cash provided by operations: change in deferred charges, change in minority equity in foreign subsidiaries.

7. Explain your treatment of the change in foreign currency translation adjustment account. Describe and justify, without using numbers, an alternative, preferable treatment for that change in balance sheet account.

GOODYEAR TIRE & RUBBER COMPANY

DECEMBER 31, Numbers in millions of dollars

Balance Sheet Accounts Debit balances without parentheses, credit balances in parentheses	19X2	19X1	Change ( ) = decrease in debit balance or increase in credit balance
Asset account balances			
Cash and short-term securities	$ 139.0	$ 143.4	$ (4.4)
Accounts and notes receivable	957.4	1,370.1	(412.7)
Inventories	1,378.5	1,333.4	45.1
Prepaid expenses	83.3	53.6	29.7
Investments in nonconsolidated subsidiaries	181.3	158.2	23.1
Long-term accounts receivable	126.8	39.6	87.2
Investments and miscellaneous assets	30.6	25.5	5.1
Deferred charges	31.6	33.8	(2.2)
Properties and plants	6,919.4	5,854.2	1,065.2
less accumulated depreciation	(2,894.4)	(2,817.5)	(76.9)
Liability and stockholders' equity account balances			
Accounts payable	$ (657.4)	$ (582.5)	$ (74.9)
Accrued payroll	(347.4)	(298.4)	(49.0)
Other current liabilities	(219.1)	(192.4)	(26.7)
Current taxes payable	(173.2)	(204.6)	31.4
Deferred taxes—current	(58.8)	(84.3)	25.5
Notes payable	(116.3)	(157.4)	41.1
Long-term debt due in one year	(35.2)	(38.8)	3.6
Long-term debt and leases	(997.5)	(656.8)	(340.7)
Other long-term liabilities	(301.6)	(293.9)	(7.7)
Deferred income taxes	(475.3)	(448.9)	(26.4)
Minority equity in foreign subsidiaries	(64.3)	(65.0)	0.7
Common stock at par	(94.1)	(92.5)	(1.6)
Capital surplus (in excess of par value)	(655.4)	(613.6)	(41.8)
Retained earnings	(3,172.2)	(2,931.1)	(241.1)
Cumulative foreign currency adjustment	414.3	465.9	(51.6)

2.3 WESTINGHOUSE ELECTRIC CORPORATION I

Statement of cash flows

Westinghouse manufactures, sells, and services electronic equipment and components for the generation, transmission, distribution, utilization, and control of electricity. The company also operates broadcasting and cable television stations, develops land, bottles and distributes beverages, and provides financing services. Listed on the New York Stock Exchange (Ticker = WX).

Based on the attached summary of the changes in the December 31, 19X3 and December 31, 19X2 balance sheet amounts for Westinghouse and the additional information below, calculate:

1. Cash and marketable securities from operating activities
2. Net change in working capital (current assets less current liabilities)
3. Common stock issued, other than for conversions
4. Net cash from sale and purchase of plant and equipment and intangibles (one number)
5. Reduction in short- and long-term debt
6. Cash dividends paid
7. Investments purchased for cash
8. Book value of intangibles sold
9. Treasury stock purchases
10. Working capital from operating activities (cash from operating activities less current asset and current liability adjustments relating to operating activities)

WESTINGHOUSE ELECTRIC CORPORATION
Balance Sheets

Dollars in millions	December 31 19X3	December 31 19X2	Change from 19X2 to 19X3
ASSETS			
Cash	$ 163.1	$ 150.2	$ 12.9
Marketable equity securities	434.4	551.9	(117.5)
Receivables	1,905.2	2,032.3	(127.1)
Inventories	1,161.6	1,109.5	52.1
Cost of uncompleted contracts in excess of progress billings (current)	229.8	152.2	77.6
Prepaid current assets	741.2	624.8	116.4
Investments (noncurrent)	893.6	762.3	131.3
Plant and equipment, net of accum. depr.	2,188.7	3,300.2	(1,111.5)
Intangible assets, net of accum. amort.	764.2	1,027.9	(263.7)
TOTAL ASSETS	$ 8,481.8	$ 9,711.3	$ (1,229.5)
Liabilities and owners' equity			
Short-term debt	596.9	2,039.2	(1,442.3)
Accounts payable	646.1	625.5	20.6
Progress billings in excess of inventoried costs (current)	1,129.5	1,096.8	32.7
Accrued current expenses	1,823.9	1,491.8	332.1
Long-term debt	518.2	525.3	(7.1)
Deferred taxes (noncurrent)	734.0	664.9	69.1
Preferred stock	23.6	33.1	(9.5)
Common stock at par value	183.1	180.6	2.5
Common stock in excess of par value	745.6	672.8	72.8
Common stock in Treasury, at cost	(1,801.3)	(1,023.7)	(777.6)
Retained earnings	3,882.2	3,405.0	477.2
TOTAL EQUITIES	$ 8,481.8	$ 9,711.3	$ (1,229.5)

Additional information for the year ended December 31, 19X3:

1. Net earnings, $681.4.
2. Included in net earnings: Plant and equipment writedowns due to restructuring, $251.0; Depreciation of plant and equipment, $300.0; Amortization of intangibles, $71.0.
3. Plant and equipment purchases, $440.0.
4. Gain on sale of plant and equipment *and* intangibles, $651.2 (included in net earnings). Derive cash from sale of plant and equipment and intangibles as one number.
5. Preferred stock conversions to common stock (at par plus capital in excess of par value), $9.5.
6. Investments purchased for cash, $131.3.

3

Receivables

3.1 BANKAMERICA CORPORATION

Allowance for credit losses

BankAmerica Corporation provides a diversity of financial services to its customers throughout the world. It is the largest bank holding company in California (based on assets and sales revenue). Listed on the New York Stock Exchange (Ticker = BAC).

Study the notes on Loans and Allowance for Credit Losses from the December 31, 19X2 financial statements. The aggregate amounts for these accounts are shown as asset and contra asset accounts on the balance sheet, respectively. The bank uses the "allowance method" of accounting for loan loss expense, one that is similar to the allowance method applied to trade receivables.

According to the bank's 19X2 financial statements, "Management performs quarterly assessment of the credit portfolio in order to determine the appropriate level of the allowance. The factors considered in this evaluation include, but are not necessarily limited to, estimated losses from loan and off-balance-sheet arrangements; general economic conditions; deteriorations in credit concentrations or pledged collateral; international lending risk; historical loss experience; and trends in portfolio volume, maturity, composition, delinquencies, and nonaccruals."

According to the consolidated statement of cash flows, in 19X2 the bank collected principal on loans of $264,671 million and originated long-term loans and net short-term loans of $269,041 million and $564 million, respectively.

Assume that the "Other additions (deductions)" amount of $(124) million shown in the 19X2 allowance account represents the cumulative amount of credit loss relating to loans swapped or sold to third parties. Such loans are carried at the lower fair market value of the assets received in the exchange.

1. Prepare journal entries to record the entries that were made in the Loan and Allowance for Credit Losses (contra asset) accounts for the year ended December 31, 19X2. Use the aggregate numbers.

2. Based on the journal entries in Part 1, state the amount of *expense* that the company recognizes in 19X2 as a result of credit losses on loans.

3. Using the information given above and in the following notes, reconcile the opening and closing balances for the asset account Loans (use the total amounts only).

BANKAMERICA CORPORATION

LOANS:

The following is a summary of loans (net of unearned income):

	As of December 31	
Dollar amounts in millions	19X2	19X1
Domestic loans		
Commercial, industrial, and financial institutions	$ 16,577	$ 15,523
Real estate—construction and development	2,677	3,252
Real estate—mortgage	13,898	12,438
Consumer	14,571	12,058
Agricultural	956	1,029
Lease financing	822	839
Other	876	864
Foreign loans	18,645	18,505
Total loans	$ 69,022	$ 64,508

Unearned income at December 31, 19X2 and 19X1 was $632 million and $518 million, respectively.

ALLOWANCE FOR CREDIT LOSSES:

The following is a summary of changes in the allowance for credit losses:

	For year ended December 31		
Dollar amounts in millions	19X2	19X1	19X0
Balance, beginning of year	$ 3,263	$ 2,172	$ 1,584
Credit losses	(642)	(1,275)	(1,749)
Credit loss recoveries	460	432	330
Net credit losses	(182)	(843)	(1,419)
Provision for credit losses	645	1,951	2,004
Other additions (deductions)	(124)	(17)	3
Balance, end of year	$ 3,602	$ 3,263	$ 2,172

3.2 NATIONAL SEMICONDUCTOR CORPORATION

*Accounts receivable, allowances for sales
and doubtful debts*

National Semiconductor Corporation designs, manufactures, and markets semiconductor devices and related technologies. The company is among the largest manufacturers of integrated circuits in the United States. Listed on the New York Stock Exchange (Ticker = NSM).

Study the excerpt from National Semiconductor's 19X0-19X2 Consolidated Statements of Operations and the note relating to receivables explaining the amounts reported in the consolidated balance sheets. Assume all sales are made on credit.

1. Assume that National Semiconductor estimates returns and allowances on 19X1 and 19X2 sales to be $50 million for each year. Also, assume that the company estimates that doubtful accounts will be 1 percent of 19X2 *gross* sales, and that the company deducts both doubtful accounts and estimated returns and allowances from gross sales revenues to arrive at net sales. Calculate the amount of cash paid by customers (trade credit and other) to the company during the fiscal year ended May 31, 19X2.

2. Assume that on May 31, 19X2, the company recovered $3 million cash from a group of customers whose original $3 million accounts had been viewed as doubtful on May 31, 19X0, and whose accounts had been written down as only 25 percent collectable on May 31, 19X1. Prepare journal entries to record the transactions as of May 31, 19X0, 19X1, and 19X2. The company wishes to reflect as accurately as possible the May 31, 19X2 balance of allowance for doubtful debts.

3. Calculate the average collection period in days defined as the ratio of net accounts receivable to average daily net sales for 19X1 and 19X2. Use end-of-year balances in your calculations and assume 365 days per year. Estimate the cash cost (or cash benefit) to the company had the average collection period for 19X1 been maintained at the same level for 19X2. Assume only that all other aspects of credit policy (e.g., actual and doubtful amounts, allowance account balances) remained unchanged. If necessary, assume a 10 percent interest rate in calculating the cash cost (or cash benefit).

NATIONAL SEMICONDUCTOR CORPORATION
Consolidated Statements of Operations
(In millions)

Years ended May 31,	19X2	19X1	19X0
NET SALES	$ 1,867.9	$ 1,478.1	$ 1,787.5
Operating costs			
Cost of sales	1,319.1	1,096.9	1,258.5
Research and development	218.9	222.4	204.6
Selling, general, and administrative	310.3	276.5	264.9
Restructuring of operations	15.0		
Total operating costs	1,863.3	1,595.8	1,728.0
OPERATING INCOME (LOSS)	4.6	(117.7)	59.5
Interest (net)	13.9	16.1	7.7
Earnings (loss) before income taxes, extraordinary credit, and cumulative effect of accounting change	(9.3)	(133.8)	51.8
Income taxes	19.5	14.5	17.4
Earnings before extraordinary credit and cumulative effect of accounting change	(28.8)	(148.3)	34.4
Extraordinary credit—tax benefits resulting from utilization of operating loss carryforwards	4.2	5.6	8.8
Earnings before cumulative effect of accounting change	(24.6)	(142.7)	43.2
Cumulative effect for years prior to 19X1 of changing revenue recognition policy on semiconductor distributor shipments (net of tax effect of $14.8 million)		51.2	
NET EARNINGS (LOSS)	$ (24.6)	$ (91.5)	$ 43.2

NOTE ON RECEIVABLES
RECEIVABLES COMPRISE (in thousands):

Years ended May 31,	19X2	19X1
Trade and other	$ 335,600	$ 276,100
Less allowances		
Doubtful accounts	22,349	24,771
Returns and allowances	44,051	30,529
NET RECEIVABLES	$ 269,200	$ 220,800

3.3 ORACLE CORPORATION

Revenue recognition and revenue growth rates

Oracle Corporation develops and markets an integrated line of software products for database management, applications development, decision support and office automation, as well as a complete suite of financial applications packages. Listed on the NASDAQ Exchange (Ticker = ORCL).

Study the notes of revenue recognition and unbilled receivables and the balance sheet data on receivables excerpted from Oracle's 19X4 annual financial report. Quarterly sales figures are provided also.

1. Identify and explain the accounting principles used for recognizing revenue from license fees from end-users, license and sublicense fees from OEMs and VARs, maintenance agreements, and consulting and training services.

2. What is an "unbilled" receivable? Describe how the company (most likely) accounts for such amounts. Calculate the percentage of receivables stated on the 19X4 balance sheet that are "unbilled." From the company's standpoint, advance an argument to support the use of this method of revenue recognition that should be acceptable to the independent auditor, Arthur Andersen & Co.

3. Given your knowledge about revenue recognition principles, as well as what the company states, comment on ways in which Oracle might apply such principles in order to maintain its growth in quarterly sales. More generally, comment on the "accounting risk" inherent in the company's reported revenues. Use the table showing reported quarterly revenues from August 19X2 to May 19X5 to examine possible trends in historical quarterly revenues growth rates. One approach is to calculate the compound growth rate using the logarithmic regression formula: $y = mb^x$, where $y =$ quarterly sales revenue; $x =$ quarter 1, 2, 3, etc.; $b = (1 +$ average compound growth); and $m =$ sales revenue for initial quarter, namely $17,611,000.

ORACLE CORPORATION

REVENUE RECOGNITION

The company generates several types of revenue including the following:

License Fees from End-users The company licenses Oracle products to end-users under noncancelable license agreements. The company generally recognizes revenue from these license agreements upon shipment of the product.

License and Sublicense Fees from OEMs and VARs The company has also entered into agreements whereby the Company licenses Oracle products and receives license and sublicense fees from original equipment manufacturers ("OEMs") and software, value-added relicensors ("VARs"). The minimum amount of license and sublicense fees specified in the agreements is recognized at the time such agreements are effective (which in most cases is the date of the agreement) if the customer is creditworthy and the terms of the agreement are such that the amounts due within one year are nonrefundable, and the agreements are noncancelable. The company recognizes revenue at such time it has substantially performed all of its contractual obligations. Additional sublicense fees are subsequently recognized as revenue at the time such fees are reported to the company by the OEMs and VARs.

Maintenance Agreements Maintenance agreements generally call for the company to provide technical support and certain systems updates to customers. Revenue related to providing technical support is recognized proportionately over the maintenance period which in most instances is one year, while the revenue related to systems updates is recognized at the beginning of each maintenance period.

Consulting, Training and Other Services The company provides consultation to its customers; revenue from such services is generally recognized under the percentage of completion method.

UNBILLED RECEIVABLES

Unbilled receivables represent amounts where revenues have been recognized for the financial statements but payment terms of the customer agreements call for extending credit and invoicing the customer at a later date. Trade receivables include unbilled receivables at May 31, 19X4 and 19X3 of $27,740,000 and $16,194,000.

ORACLE CORPORATION

CONSOLIDATED BALANCE SHEETS

Dollars in thousands	May 31	
	19X4	19X3
ASSETS		
CURRENT ASSETS:		
Cash and short-term investments	$ 48,610	$ 37,557
Receivables:		
Trade, net of allowance for doubtful accounts of $10,102 in 19X4 and $6,628 in 19X3	129,999	65,205
Other	9,378	4,014
Prepaid expenses and supplies	3,840	2,362
Total current assets	191,827	109,138
OTHER ASSETS:	57,741	34,654
TOTAL ASSETS	$ 249,568	$ 143,792
LIABILITIES AND STOCKHOLDERS' EQUITY		
CURRENT LIABILITIES:	102,183	48,125
OTHER LIABILITIES:	12,742	13,011
STOCKHOLDERS' EQUITY:	$ 134,643	$ 82,656

QUARTERLY SALES REVENUES

Fiscal year-quarter		Revenue for the quarter ended	Dollars in thousands
1.	Fiscal 19X3-1	August 31, 19X2	$ 17,611
2.	Fiscal 19X3-2	November 30, 19X2	28,352
3.	Fiscal 19X3-3	February 28, 19X3	34,911
4.	Fiscal 19X3-4	May 31, 19X3	50,397
5.	Fiscal 19X4-1	August 31, 19X3	41,274
6.	Fiscal 19X4-2	November 30, 19X3	60,306
7.	Fiscal 19X4-3	February 29, 19X4	76,340
8.	Fiscal 19X4-4	May 31, 19X4	104,193
9.	Fiscal 19X5-1	August 31, 19X4	90,640
10.	Fiscal 19X5-2	November 30, 19X4	123,744
11.	Fiscal 19X5-3	February 28, 19X5	153,354
12.	Fiscal 19X5-4	May 31, 19X5	215,935

3.4 LINCOLN SAVINGS & LOAN ASSOCIATION

Real estate land sales

On February 22, 1984, Lincoln Savings & Loan was acquired by American Continental Corporation. On that date, Lincoln's total assets of $1.2 billion comprised residential loans (41 percent), "risk" assets (28 percent), brokered deposits (6 percent) and other (25 percent). Between that date and April 14, 1989, when Lincoln was placed in conservatorship by the Federal Home Loan Bank Board and other government regulatory agencies, the Association grew to a size of approximately $4.6 billion in assets, comprising residential loans (2 percent), risk assets (64 percent), and brokered deposits (34 percent). Also, during that time, Lincoln engaged in increasing levels of lending and (direct) investing in land development and construction activities, principally in Arizona, and was able to report cumulative pretax profits of $238,633,000.

However, as a result of a special investigation, initiated in 1987 by the Federal Home Loan Bank Board, San Francisco, public accountants Kenneth Leventhal & Company concluded in 1989 that more than 50 percent of the $238.6 million in profits had arisen due to the improper use of the accrual method of accounting for various real estate transactions. Specifically, based on 15 transactions that were analyzed, Kenneth Leventhal & Company calculated that Lincoln had improperly recognized as profit the amount of $135,269,000.

This case examines a series of transactions involving the sale of real estate in the Hidden Valley area, a 26 square mile block of vacant, undeveloped land in western Maricopa County (which is situated about 35–40 miles west of Phoenix, Arizona). Lincoln had purchased the land in 1985 and 1986 and intended to develop this land over 20–30 years, along with other land nearby, into a modern city of about 200,000 people.

The specific debits and credits of each transaction are analyzed as the basis for understanding differences between the accounting and economic realities represented by such transactions. All materials used in this case have been extracted from the Hearing before the Committee on Banking, Finance and Urban Affairs, House of Representatives, One Hundred First Congress, *Investigation of Lincoln Savings & Loan Association*, Serial 101-59, November 14, 1989.

Prior to 1989, the Association was traded as an over-the-counter security, with ticker symbol = LSLA; American Continental's ticker = AMCC.

1. Lincoln purchases the land in a series of transactions summarized as follows:

Date	Net acres	Purchase price	Price per net acre§	Seller
6/25/1985	2,426	$ 7,802,010*	$ 3,216	Hardesty Bros. and G-P Farms
5/16/1986	6,070	18,062,740†	2,976	Wolfswinkel
4/21/1987	40	320,000*	8,000	Hardesty/Shelton
5/31/1988	40	400,000*	10,000	State of Arizona
Total	8,576	$ 26,584,750	$ 3,100	

* Purchased by Lincoln for cash.
† Purchased by Lincoln for $12.6 million in cash and the balance as assumption of liens, which were paid off by Lincoln on December 31, 1986. Wolfswinkel originally purchased the land in May 1985 for $6.9 million with funds borrowed from Lincoln Savings & Loan.
§ Purchase price ÷ net acres.

Record the acquisition of the Hidden Valley land and the payment of the liens in Lincoln's books on the assumption that all transactions are independent, bona fide, third party transactions.

2. Lincoln sells 1,000 net acres of Hidden Valley land to the West Continental Mortgage Corporation (Westcon).

  a. March 30, 1987

   Lincoln provides a $30 million loan commitment to ECG Holdings, Incorporated, secured by the stock in that company. ECG Holdings is a corporation controlled by Mr. E. C. Garcia, a local real estate developer. On that same day, Mr. Garcia draws a check for $19.6 million of the loan commitment. Also, on that same day, Mr. Garcia lends $3.5 million to the West Continental Mortgage Corporation (Westcon) on a nonrecourse basis. Westcon's balance sheet at the time shows total assets of $87,000 and owners' equity of $30,000.

  b. March 31, 1987

   Westcon purchases from Lincoln 1,000 net acres of Hidden Valley land for $14 million. Westcon pays for the land with $3.5 million cash (the cash received from Mr. Garcia the day before) and the balance is financed by Lincoln as a loan to Westcon of $10.5 million. Since the recorded cost of the land was $2.9 million, the pretax profit to Lincoln on this transaction was $11.1 million.

   i. Record the March 30 and March 31, 1987 transactions in Lincoln's books on the assumption that all transactions are independent, bona fide, third party transactions.

   ii. Record also the March 30 and March 31, 1987 transactions from the standpoint of Mr. Garcia (and his company) on the assumption that all transactions are independent, bona fide, third party transactions.

c.   December 31, 1987 (assumed: the actual date is unknown)

American Continental Corporation, the owner of Lincoln Savings & Loan, receives from Lincoln the amount of 40 percent of the profit on the sale of land to Westcon. This amount is due to American Continental under a tax sharing arrangement, whereby Lincoln's owner (American Continental) assumes the tax liability for Lincoln and files a consolidated tax return with the Internal Revenue Service.

Record the cash payment to American Continental in Lincoln's books.

d.   June 1988

Mr. E.C. Garcia purchases the 1,000 acres from Westcon and assumes the $10.5 million note that Westcon had agreed to pay Lincoln. (The actual purchase price is unclear from the Congressional record. Assume the original price is used.) Since essentially no interest payments have been made to Lincoln by either Westcon or Mr. Garcia, Lincoln must place the $10.5 million note on the nonaccrual status.

Record the June 1988 transaction in Mr. Garcia's books on the assumption that the purchase of the note is an independent, bona fide, third party transaction. What transactions, if any, should Lincoln make when it places the note on the nonaccrual status?

3.   Summarize the transactions in Part 2 from the standpoint of Lincoln Savings & Loan in terms of the following classifications:

a.   How much pretax profit was recognized by Lincoln due to the series of transactions?

b.   How much cash did Lincoln receive or pay due to the series of transactions?

c.   Other than cash, what assets and liabilities does Lincoln show on its books?

4.   Finally, comment on the following statements made at the Hearing before the Committee on Banking, Finance and Urban Affairs, House of Representatives, One Hundred First Congress, *Investigation of Lincoln Savings & Loan Association*, Serial No. 101-59, November 14, 1989.

Statement #1

Congressmen, seldom in our experience as accountants have we experienced a more egregious example of the misapplication of generally accepted accounting principles. This association [Lincoln] was made to function as an engine, designed to funnel insured deposits to its parent in tax allocation payments and dividends. To do this it had to generate reportable earnings, and it generated earnings by making loan or other reportable transfers of cash or property to facilitate sham sales of land.

Roger A. Johnson
Partner
Kenneth Leventhal & Company

Statement #2

Lincoln was an institution with over $4 billion of assets. An institution of this size conducts thousands of transactions, many of which could individually be called major. Kenneth Leventhal, at the request of the lawyers for the Federal Home Loan Bank Board [of San Francisco] reviewed just 15 of the transactions that occurred in three different fiscal years, 1986, 1987, and 1988...

Based on this limited review, its report reached sweeping, and we believe, unsupported conclusions. We recognize that different accountants can and do reach different conclusions. When an audit involves complex transactions and requires judgment calls on the accounting for many of those transactions, the difference of opinion may legitimately occur. We do not share Kenneth Leventhal's confidence that theirs is the only correct application of the 200 pages of accounting principles attached to its report...

Others that examined Lincoln and ACC [American Continental] in 1986 and 1987 did not reach the same sweeping conclusions. While the Federal Home Loan Bank Board [Washington, D.C.] received critical comments from the San Francisco Bank [Board] and others, it did not move to take over Lincoln until April 1989, after American Continental had declared bankruptcy.

William L. Gladstone

Co-Chief Executive
Ernst & Young

4

Inventory

4.1 DAYCO CORPORATION

LIFO inventories and tax savings

Dayco is a worldwide distributor and manufacturer of rubber and plastic products. Prior to 1989, listed on the New York Stock Exchange (Ticker = D.DPI).

Study Dayco's balance sheet for 19X2–19X3. Dayco's 19X3 net earnings *before* taxes was $9,280,000. Footnote A, Inventories, reads as follows:

Substantially all inventories are stated at the lower of LIFO cost or market. If the FIFO method had been used, inventories would have been approximately $53,198,000 higher than reported at October 31, 19X3 ($58,488,000 higher at October 31, 19X2). During recent years, in reaction to downturns in demand for certain products, the Corporation reduced inventory levels related to these products. These reductions resulted in a liquidation of LIFO inventories carried at costs prevailing in prior years. Without these reductions of inventories, costs of sales (net of taxes) would have been higher by approximately $2,041,000 ($2,568,000 and $1,532,000 in 19X2 and 19X1).

---

1. If Dayco had used FIFO in 19X3, how much higher or lower would earnings before taxes have been? Restate 19X3 pretax earnings on a FIFO basis.

2. Management states elsewhere in the October 31, 19X3 annual report that the existing tax savings from being on LIFO are $24,471,000. Approximately, what tax rate is management using in its calculation? Show your own calculations. Is the term "tax savings" an appropriate description of the LIFO benefit?

DAYCO CORPORATION
Balance Sheet as of

October 31,	19X3	19X2
ASSETS		
Current assets		
Cash and cash equivalents	$ 19,231,000	$ 5,193,000
Marketable securities	2,186,000	8,761,000
Accounts receivable, less allowances		
1983—$6,017,000; 1982—$5,728,000	141,913,000	120,096,000
Federal income taxes recoverable	389,000	3,397,000
Inventories		
Finished goods	64,564,000	69,813,000
Work in process	8,866,000	8,644,000
Raw materials and supplies	12,540,000	13,481,000
	85,970,000	91,938,000
Deferred federal income taxes	2,166,000	3,713,000
Prepaid expenses	6,151,000	8,523,000
Total current assets	258,006,000	241,630,000
Property, plant and equipment		
Land and land improvements	4,471,000	4,516,000
Buildings	56,826,000	62,239,000
Machinery and equipment	209,317,000	203,713,000
Construction in process	5,044,000	47,715,000
Allowances for depreciation and amortization (deduction)	(129,954,000)	(121,099,000)
	145,704,000	154,084,000
Excess of cost over market value of net assets of business purchased	17,940,000	17,999,000
Notes receivable	4,399,000	6,466,000
Other assets	8,691,000	17,045,000
	$434,740,000	$437,224,000

4.2 CHAMPION SPARK PLUG COMPANY

FIFO vs. LIFO inventory valuation,
cumulative and specific-year effects

Champion Spark Plug Company is a worldwide firm involved principally in the manufacture, distribution, and marketing of spark plugs, windshield wipers, and other automotive components. Through subsidiaries, Champion is also engaged in manufacturing coating application equipment, health-care equipment, and cold-drawn steel. Listed on the New York Stock Exchange Prior to 1989 (Ticker = CHM).

Study Champion's Consolidated Statements of Earnings for 19X1–19X3, Consolidated Balance Sheets for 19X2–19X3 and 19X1–19X2 (assets section only), and note to the 19X3 Financial Statements, "Inventories: Change to LIFO in 19X2."

1. Using the financial statements provided, identify the unknowns in the table below. Assume that the effective tax rate for Champion during 19X2 and 19X3 was 46 percent. (Since it is actually a fraction less than 46 percent, any minor "unexplained" differences can be attributed to rounding errors.)

	19X3	19X2	19X1
Inventories on LIFO basis	a	b	N.A.*
Inventories on FIFO basis	c	d	e
Cumulative impact of switch to LIFO as of December 31 on pretax basis	f	g	N.A.
Specific-year impact of switch to LIFO on pretax basis	h	j	N.A.
Specific-year impact of switch to LIFO on after-tax basis	i	k	N.A.

*Not applicable

2. Using a journal entry, show the effects on the December 31, 19X2 balance sheet of the 19X2 change in Champion's method of pricing inventory from FIFO to LIFO.

3. Champion's operating earnings decreased slightly from $118.2 million in 19X1 to $114.1 million in 19X2. After fully recognizing the effects of the switch to LIFO on 19X1 and 19X2 income, assess the extent of change in operating earnings. In other words, of the earnings change, how much appears to be due to change in accounting rules for inventories and how much appears to be due to other economic activity? (Note: A precise numerical solution is not possible.)

4. In nontechnical language, explain what the company is trying to tell its stockholders in the third paragraph of the note entitled "Inventories: Change to LIFO in 19X2."

CHAMPION SPARK PLUG COMPANY
Consolidated Statements of Earnings

Years ended December 31 (In millions, except per share)	19X3	19X2	19X1
Net sales	$ 799.8	$ 806.5	$ 692.6
Costs and expenses:			
Cost of goods sold	535.9	516.0	421.4
Selling, administrative and general expense	190.6	176.4	153.0
	726.5	692.4	574.4
Operating earnings	73.3	114.1	118.2
Other income:			
Interest and dividends	4.5	6.0	4.3
Sundry–net	2.9	1.5	.8
	7.4	7.5	5.1
	80.7	121.6	123.3
Other deductions:			
Interest expense	11.4	7.3	6.3
Amortization of goodwill	.8	.8	.7
Prior year loss arising from translation of a capitalized foreign lease	-	-	1.3
Net loss due to foreign currency fluctuations	1.9	.9	.1
	14.1	9.0	8.4
Earnings before taxes based on income	66.6	112.6	114.9
State and local taxes based on income	2.2	5.0	5.2
Earnings before federal and foreign income taxes	64.4	107.6	109.7
Federal and foreign income taxes	25.5	49.0	52.9
Net earnings before minority interests	38.9	58.6	56.8
Minority interests in net earnings of consolidated subsidiaries	2.0	1.7	1.5
Net earnings	$ 36.9	$ 56.9	$ 55.3
Net earnings per share	$ .96	$ 1.49	$ 1.45

CHAMPION SPARK PLUG COMPANY
Consolidated Balance Sheets

ASSETS December 31 (Dollars in millions)	19X3	19X2
Current assets:		
Cash	$ 8.1	$ 10.6
Marketable securities, at cost which approximates market	12.4	32.8
Accounts receivable, less allowances of $4.1 million and $3.1 million	136.0	125.8
Current portion of notes receivable	1.3	1.3
Inventories	261.4	240.8
Prepaid expenses	8.9	5.9
Total current assets	428.1	417.2
Notes receivable and other assets	9.5	11.1
Property, plant and equipment, at cost:		
Land and land improvements	8.3	8.2
Buildings	105.0	94.1
Machinery and equipment	188.5	175.6
Construction in progress	17.6	9.2
	319.4	287.1
Less accumulated depreciation and amortization	138.1	122.6
Net property, plant and equipment	181.3	164.5
Intangible assets, at amortized cost	17.3	18.0
	$ 636.2	$ 610.8

CHAMPION SPARK PLUG COMPANY
Consolidated Balance Sheets

LIABILITIES AND STOCKHOLDERS' EQUITY

(Dollars in millions)	19X3	19X2
Current liabilities:		
Notes payable to banks	$ 40.9	$ 19.3
Current portion of long-term debt	5.4	5.0
Accounts payable	52.3	52.3
Accrued expenses:		
Salaries and wages	14.4	12.9
Taxes, other than federal and foreign income taxes	9.1	9.8
Pension and other	26.2	20.9
Federal and foreign income taxes	14.6	19.7
Total current liabilities	162.9	139.9
Non-current portion of long-term debt:		
5-7/8% debentures due September 15, 1992 (net of $4.1 million and $5.5 million reacquired)	13.9	14.0
Unsecured notes payable	6.0	9.0
Capital lease obligations and other	21.5	21.4
Total non-current portion of long-term debt	41.4	44.4
Deferred income	7.3	8.1
Deferred federal and foreign income taxes	10.6	12.7
Minority interests in subsidiary companies	8.1	6.5
Stockholders' equity:		
Common stock of 30¢ par value per share		
Authorized 40,000,000 shares; issued 38,292,757 and 38,260,728 shares	11.5	11.5
Capital in excess of par value	18.4	18.0
Retained earnings	376.0	369.7
Total stockholders' equity	405.9	399.2
	$ 636.2	$ 610.8

CHAMPION SPARK PLUG COMPANY
Consolidated Balance Sheets

ASSETS ended December 31,	19X2	19X1
Current assets:		
Cash	$ 10,594,055	$ 12,137,198
Marketable securities, at cost which approximates market	32,776,831	32,183,253
Accounts receivable, less allowances of $3,126,000 and $2,488,000	125,825,970	113,110,560
Current portion of notes receivable	1,246,400	1,246,400
Inventories	240,812,523	227,091,343
Prepaid expenses	5,938,104	5,801,327
Total current assets	417,193,883	391,570,081
Notes receivable and other assets	11,098,313	9,469,437
Property, plant and equipment, at cost:		
Land and land improvements	8,232,174	8,174,386
Buildings	94,085,302	89,513,229
Machinery and equipment	175,611,880	164,182,022
Construction in progress	9,160,076	5,980,900
	287,089,432	267,850,537
Less accumulated depreciation and amortization	122,605,393	108,800,675
Net property, plant and equipment	164,484,039	159,049,862
Intangible assets, at amortized cost	18,022,323	20,043,789
	$ 610,798,558	$ 580,133,169

INVENTORIES: CHANGE TO LIFO IN 19X2

In 19X2 the Company adopted the last-in, first-out (LIFO) method of determining costs for substantially all of its U.S. inventories. In prior years, inventory values were principally computed under the lower of cost or market, first-in, first-out (FIFO) method. The effect of the change on the operating results for 19X2 was to reduce net earnings by $5.8 million, or $.15 per share.

Inventory balances at December 31, 19X3 and 19X2 would have been $26.8 million and $10.7 million higher, respectively, if U.S. inventory costs had continued to be determined principally under FIFO rather than LIFO. Net earnings on a primarily FIFO method basis would have been $45.6 million or $1.19 per share in 19X3 compared to $62.7 million or $1.64 per share in 19X2.

During 19X3 certain inventory balances declined below the levels at the beginning of the year resulting in a smaller increase in the LIFO reserve than would have occurred if these inventory levels had not declined. Net earnings in 19X3 would have been $1.3 million ($.03 per share) lower had the LIFO reserve addition not been affected by reduced inventories.

It was not practical to determine prior year effects of retroactive LIFO application.

4.3 USX CORPORATION

Inventory valuation

USX is a diversified energy and resource company with operations in steel (USS, formerly United States Steel), oil (Marathon Oil and Texas Oil and Gas), and other related businesses. Listed on the New York Stock Exchange (Ticker = X).

Use the footnote below regarding inventories from its 19X3 financial report to answer the following questions:

1. Provide journal entries that would have been made in the Inventory market valuation reserve account on December 31, 19X3 and December 31, 19X2.

2. Provide a journal entry to be made on January 1, 19X4 in the event that the *realizable market value* of the December 31, 19X3 inventories suddenly jumped to $1,700 million.

3. If USX had valued its inventories consistently using *current acquisition costs* instead of the LIFO cost method (and other cost methods for the remaining inventories), how much would 19X3 pretax operating income have been? USX reported total pretax operating income of $267 million in 19X3. Ignore the effects of the adjustments in (1).

4. Explain how it is possible that, for both years, operating income *increased* as a result of LIFO liquidations while the changes in the Inventory market valuation reserve account had the opposite effect on operating income.

USX CORPORATION
Inventories
(Dollars in millions)

| INVENTORIES: | December 31 | |
	19X3	19X2
Raw materials	$ 440	$ 538
Semi-finished products	168	40
Finished products	830	770
Supplies and sundry items	243	283
Total (at cost)	1,681	1,631
Inventory market valuation reserve	(308)	(300)
Net inventory carrying value	$ 1,373	$ 1,331

At December 31, 19X3 and December 31, 19X2, respectively, the LIFO method accounted for 80% and 72% of total inventory value. Current acquisition costs are estimated to exceed the above "at cost" values at December 31 by approximately $270 million in 19X3 and $480 million in 19X2.

Cost of sales has been reduced and operating income increased by $113 million in 19X3 and $334 million in 19X2 as a result of liquidations of LIFO inventories.

In 19X2, market values of crude oil were very volatile and declined to the extent that cost of oil and gas inventories exceeded realizable (market) value at December 31, 19X2. Consequently, a market inventory valuation reserve was established in 19X2, which increased total operating costs and reduced net income. In 19X3, the reserve was increased by $8 million.

4.4 UPJOHN COMPANY

*Inventory valuation at historical
and current cost values*

Upjohn engages in the research, development, production, and sale of prescription pharmaceuticals. The company also manufactures nonprescription drugs and chemicals, furnishes home health care and staffing services for hospitals, and develops and produces vegetable and agronomic seeds and animal pharmaceutical products. Listed on the New York Stock Exchange (Ticker = UPJ).

Study the Consolidated Balance Sheets for December 31 19X4 and 19X3 and Notes A, B, and C on inventories, investments, and changing prices, respectively, to those financial statements. Unless otherwise stated, numbers are in thousands of dollars.

1. Identify or calculate the following measures for *inventories* that would be shown in the December 31, 19X4 balance sheet:

   a. As reported—on a combination of the LIFO (domestic inventories) and FIFO (foreign inventories) bases;
   b. On a replacement cost or FIFO basis; and
   c. On a current cost value basis.

2. Identify the valuation method (either a, b, or c) that would allow the company to show the greatest total value for stockholders' equity as of December 31, 19X4. Explain why.

3. Assume that the company considered changing to FIFO (approximates current replacement cost) for worldwide inventories beginning on January 1, 19X4. What would have been reported in the statement of income as net profit for fiscal year 19X4? Assume that the company followed generally accepted accounting principles with respect to the reporting of an accounting change. Reported 19X4 net income was $173,272. Assume a 40 percent tax rate in your calculations.

4. Why does the company report its investments at cost when the market value of those investments is less than cost? What would be the change in pretax net income for 19X4 if the lower of cost or market rule had been applied to investments, assuming unrealized gain and losses are charged to the income statement? Provide a journal entry to record the change in market value of the investments during 19X4.

THE UPJOHN COMPANY AND SUBSIDIARIES
Consolidated Balance Sheets
Dollar amounts in thousands

December 31	19X4	19X3
Current assets:		
Cash and cash items	$ 44,487	$ 61,898
Trade accounts receivable, less allowances of $8,959 (19X3: $9,004)	373,532	379,207
Other accounts receivable	38,007	36,822
Inventories	377,203	345,362
Deferred income taxes	53,687	60,994
Other	72,862	55,264
Total current assets	959,778	939,547
Investments at cost	400,594	410,404
Property, plant and equipment at cost:		
Land	24,301	24,119
Buildings and utilities	511,773	457,871
Equipment	675,456	607,681
Leasehold improvements	6,384	6,043
Construction in process	72,105	90,771
	1,290,019	1,186,485
Less allowance for depreciation	480,485	431,531
	809,534	754,954
Other noncurrent assets	78,457	90,143
Total assets	$ 2,248,363	$ 2,195,048

THE UPJOHN COMPANY AND SUBSIDIARIES
Notes to Consolidated Financial Statements
Dollar amounts in thousands, except per-share data

Note A: Inventories

December 31	19X4	19X3
Estimated replacement cost (FIFO basis):		
Pharmaceutical and chemical finished products	$ 134,810	$ 122,329
Seeds	99,042	93,274
Raw materials, supplies, and work in process	262,874	253,432
	496,726	469,035
Less reduction to LIFO cost	119,523	123,673
	$ 377,203	$ 345,362

Inventories valued on the LIFO method had an estimated replacement cost (FIFO basis) of $283,693 at December 31, 19X4, and $288,854 at December 31, 19X3.

THE UPJOHN COMPANY AND SUBSIDIARIES
Notes to Consolidated Financial Statements, contd.
Dollar amounts in thousands, except per-share data

Note B: Investments

Investments at cost held by a subsidiary operating in Puerto Rico were:

December 31	19X4	19X3
Government issued or guaranteed	$ 112,839	$ 117,404
Corporate preferred securities	116,330	120,715
Other	171,425	172,285
Total cost	400,594	410,404
Estimated market value	$ 385,600	$ 388,400

The company expects to hold these investments until their maturity.

Note C: Schedule of Consolidated Earnings Restated for Changing Prices

For the Year Ended December 31, 19X4 Millions of Average 19X4 dollars	Historical Cost	(Unaudited) Restated to Current Cost
Operating revenue	$ 2,188	$ 2,188
Operating costs and other deductions:		
Products and services sold, excluding depreciation	922	919
Depreciation expense	66	103
Other operating expenses	917	917
Other deductions, net	22	22
Provision for income taxes	88	88
Total	$ 2,015	$ 2,049
Net earnings	173	139
Purchasing power gain on net monetary liabilities		3
Increase in current cost value of inventory, property, plant, and equipment held during the year*		104
Increase due to general inflation		63
Excess of increase in specific prices over increases in general inflation		41
Translation adjustment		$ (181)

*At December 31, 19X4, the current cost value of inventory was $530 and the current cost value of property, plant and equipment, less accumulated depreciation, was $1,113.

4.5 U & I INCORPORATED

Inventory cost flow, impact of changing prices, discontinuance

U & I Incorporated operates in two principal industries: farming and related processing, and warehousing and distribution. Previously involved in sugar-processing operations, the company announced in November 19X4 that its sugar factories and terminals were for sale. Sugar inventories were liquidated mainly during fiscal years 19X6 and 19X7.

Study the accompanying portions of U & I Incorporated's financial statements from: (1) Consolidated Statements of Financial Position for 19X0–19X1 and 19X1–19X2, and Notes D and B to those respective statements; (2) Consolidated Statements of Earnings and Earnings Retained for Use in the Business for 19X0–19X1; and (3) Consolidated Statements of Financial Position for 19X6–19X7, Consolidated Statements of Operations for 19X5–19X7, and Notes B and D to those 19X7 statements.

1. Identify or compute the end-of-year values for inventories on the LIFO and FIFO accounting methods. Prepare your answer in a tabular format such as the following:

Inventories	Year Ended February 28(29)th		
	19X2	19X1	19X0
FIFO valuation			
LIFO valuation			
Difference (FIFO - LIFO)			

2. a. If U & I had used FIFO instead of LIFO for the granulated sugar part of the inventory, what effect would this have had on the 19X1 and 19X2 Statements of Financial Position? Ignore tax effects.

   b. If U & I had used FIFO instead of LIFO for the granulated sugar part of the inventory, what effect would this have had on the 19X1 and 19X2 Earnings before Taxes? Ignore tax effects.

3. a. Assume that U & I pays taxes on profits at the rate of 40 percent. What effect would the use of FIFO have on the 19X1 and 19X2 Statements of Financial Position? (Note: This is the same question as 2a except that the tax rate is assumed to be 40 percent.)

Based on an earlier case by Robert K. Jaedicke and James M. Patell.

b. Assume that U & I pays taxes on profits at the rate of 40 percent. What effect would the use of FIFO have on the 19X1 and 19X2 Earnings before Taxes, Taxes, and Earnings after Taxes?

4. Comment on the nature and impact of sugar price movements during 19X0–19X2. Did U & I make a sound business decision to adopt the LIFO method for valuing sugar inventories prior to 19X0? Aside from tax considerations, what other factors might have influenced the firm's decision at the time?

5. From 19X2 to 19X7, U & I reduced its inventories of sugar and sugar-related products substantially. In 19X2, for instance, sugar inventories on a LIFO basis were $38,505,138, whereas in 19X6 and 19X7 sugar inventories on a LIFO basis were $1,585,000 and $900,000, respectively (Note: The $1,585,000 amount excludes inventories of $5,455,000 relating to the discontinued operations). If U & I had used FIFO consistently during 19X2–19X7, how much different would "cumulative earnings before taxes" have been as of February 28, 19X7? Cumulative earnings represents the sum of earnings for those years. It is not necessary to calculate each year's change individually.

6. a. If U & I had used FIFO during 19X7 and earlier, what would the Gain (Loss) on Disposal After Income Taxes have been? Refer to Note B, "Discontinuance of Sugar Processing Operations" and in your calculations use a 40 percent tax rate, excluding investment tax recapture of $1,244,000, which is assumed to remain unchanged if the gain (loss) were reported on a FIFO basis.

   b. Restate 19X7 Net Earnings (Loss) on the FIFO basis, assuming that FIFO had been used during 19X6, 19X7, and earlier.

U & I INCORPORATED
Consolidated Statements of Financial Position

	February 28	
	19X1	19X0 (Restated)
Inventories (first-in, first-out method would be $105,466,988 higher in 19X1 and $18,723,033 higher in 19X0)—Note D	$ 44,846,014	$ 42,114,796

Note D—Inventories and Change in Accounting Principle

	February 28 19X1	February 28 19X0 (Restated)
Granulated sugar, thick juice, beets and molasses: at lower of cost (last-in, first-out method) or market	$ 30,210,363	$ 31,625,017
Dried beet pulp, operating materials and supplies, farm products and other inventories—at lower of cost (first-in, first-out method) or market	$ 14,635,651	$ 10,489,779
	$ 44,846,014	$ 42,114,796

Effective March 1, 19X0, the Company changed to the dollar-value method (from the specific-goods method) of determining last-in, first-out (LIFO) inventory valuations.

U & I INCORPORATED
Consolidated Statements of Financial Position

	February 29 19X2	February 28 19X1 (Restated)
Inventories (first-in, first-out method would be $49,788,076 higher in 19X2 and $105,466,988 higher in 19X1)—Note B	$ 55,772,773	$ 44,846,014

Note B—Inventories
Inventories at each year end were as follows:

	February 29 19X2	February 28 19X1 (Restated)
Granulated sugar, thick juice, beets and molasses: at lower of cost (last-in, first-out method) or market	$ 38,505,138	$ 30,210,363
Dried beet pulp, operating materials and supplies, farm products and other inventories: at lower of cost (first-in, first-out method) or market	17,267,635	14,635,651
	$ 55,772,773	$ 44,846,014

U & I INCORPORATED
Consolidated Statements of Earnings and Earnings
Retained for Use in the Business

	February 28 19X1	February 28 19X0 (Restated)
Earnings Before Income Taxes	$ 9,199,022	$ 10,257,517
Income Taxes		
Current federal and state income taxes	2,698,503	4,305,825
Deferred federal income taxes	759,623	517,963
	3,458,126	4,823,788
NET EARNINGS	$ 5,740,896	$ 5,433,729

U & I INCORPORATED
Consolidated Statements of Financial Position

	February 28 (29)	
	19X7	19X6
TOTAL ASSETS APPLICABLE TO CONTINUING OPERATIONS	$109,326,000	$ 94,735,000
ASSETS APPLICABLE TO DISCONTINUED OPERATIONS—NOTE B		
Inventories	-	5,455,000
Property, plant, and equipment:		
Land	-	2,209,000
Plant and equipment	-	83,621,000
Less net proceeds from assets sold and allowances for depreciation	-	(73,981,000)
		11,849,000
Total Assets Applicable to Discontinued Operations		$ 17,304,000

U & I INCORPORATED
Consolidated Statements of Operation

	February 28 19X7	February 29 19X6	February 28 19X5
Earnings (Loss) from Continuing Operations Before Income Taxes (Credits)	$ 1,873,000	$ (3,558,000)	$ 1,517,000
Income Taxes (Credits)	(2,408,000)	(2,900,000)	700,000
Earnings (Loss) from Continuing Operations	4,281,000	(658,000)	817,000
Discontinued Sugar Processing Operations Note B: Loss from operations less applicable income tax credits			(8,852,000)
Gain on disposal, less provision for estimated additional costs and applicable income taxes	802,000		
NET EARNINGS (LOSS)	$ 5,083,000	$ (658,000)	$ (8,035,000)

U & I INCORPORATED
Notes to 19X7 Consolidated Financial Statements

Note B: Discontinuance of Sugar Processing Operations

The company announced in November 19X4 that its sugar factories and terminals were for sale and, in January 19X5, that it would close those sugar facilities for which it was unable to find buyers. In February 19X5, the company adopted a plan for the sale or other disposal of the company's sugar facilities.

A substantial part of the sugar inventory associated with the discontinuance was sold during the year ended February 29, 19X6 in accordance with the company's normal terms and prices. The remaining sugar inventory was sold during the year ended February 28, 19X7 in the same manner. Since March 19X5 the company has proceeded with its plan to sell or salvage sugar processing assets related to the discontinuance.

In accordance with Opinion No. 30 of the Accounting Principles Board of the American Institute of Certified Public Accountants, the recognition of the gain on disposal has been deferred until actually realized. Accordingly, the gain from the disposal of discontinued sugar processing assets over the last two years is shown in the accompanying Statements of Operations within the year ended February 28, 19X7. Details of the gain are as follows:

Revenues	$ 134,888,000
Costs and expenses, including provision for estimated additional phase-out costs of $2,600,000	93,913,000
	40,975,000
Write-off of unsold assets	37,816,000
Gain on disposal before income taxes	$ 3,159,000
Income taxes, incl. inv. tax credit recapture of $1,244,000	2,357,000
Gain on disposal	$ 802,000

The above costs and expenses include sugar inventories valued at LIFO cost which was $48,804,000 less than FIFO cost. Certain assets with a net book value of approximately $2,630,000 were sold to another corporation in which a director of the company is a principal officer. For the year ended February 28, 19X5, discontinued sugar processing operations had revenues of approximately $134,000,000 and $8,900,000 in tax benefits from losses for discontinued operations.

Management is continuing to sell or salvage the remaining sugar processing assets at as favorable a return to the company as is practical. Management is unable to predict when all of the remaining assets will be sold.

Note D: Inventories

Inventories are comprised of the following:	February 28 19X7	February 29 19X6
Potatoes and farm products	$ 20,542,000	$ 10,676,000
Livestock, operating materials and supplies and other inventories	3,430,000	3,269,000
Sugar and related sugar products	900,000	1,585,000
	$ 24,872,000	$ 15,530,000

Inventories when valued at FIFO cost exceed the LIFO cost method by $3,104,000 at February 28, 19X7 and $2,651,000 at February 29, 19X6.

5

Other Current Assets

5.1 ELGIN NATIONAL INDUSTRIES, INC.

Construction receivables and revenue recognition

Elgin National Industries' business is concentrated in two basic areas: (1) specialized engineering, manufacturing, and construction and (2) clocks and watches. Elgin is the official manufacturer and distributor of Mickey Mouse and other Disney fanciful character watches and clocks. Listed on the New York Stock Exchange (Ticker = ENW).

Study Elgin's Consolidated Statements of Income for 19X0–19X2, Consolidated Balance Sheets for 19X1–19X2, and Notes 1 and 2 to the financial statements.

1. What method of accounting for construction contracts does Elgin use for financial reporting purposes? In what way might that method illustrate the concept of conservatism?

2. Another distinct method of accounting for construction contracts is the completed contract method. What would be the likely effect on Elgin's reported pretax profits and cash flows if it were to have adopted such a method for tax purposes in 19X2 and earlier years while maintaining the method identified in Part 1 for financial reporting purposes?

3. Assume that Elgin's costs of production and construction average 80 percent of sales and construction revenues and that other expenses such as selling, general, administrative, and interest expenses are fixed. Calculate what Elgin's 19X2 Income before Taxes on Income would have been had the company used for reporting purposes the method of accounting for construction contracts used for tax purposes. Provide journal entries that would restate the 19X2 pretax profits on the alternative basis. Assume that unbilled and retainage amounts in 19X1 are billed in 19X2.

ELGIN NATIONAL INDUSTRIES, INC.
Consolidated Statements of Income

	Year Ended December 31,		
	19X2	19X1	19X0
Net sales and construction revenues including agency sales (Note 1)	$ 210,768,316	$ 207,527,696	$ 208,616,421
Revenues:			
Net sales and construction revenues	$ 200,346,720	$ 207,527,696	$ 189,282,849
Interest income	3,677,064	1,070,431	276,970
Other income	415,239	145,209	—
Costs and expenses:			
Cost of sales and cost of construction	$ 162,588,944	$ 171,109,354	$ 153,069,273
Selling, general and administrative expenses	21,831,209	20,110,901	19,228,221
Interest expense	373,921	315,055	655,150
	$ 184,794,074	$ 191,535,310	$ 172,952,644
Income before Taxes on Income:	$ 19,644,949	$ 17,208,026	$ 16,607,175
Tax provision on above income	9,297,000	7,924,000	8,319,000
Net Income:	$ 10,347,949	$ 9,284,026	$ 8,288,175
Primary income per share	$ 3.46	$ 3.13	$ 2.83
Fully diluted income per share	$ 3.37	$ 3.03	$ 2.71

ELGIN NATIONAL INDUSTRIES, INC.
Consolidated Balance Sheets

	December 31,	
	19X2	19X1
ASSETS		
CURRENT ASSETS:		
Cash	$ 2,316,939	$ 7,363,746
Short-term investments (at cost which approximate market)	29,200,000	21,900,000
Accounts and notes receivable (Note 2)	46,529,208	50,611,335
Receivable—sale of companies	605,000	-
Inventories	16,900,866	16,237,155
Prepaid expenses and other current assets	576,845	728,903
TOTAL CURRENT ASSETS	$ 96,128,858	$ 96,841,139
PROPERTY, PLANT AND EQUIPMENT	$ 9,492,770	$ 9,686,583
OTHER ASSETS:		
Receivable—sale of companies	$ 258,000	$ 508,000
Excess of cost over net assets acquired	6,153,046	6,322,750
Other	478,563	530,443
	$ 6,889,609	$ 7,361,193
	$ 112,511,237	$ 113,888,915
LIABILITIES AND STOCKHOLDERS' INVESTMENT		
CURRENT LIABILITIES:		
Trade payables	$ 9,740,429	$ 12,548,026
Accrued liabilities and taxes	26,285,230	27,896,022
Federal income taxes payable:		
Current	4,335,000	3,965,000
Deferred (Note 1)	14,387,333	16,783,598
Current portion of long-term debt	498,780	440,736
TOTAL CURRENT LIABILITIES	$ 55,246,772	$ 61,633,382
LONG-TERM DEBT	$ 2,438,128	$ 3,319,604
LOAN GUARANTEE—EMPLOYEE STOCK OWNERSHIP TRUST	$ 5,203,582	$ 6,562,370
CONTINGENT LIABILITIES		
STOCKHOLDERS' INVESTMENT		
Preferred stock, par value $1 per share; authorized 1,000,000 shares; none issued	$ -	$ -
Common stock, par value $1 per share; authorized 7,500,000 shares; issued 4,621,724 in 19X2, 4,599,008 in 19X1	4,621,724	4,599,008
Paid-in surplus	51,486,105	51,168,485
Retained earnings	13,659,465	8,109,393
	$ 69,767,294	$ 63,876,886
Less:		
Cost of 1,612,894 shares of common stock in treasury	14,940,957	14,940,957
Deferred charge—Employee Stock Ownership Trust	5,203,582	6,562,370
	$ 49,622,755	$ 42,373,559
	$ 112,511,237	$ 113,888,915

ELGIN NATIONAL INDUSTRIES, INC.
Notes to Consolidated Financial Statements

1. *Summary of significant accounting and reporting policies:*

   a. Principles of consolidation: The consolidated financial statements include the accounts of the Company and its wholly-owned subsidiaries. All significant intercompany profits, transactions and balances have been eliminated in consolidation.

   b. *Accounting for construction contracts:* The length of the Company's construction contracts varies but is typically longer than one year. Therefore, contract related assets and liabilities are classified as current in the accompanying consolidated balance sheets. For financial statement purposes, profits on uncompleted contracts are determined by applying the percentage of completion to the engineering estimate of total profit on each contract. The percentage of completion is determined by comparing costs incurred to date with total estimated costs on each project. The Company's contract cost estimates include amounts related to plant start-up, customer acceptance, and other construction uncertainties. Favorable adjustments to these estimates are made and the effect on income is recorded only when construction progress reaches the point where experience is sufficient to estimate final results with reasonable accuracy; unfavorable adjustments are recorded as soon as they are apparent. Other adjustments of cost estimates, if required, are recorded in the periods when they become known. Estimated losses on uncompleted contracts are provided in full.

2. *Accounts and notes receivable:*

   Accounts and notes receivable consist of the following:

	December 31,	
	19X2	19X1
Trade accounts	$ 12,944,961	$ 9,649,369
Construction contracts:		
Billed	$ 16,278,687	$ 25,806,240
Recoverable costs and accrued profits on contracts in process—unbilled	2,608,519	1,986,061
Retainage due upon completion of contracts	14,572,109	12,614,155
	$ 33,459,315	$ 40,406,456
Other	989,385	1,198,502
	$ 47,393,661	$ 51,254,327
Less allowance for doubtful accounts	864,453	642,992
	$ 46,529,208	$ 50,611,335

It is estimated that approximately $13,500,000 of the retainage balance at December 31, 19X2, will be collected in 19X3.

The unbilled recoverable costs and accrued profits on contracts in process represent revenues which have been recognized in the financial statements because the related costs have been incurred but which were not yet billed to customers under the terms of the contract.

5.2 MCDONNELL DOUGLAS CORPORATION

Revenue recognition and government contracts

McDonnell Douglas Corporation is a world leader in the development and application of aerospace technology and is a significant supplier of information-related products and services. The company's major segments include combat aircraft, transport aircraft, space systems, and missiles. Listed on the New York Stock Exchange (Ticker = MD).

The company in its December 31, 19X8 financial statements provides the following information about its various accounts. Dollars are in millions.

1. Contracts in Process and Inventories:

	19X8	19X7
Government contracts in process	$ 5,275	$ 5,968
Commercial products in process	2,081	1,700
Material and spare parts	1,349	1,353
Progress payments to subcontractors	1,581	1,339
Progress payments received	(6,007)	(6,567)
	$ 4,279	$ 3,793

Commercial products in process at December 31, 19X8 include $74 million of tooling and $349 million of production costs related to the MD-11 tri-jet that will be accounted for under the program-average cost method. Production costs incurred on early production aircraft in excess of the estimated average cost of aircraft in the program will be finalized prior to the first delivery of aircraft scheduled for 19X10. At December 31, 19X8, there were 88 firm orders and 162 options and reserves for the MD-11.

2. Accounts receivable:

Accounts receivable consist of the following at December 31.
U.S. Government—primarily from long-term contracts

	19X8	19X7
Billed	$ 676	$ 642
Unbilled	210	163
	886	805
Commercial and other governments	534	610
	$ 1,420	$ 1,415

Unbilled amounts represent the estimated sales value of items delivered or other work performed which lack contractual documentation to permit billing. Unbilled amounts at December 31, 19X8 also include $76 million of receivables estimated to be recoverable under cost-sharing agreements for which funding has not been appropriated. Approximately $38 million of the 19X8 unbilled amount is expected to be collected after one year.

3. Balance sheet information:

	19X8	19X7
Contracts in process and inventories	$ 4,279	$ 3,793
Total assets	11,885	10,624
Liabilities and shareholders' equity		
Liabilities	8,699	7,654
Advances and billings in excess of related costs	1,449	950
Shareholders' equity	3,186	2,970
Retained earnings	2,859	2,607

4. Income statement information:

	19X8	19X7
Combat aircraft	$ 6,070	$ 5,925
Transport aircraft	4,877	3,977
Space systems and missiles	2,368	2,146
Information systems	1,295	1,241
Financial services	423	353
Other	36	31
Non-operating revenue	3	3
Total revenues	$ 15,072	$ 13,676
Operating earnings	710	594
Earnings before income taxes	507	457
Net earnings	$ 350	$ 313

5. Other information from the notes to the financial statements:

   a. **Revenue recognition.** Revenues and earnings on cost-reimbursement and fixed-price government contracts are generally recognized on the percentage of completion method of accounting as costs are incurred (cost-to-cost basis). Revenues include costs incurred plus a portion of estimated fees or profits based on the relationship of costs incurred to total estimated costs.

   Revenues relating to contracts or contract changes that have not been completely priced, negotiated, documented, or funded are not recognized unless realization is considered probable.

   Revenues, costs, and earnings on government contracts and commercial aircraft programs are determined, in part, based on estimates. Adjustments of such estimates are made on a cumulative basis whereby the effect of such changes is recognized currently. Any losses anticipated on government contracts or commercial programs are charged to operations in full when determined.

b. **Contracts in process and inventories**. Government contracts in process are stated on the basis of incurred costs plus estimated earnings, less amounts billed to customers when items are completed and delivered. Incurred costs include production costs and related overhead. Commercial products in process on the basis of the production and tooling costs incurred, less the cost allocated to the delivered items, reduced to realizable value, where applicable.

Based on the preceding information, answer the following questions.

1. Provide a journal entry to record revenues associated with (a) combat aircraft, assumed derived solely on the basis of cost reimbursement and fixed-price government contacts, and (b) transport aircraft, assumed based on the sales prices of such aircraft at the time of delivery.

2. Assume that 19X7 combat aircraft production of $5,925 million was completed and delivered on January 1, 19X8 without additional cost. No progress payments had been made with respect to that production. Provide an entry to record the completion and shipping on January 1, 19X8 of the 19X7 combat aircraft production.

3. Provide an entry to record the amount of progress payments received during 19X8 applicable to contracts in process and inventories on hand at December 31, 19X8.

4. Estimate the effect on the company's 19X8 pretax earnings had the tooling and production costs relating to the MD-11 tri-jet been written off as incurred rather than been accounted for on the program-average cost method. Assume that the program-average cost method was applied to the MD-11 tri-jet beginning on January 1, 19X8. Comment on the reasonableness of the cost projections inherent in this accounting policy.

5. With respect to the recognition of estimated revenue, compare the use of the account Unbilled Receivable with the Contracts in Process account.

6

Property, Plant, and Equipment

6.1 IDS, INC.

Depreciation and gains and losses

Review the 19X2–19X3 Statement of Income and Retained Earnings for IDS, Inc. Review also the note that describes the special credit amount of $278,331. Show using journal entry (or entries) or T accounts how IDS would have recorded the sale of land and buildings described in the Note.

STATEMENT OF INCOME AND RETAINED EARNINGS
Years Ended June 30, 19X3 and 19X2

	19X3	19X2
Net sales	$ 5,633,208	$ 2,539,230
Operating costs and expenses		
Cost of sales	5,008,041	2,165,541
Selling, general, and administrative expenses	335,286	209,541
Operating profit	$ 289,881	$ 164,148
Other income	8,301	0
Interest expense	(91,098)	(26,976)
Income before federal income tax	207,084	137,172
Provision for federal income tax (after reduction of $55,956 in 19X3 and $57,057 in 19X2 for net operating loss carryforward)	44,814	0
Net income	$ 162,270	$ 137,172
Special credit—gain on sale of land and building (less applicable federal income tax of $95,778 —refer to Note)	287,331	0
Net income and special credit	449,601	137,172
Retained earnings (deficit) at beginning of year	(111,897)	(249,069)
Retained earnings (deficit) at end of year (refer to Note)	$ 337,704	$ (111,897)

Depreciation deducted in the above statement:
19X3—$43,548; 19X2—$25,416

Note: During 19X3, the Company entered into agreements providing for the sale of a major portion of its land and buildings at a sales price of $1,439,892. This amount exceeded the depreciated cost of the assets involved, after applicable income taxes, by $287,331 which has been treated as a special credit to Income. The original cost of the fixed assets sold was about $1,800,000.

6.2 CONAGRA, INC. I

Gains and losses on disposal,
and accumulated depreciation

ConAgra, Inc., conducts operations across the food chain in agriculture, grain, and food. ConAgra manufactures and markets agricultural chemicals, formula feeds and fertilizers, grain milling and merchandising, poultry products, prepared food, and seafood. Listed on the New York Stock Exchange (Ticker = CAG).

Refer to the company's Consolidated Statement of Earnings for years ended June 29, 19X2 and June 30, 19X1 and the note on property, plant, and equipment from the company's 19X2 annual report. Also, the statement of cash flow for the company discloses that depreciation expense for 19X2 and 19X1 was $4,383,108 and $4,200,843, respectively, and that during both fiscal years no purchases of property, plant, and equipment had been made.

Note that since the provision for loss on disposal of non-operating properties is shown above the account provision for taxes, the loss on disposal amount is presumed reported on a pretax basis. Use this information and the statements below to answer the following questions:

1. Calculate the combined historical cost (original purchase price) of the assets disposed, namely sold or written down, during fiscal year 19X2.

2. Calculate the combined amount of accumulated depreciation relating to the assets disposed, during fiscal year 19X2.

3. Calculate the amount of cash (or other assets) that the company received for the property, plant, and equipment disposed in fiscal 19X2.

4. Provide a journal entry (or entries) dated June 30, 19X2 that account fully for the provision for loss, the gain on disposal, and the amounts calculated in Parts 1, 2, and 3.

CONAGRA, INC.
Consolidated Statement of Earnings for
Years Ended June 29, 19X2 and June 30, 19X1

	52 weeks ended June 29, 19X2	52 weeks ended June 30, 19X1
Net sales	$ 573,543,906	$ 633,643,845
Cost of goods sold	531,656,040	603,739,970
Selling and administrative expenses	25,711,851	26,637,910
Operating income	$ 16,176,015	$ 3,265,965
Other income:		
Gain on disposal of assets	4,472,135	0
Sundry	1,210,547	1,060,402
	$ 21,858,697	$ 4,326,367
Other deductions		
Interest	13,427,772	16,025,542
Provision for loss on disposal of non-operating properties (loss on disposition of assets in 19X1)	3,650,000	1,426,394
Sundry	184,608	247,449
Earnings (loss) before income taxes	$ 4,596,317	$ (13,373,018)
Income taxes		
Current (recoverable)	525,000	(1,029,286)
Deferred (reduction)	0	(490,614)
Net earnings (loss)	$ 4,071,317	$ (11,853,118)
Earnings (loss) per common share	$ 1.14	$ (3.88)

CONAGRA, INC.
Property, plant, and equipment

The major categories of property, plant and equipment are summarized as follows:

	June 29 19X2	June 30 19X1
Land	$ 1,823,079	$ 2,156,079
Buildings, machinery and equipment	65,429,084	79,743,575
Furniture and fixtures	1,254,072	1,380,865
Autos, trucks, trailers, etc.	1,668,143	3,302,838
Construction in progress	1,041,452	895,577
	71,215,830	87,478,934
Less accumulated depreciation	28,679,872	29,046,314
	$ 42,535,958	$ 58,432,620

During the year ended June 29, 19X2, the Company began a program of evaluating its operating facilities. Property, plant, and equipment which no longer met earnings requirements, or were not compatible with the company's long-range plans, were considered for disposal.

As of June 29, 19X2 the company had completed the evaluation and has disposed of several facilities at a net gain of $4,472,135. Additional facilities not used in the business remained unsold at year end. These assets have been written down by $3,650,000 to more fairly reflect their realizable value. Sale of these facilities is being actively pursued.

6.3 GENERAL MOTORS CORPORATION I

Depreciation and amortization

General Motors Corporation is the largest automotive manufacturer in the United States and one of the largest in the world. Listed on the New York Stock Exchange (Ticker = GM).

In the third quarter of 19X2, General Motors revised the estimated service lives of its plants and equipment and special tools retroactive to January 1, 19X2. The Company based those revisions on studies of actual useful lives and periods of use and recognized current estimates of service lives. Their effect was to add $1,236.6 million to pretax operating income for the year, $2.55 per share to annual earnings per share, and according to the *Wall Street Journal*, October 28, 19X2, $536.9 million to the reported third quarter, pretax operating income of $356.8 million.

According to the *Wall Street Journal*, the accounting change had been widely anticipated by financial analysts, who had been informed in a press conference two weeks prior to the third quarter's earnings announcement by Chairman Roger Smith that he expected the change to occur for the third quarter report. Even earlier, *Forbes*, August 24, 19X2, had reported analysts' predictions of the effects of the accounting change (as much as $4 per share).

The company announced third quarter earnings on October 27, 19X2. In addition to the company's statements about the reasons for the move, the general view was that General Motors' accounting moves would place it more in line with the estimated useful lives that Ford and Chrysler use and would enable General Motors' future earnings to better cope with the depreciation effects of the company's increased future capital spending.

Use the information in the table below, which has been extracted from the 19X2 and 19X1 financial statements, to answer the following questions.

1. Reconstruct the aggregate journal entries for fiscal years 19X1 and 19X2 that would account for the changes in the Real estate, plants, and equipment (cost and accumulated depreciation) and Special tools accounts. Assume that all expenditures and disposals are for cash and that the disposals produced no gains or losses.

2. General Motors records the change in depreciation as a change in an accounting estimate. In general terms, state how such a change should affect the fiscal year 19X2 and 19X1 financial statements, including which accounts would be involved. State what adjustments would have been made at the time of the change—the end of the third quarter of 19X2.

3. Calculate the impact of the change in accounting method on pretax operating income and net income after taxes in terms of the percentage change in earnings with and without the accounting change.

4. On the day that General Motors released its third quarter 19X2 earnings, which included the effects of the accounting change, its stock price jumped $3.875 to close at $59.375 per share. Comment on the extent to which this positive stock market response suggests that the market in part responded favorably to increased earnings due to the accounting change. The stock price data in the table that follows describe the market behavior of General Motors and the Dow Jones 30 index.

Information on asset (and contra asset) balances:

REAL ESTATE, PLANTS, AND EQUIPMENT

Dollars in millions	Fiscal 19X1		Fiscal 19X2	
	Cost	Accumulated Depreciation	Cost	Accumulated Depreciation
Balance at January 1	$47,267.1	$ 4,325.0	$55,240.7	$27,658.0
Foreign Currency adjustments	1,437.9	850.8	1,461.4	1,180.4
Depreciation		3,469.6		3,417.5
Expenditures	8,086.3		4,711.2	
Disposals	(1,550.6)	(987.4)	(1,603.9)	(1,279.9)
Balance at December 31	$55,240.7	$27,658.0	$59,809.4	$30,976.0

SPECIAL TOOLS

Dollars in millions	Fiscal 19X1 Net book value	Fiscal 19X2 Net book value
Balance at January 1	$ 1,710.9	$ 2,793.7
Foreign Currency adjustments	53.6	222.6
Amortization	(2,596.1)	(2,155.5)
Expenditures	3,625.3	2,346.2
Disposal		
Balance at December 31	$ 2,793.7	$ 3,207.0

Other information:

Dollars in millions	Fiscal 19X1	Fiscal 19X2
Depreciation and amortization expense	$ 6,065.7	$ 5,573.0
Operating income before income tax	1,430.9	2,569.4
Net income available for common shares	2,933.9	3,537.2
Average number of shares (millions)	315.8	317.6

General Motors and Dow-Jones 30 Industrials Index: September 30, 19X2 to November 30, 19X2

Date	Volume of trading	Closing price	Dow Jones industrials
9/30/19X2	2,244,000	83	2,596.28
10/1/19X2	1,605,000	84.25	2,639.20
10/2/19X2	1,472,800	82.5	2,640.98
10/5/19X2	2,266,000	81.376	2,640.18
10/6/19X2	2,220,000	80	2,548.63
10/7/19X2	2,976,000	78.25	2,551.08
10/8/19X2	4,138,000	76.25	2,516.64
10/9/19X2	3,710,000	74.5	2,482.21
10/12/19X2	3,124,000	73.875	2,471.44
10/13/19X2	2,436,000	75.375	2,508.16
10/14/19X2	2,678,000	73	2,412.70
10/15/19X2	4,504,000	70.875	2,355.09
10/16/19X2	5,260,000	66	2,246.73
10/19/19X2	8,470,000	60	1,738.74
10/20/19X2	9,058,000	59.75	1,841.01
10/21/19X2	5,606,000	62.25	2,027.85
10/22/19X2	5,076,000	58	1,950.43
10/23/19X2	3,236,000	57.5	1,950.76
10/26/19X2	2,324,000	55.5	1,793.93
10/27/19X2	3,584,000	59.375	1,846.49
10/28/19X2	2,584,000	57.875	1,846.82
10/29/19X2	1,864,000	59.125	1,938.33
10/30/19X2	3,390,000	58.875	1,993.53
11/2/19X2	1,918,000	58.625	2,014.09
11/3/19X2	3,362,000	58.75	1,963.53
11/4/19X2	5,608,000	60.25	1,945.29
11/5/19X2	2,782,000	60.125	1,985.41
11/6/19X2	1,804,000	58.75	1,959.05
11/9/19X2	2,053,400	58	1,900.20
11/10/19X2	1,840,800	57.375	1,878.15
11/11/19X2	1,208,400	57.75	1,899.20
11/12/19X2	3,028,200	60.375	1,960.21
11/13/19X2	1,396,200	59	1,935.01
11/16/19X2	1,726,600	60	1,949.10
11/17/19X2	1,494,200	59.75	1,922.25
11/18/19X2	1,920,200	61	1,939.16
11/19/19X2	2,002,600	59.25	1,895.39
11/20/19X2	1,823,000	60.625	1,913.63
11/23/19X2	1,260,000	60.125	1,923.08
11/24/19X2	1,518,000	59.875	1,963.53
11/25/19X2	1,600,000	59.25	1,946.95
11/26/19X2	Holiday	0	0.00
11/27/19X2	743,400	58.5	1,910.48
11/30/19X2	3,220,600	56.375	1,833.55

6.4 PORTLAND GENERAL CORPORATION

Interest capitalization, allowance for funds used during construction, tax benefits

Serving more than one million people, Portland General is Oregon's largest supplier of electricity. The company's wholly-owned regulated utility, Portland General Electric Company, is the largest utility in the state and serves approximately 45 percent of state's population in a 3,170 square-mile area. Listed on the New York Stock Exchange (Ticker = PGN).

Public utility companies such as Portland include in the cost of additions to plant and equipment an allowance for funds used during the construction of the plant and equipment (AFDC). The AFDC amount includes interest on borrowed funds and an *imputed* interest on equity funds used during construction to conform with Federal Energy Regulatory Commission pronouncements.

Study Portland General's Consolidated Statements of Income for 19X5–19X9, Consolidated Statements of Changes in Financial Position for 19X5–19X9, and portions of Notes 1 and 2 to the 19X9 financial statements.

1. For 19X8 and 19X9, provide journal entries that record outlays for interest costs (exclude Other Interest and Amortization and non-cash amounts credited to income for Allowance for Funds Used during Construction).

2. If Portland General had not capitalized interest (i.e., credited Allowance for Funds Used during Construction to income) in years 19X5–19X9, what would Net Income before Taxes on Income have been for those years?

3. It has been suggested that investors value AFDC credits differently from equal amounts of normal or regular operating earnings. As an investor or analyst attempting to assess Portland General as an investment opportunity, how would you treat such credits in your calculations (for example, in a valuation equation)?

4. Explain why in the 19X5–19X9 Consolidated Statements of Changes in Financial Position Portland General subtracts out only one of the two AFDC credits that appear in the Statements of Income.

5. Note 1 states that the allowance for funds using during construction "is not capitalized for income tax purposes." Using information in Note 2, explain from the standpoint of an investor the general effect of this different method of accounting for tax purposes.

PORTLAND GENERAL CORPORATION
Consolidated Statements of Income

For the Years Ended December 31	19X9	19X8	19X7	19X6	19X5
	(Thousands of Dollars)				
Operating Revenues	$349,981	$ 303,678	$ 253,073	$ 217,787	$ 179,942
Taxes on income (included in operating exps.)	12,300	4,968	5,006	4,510	1,493
Operating Expenses	284,692	220,439	179,946	135,110	117,780
Operating Income	65,289	83,239	73,127	82,677	62,162
Other Income					
Allowance for equity funds used during construction (Note 1)	27,445	9,058	5,089	4,360	6,317
Other income and deductions	1,270	5,325	541	988	(641)
	28,715	14,383	5,630	5,348	5,676
Interest Charges					
Interest on long-term debt	70,326	58,206	48,528	40,711	28,519
Interest on short-term borrowings	9,096	8,973	4,794	5,447	9,211
Other interest and amortization	1,030	1,183	846	899	347
Allowance for borrowed funds used during construction (Note 1)	(32,570)	(19,524)	(12,399)	(11,053)	(16,242)
	47,882	48,838	41,769	36,004	21,835
Income before cumulative effect of change in accounting policy	46,122	48,784	36,988	52,021	46,003
Cumulative effect to January 1, 19X8 of accounting estimated unbilled revenues–less income taxes of $8,503 (Note 1)	-	7,845	-	-	-
Net Income	$ 46,122	$ 56,629	$ 36,988	$ 52,021	$ 46,003
Preferred Dividend Requirement	13,830	14,175	13,657	11,812	9,818
Common Stock					
Income available	32,292	42,454	23,331	40,209	36,185
Average shares outstanding	30,403,911	24,709,977	21,414,344	17,687,41	14,333,33
Earnings per share					
Before cumulative effect of change in accounting policy	$1.06	$1.40	$1.09	$2.27	$2.52
Cumulative effect to January 1, 19X8 of accruing estimated unbilled revenues–net	-	.32	-	-	-
Earnings per share	$1.06	$1.72	$1.09	$2.27	$2.52
Dividends declared per share	1.70	1.70	1.70	1.64	1.58

PORTLAND GENERAL CORPORATION
Consolidated Statements of Changes in Financial Position*

For the Years Ended December 31	19X9	19X8	19X7	19X6	19X5
(Thousands of Dollars)					
Source of Funds					
Current operations					
Income before cumulative effect of change in accounting policy	$ 46,122	$ 48,784	$ 36,988	$ 52,021	$ 46,003
Non-cash charges (credits) to income					
Depreciation and amortization	46,840	35,008	39,548	24,708	13,890
Deferred income taxes–net	11,293	1,018	7,683	8,167	5,129
Reserve transferred to revenue	-	-	-	-	(1,989)
Allowance for equity funds used during construction	(27,445)	(9,058)	(5,089)	(4,360)	(6,317)
Other–net	2,799	3,038	(214)	138	134
	79,609	78,790	78,916	80,674	56,850
Cumulative effect of change in accounting policy	-	7,845	-	-	-
Funds provided internally	79,609	86,635	78,916	80,674	56,850
Proceeds from external financing					
Long-term debt	102,672	116,795	157,978	120,104	122,861
Preferred stock	-	-	27,000	27,375	30,000
Common stock	93,834	68,459	62,532	65,774	29,770
Short-term borrowings–net	59,000	26,000	(25,650)	(57,284)	32,143
Sale/leaseback of assets	20,246	50,310	-	-	-
	$355,361	$348,199	$300,776	$236,643	$271,624
Application of Funds					
Gross utility construction	$254,289	$278,265	$201,896	$191,475	$182,513
Reimbursement for prior years' construction expenditures	-	-	-	(18,940)	-
Allowance for equity funds used during construction	(27,445)	(9,058)	(5,089)	(4,360)	(6,317)
	226,844	269,207	196,807	168,175	176,196
Headquarters complex construction	-	-	9,259	21,342	18,982
Dividends declared	66,960	56,689	50,156	41,776	32,728
Retirement of long-term debt and preferred stock	45,119	45,666	54,156	4,480	40,124
Miscellaneous–net	13,984	8,459	(11)	2,812	1,219
Increase (decrease) in working capital excluding current maturities, sinking funds and short-term borrowings					
Cash	522	(681)	(2,966)	(3,675)	6
Receivables	4,684	7,457	(3,981)	5,802	7,404
Estimated unbilled revenues	1,572	20,209	-	-	-
Materials and supplies	24,525	(5,776)	7,209	(13,308)	7,309
Accounts payable and accruals	(41,516)	(50,810)	(13,171)	7,886	(13,824)
Other–net	12,667	(2,221)	3,318	1,353	1,480
	$355,361	$348,199	$300,776	$236,643	$271,624

*Funds are defined as working capital, excluding current maturities of long-term debt, sinking fund payments, and short-term borrowings.

PORTLAND GENERAL CORPORATION
Notes to Financial Statements

NOTE 1: SUMMARY OF ACCOUNTING POLICIES

Allowance for Funds Used During Construction (AFDC)–AFDC represents the net cost for the period of construction of borrowed funds used for construction purposes and a reasonable rate on other funds used. AFDC is capitalized as part of the cost of the utility plant and is credited to income but does not represent current cash earnings. The allowance for borrowed funds used during construction is calculated on a pre-tax basis. AFDC is not capitalized for income tax purposes.

Effective January 1, 19X7 the Federal Energy Regulatory Commission (FERC) established a formula to determine the maximum allowable AFDC rate and ordered that the allowance for borrowed funds used during construction be credited to interest charges and that the allowance for other (equity) funds used during construction be credited to other income. A 7 percent AFDC rate was used on all construction expenditures until November 15, 19X7 when the maximum rate allowed under the FERC order was adopted for certain construction projects. Effective January 1, 19X9 the maximum rate (11.5 percent for 19X9) was adopted for all construction expenditures.

NOTE 2. INCOME TAX EXPENSE–The following table shows the detail of taxes on *utility* income.

For the Years Ended December 31	19X9	19X8	19X7	19X6	19X5
(Thousands of Dollars)					
Utility income tax expense					
Currently payable	$ 143	$ (25)	$ (1,045)	$ (1,727)	$ 3,637
Deferred income taxes					
Capitalized interest	7,943	3,342	4,433	4,013	6,529
Deferred income taxes	3,361	1,354	2,409	2,787	630
Liberalized depreciation	1,810	-	-	-	-
Other	(855)	400	(457)	(541)	(540)
Investment tax credits	(102)	(103)	(334)	(22)	1,489
Total	12,300	4,968	5,006	4,510	1,493

6.5 SACRAMENTO POWER CORPORATION

Abandonment of utility plant cost

Sacramento Power Corporation is a fictitious electric power facility operating in Sacramento County, California. Several years ago the county's supervisors voted to build a small, environmentally sound, nuclear reactor to take care of the county's growing energy needs. At that time, Sacramento Power, a privately owned company, contracted with Hullar Construction to perform the construction, which was expected to take up to six years. However, based on a recent general referendum of the voting public and various other public discussions, Sacramento Power's management decided that, on December 31, 19X2, abandonment of its nuclear power station was a most probable event. The power facility has been under construction for five years and as of December 31, 19X2, had accumulated costs in the balance sheet of $628 million. All such costs were the result of prudent operating and investment activities.

In the event of cancellation of the construction contract, Sacramento Power will be required to pay Hullar Construction contract penalties of $21.5 million, which will be paid in approximately six months' time. Sacramento's incremental annual borrowing rate is 12 percent, compounded monthly. Though it will take about 18 months to obtain a rate order, Sacramento Power's management is optimistic that it will be permitted to recover the *full* construction cost but without any amount for additional return on investment during the recovery period. The recovery period is expected to be at least than five years but less than ten.

The plant has a tax basis of $400 million, which includes the cancellation penalty levied by Hullar. Because Sacramento Power expects to receive a federal tax refund by way of a loss carryback of 34 percent of that amount, it will not be allowed recovery of such benefit. Also, certain future federal tax benefits of $32 million will be deducted by the California utilities regulators and, thus, not allowed in the computation of costs for recovery purposes. The net amount allowed—construction costs plus penalties less tax benefits—is expected to be recoverable over 60 months, with cash payments beginning at the *end* of the first month following the rate order.

1. Calculate the net loss after deferred taxes to be recorded at the time of the decision to abandon the plant, December 31, 19X2. Deferred taxes at 34 percent should be calculated for both the amount of reduction in net regulatory amount allowed to be recovered and amount of gain to reduce expected cancellation charges to their present value. Note that the latter

amount is not included in the net regulatory amount. Provide journal entries to record the loss and show any reclassifications in the balance sheet.

One year later on December 31, 19X3, Sacramento now deems that it is probable that the rate order will be forthcoming from the regulators in 12 months' time and that the recovery period will be 7 years from that date. During the time between the initial decision to abandon (December 31, 19X2) and December 31, 19X3, Sacramento has been accruing carrying charges on the recorded asset, which was stated on January 1, 19X3, at its new, written-down present value, at the rate of 12 percent compounded monthly. Those carrying charges were recorded monthly as additions to the carrying value of the abandoned plant (debit) and as estimated and actual liabilities (credit). Calculate and provide a journal entry to record the amount of loss after deferred taxes at 34 percent that Sacramento Power will record for the year ended December 31, 19X3.

One year later on December 31, 19X4, the rate order is received. The order, however, allows a recovery period of nine years. Determine the additional amount of loss after deferred taxes to be recorded at that date, namely, December 31, 19X4. Calculate also the expected amount of revenue and net income before taxes (revenue less amortization of unrecovered cost) for the first year of the rate order, January–December 19X5. Provide journal entries to record the loss recognition on December 31, 19X4 and the aggregate cash receipts from the rate order during the following year.

7

Intangibles

7.1 CAMPBELL SOUP COMPANY II

Plant assets, gains/losses on retirement, amortization of intangibles

Study Campbell's fiscal year 19X1–19X3 Consolidated Statements of Changes in Financial Position and note from the financial statements on Other Assets and Plant Assets. The numbers in this case should not be used in the Campbell Soup Company I case. Treat the cases as independent. All numbers are in thousands of dollars. Campbell's 19X3 fiscal year ended on August 2nd.

1. Estimate the historical cost of Plant Assets sold during 19X3.

2. Estimate the accumulated depreciation relating to Plant Assets sold during 19X3.

3. Estimate what the loss of retirement (i.e., loss on "sale") would have been had Campbell's actually "sold" its Plant Assets for zero dollars in 19X3. State the loss on a pretax basis.

4. Estimate the historical cost of Other Assets (intangibles plus other) sold or otherwise disposed of or retired in 19X3.

5. Assuming Other Assets sold at book value (acquisition cost less accumulated depreciation to date), what apparently was the gain or loss on Plant Assets actually sold during 19X3?

6. Assume that the intangibles are being amortized on a straight-line basis over thirty years. Approximately when (i.e., in what month) were Goodwill and Other Intangibles of $48,480 ($133,950 – $85,470) acquired?

CAMPBELL SOUP COMPANY
Consolidated Statements of Changes in Financial Position

Dollars in thousands	19X3	19X2	19X1
Additions			
Net earnings	$ 129,717	$ 121,655	$ 132,744
Items not requiring the use of working capital			
Depreciation	75,118	67,958	60,360
Amortization of intangibles	4,300	1,758	3,067
Deferred income taxes	5,692	3,534	5,747
Other	789	1,677	64
Working capital from operations	215,616	196,582	201,982
Plant and other assets sold	13,268	13,806	4,170
Conversion to equity of advance to foreign supplier		20,000	
Treasury stock issued (23,219 shares–19X3; 25,213 shares–19X2; 90,078 shares–19X1), at cost	693	827	2,766
Long-term debt incurred	36,114	109,855	5,337
Other liabilities incurred	13,421		
Additions to working capital	279,112	341,070	214,255
Deductions			
Plant assets purchased for cash	135,402	97,391	108,132
Plant assets acquired	19,873	58,405	51,471
Dividends	66,298	61,479	57,304
Advance to foreign supplier			20,000
Goodwill and other assets	49,470	69,503	3,520
Treasury stock purchased (702,200 shares–19X3; 79,600 shares–19X2; 953,748 shares–19X1)	21,754	2,405	32,849
Reduction in long-term debt	23,406	8,274	12,969
Other	291	172	194
Deductions from working capital	316,494	297,629	286,439
Increase (decrease) in working capital	$ (37,382)	$ 43,441	$ (72,184)
Increase (decrease) in working capital			
Cash and temporary investments	$ (18,059)	$ (53,515)	$ (97,742)
Accounts receivable	11,555	32,692	32,469
Inventories	(16,819)	86,883	53,954
Prepaid expenses	6,821	7,800	9,530
Notes payable	3,877	(79,289)	(26,608)
Payable to suppliers and others	(16,411)	(37,276)	(9,608)
Dividend payable		14,503	(971)
Accrued liabilities	(8,346)	(35,387)	(33,208)
	$ (37,382)	$ 43,441	$ (72,184)

CAMPBELL SOUP COMPANY
Note on Other Assets and Plant Assets
Dollars in thousands

Other Assets, At Cost	19X3	19X2
Intangibles		
Cost of investments over net assets of purchased companies	$ 128,233	$ 79,774
Other intangibles	5,717	5,696
	133,950	85,470
Accumulated amortization	(13,001)	(8,510)
	120,949	76,960
Other	1,564	755
	$ 122,513	$ 77,715

Plant Assets, At Cost	19X3	19X2
Land	$ 68,617	$ 61,175
Buildings	430,834	413,074
Machinery and equipment	783,126	729,034
Projects in progress	86,086	45,452
	1,368,663	1,248,735
Accumulated depreciation	613,643	560,730
	$ 755,020	$ 688,005

Depreciation provided in costs and expenses was $75,118 in 19X3, $67,958 in 19X2 and $60,360 in 19X1. Approximately $96,000 is required to complete projects in progress at August 2, 19X3.

7.2 CAPITAL CITIES/ABC, INC.

Television program rights and amortization

Capital Cities/ABC, Inc., is a diversified communications and entertainment corporation. The Company's broadcast operations include the ABC Television Network and the Capital Cities/ABC Broadcast Group. Capital Cities purchased American Broadcasting Companies, Inc. (ABC) on January 3, 1986. Capital Cities also publishes newspapers, shopping guides, business periodicals, and distributes information from electronic data bases. Listed on the New York Stock Exchange (Ticker = CCB).

On December 15, 1980, the *Wall Street Journal* reported: "ABC is changing the method by which it accounts for prime-time programming in a way that will enhance its earnings for the fourth quarter (of 1980) and for all of next year. In effect, the company will absorb a smaller proportion of programming costs when a show is originally broadcast than previously, while a higher proportion of costs will be charged against reruns [in future years]. 'Their business had been bad lately and this is a way of enhancing earnings,' a television-industry source contends."

Study the assets section of ABC's Consolidated Balance Sheets for 1978–1980 and Note M, Program Amortization, of ABC's notes to consolidated financial statements. Net earnings (after provision for income tax expense) for 1979 and 1980 were $159,310,000 and $146,304,000, respectively.

1. Restate 1980 Net Earnings on a basis consistent with the methods used in calculating 1979 Net Earnings. Calculate the percentage change in Net Earnings from 1979 to 1980 as reported and as if consistent methods of accounting for prime-time programming costs had been used. (Ignore the fact that 1979 earnings are for 52 weeks and 1980 earnings are for 53 weeks.)

2. Assuming that a 40 percent tax rate is applicable to pretax net income, restate the current asset account balance for Television Program Rights, Production Costs, and Advances less Amortization on a basis consistent with the methods used in 1979 (i.e., assuming amortization rates for prime-time programming costs were not modified.)

3. Provide a journal entry to recognize the change in rate of amortization in the 1980 balance sheet.

4. Why would ABC's management choose to adopt this new accounting policy? Is it in the best interests of ABC's stockholders? Explain briefly.

CAPITAL CITIES/ABC, INC.
Consolidated Balance Sheets
(Dollars in thousands)

Assets	Jan. 3, 1981	Dec. 29, 1979	Dec. 30, 1978
Current assets:			
Cash	$ 26,265	$ 16,798	$ 29,989
Marketable securities (including certificates of deposit of $44,170 in 1980, $84,275 in 1979 and $150,684 in 1978), at cost, which approximates market	121,176	196,195	220,802
Receivables, less allowances of $23,829 in 1980, $22,409 in 1979 and $29,134 in 1978	297,343	271,853	231,346
Television program rights, production costs and advances less amortization (Note M)	265,656	212,161	207,402
Inventory of merchandise and supplies, at the lower of cost (principally on the first-in first-out basis) or market	21,816	21,708	18,232
Prepaid expenses	74,942	58,280	53,481
Total current assets	807,198	776,995	761,252
Property and equipment, at cost:			
Land and improvements	29,994	28,504	23,940
Buildings and improvements	199,601	150,969	119,966
Operating equipment	281,931	234,399	172,689
Leasehold and leasehold improvements	34,393	29,094	26,073
	545,919	442,966	342,668
Less accumulated depreciation and amortization	168,131	142,898	124,492
Property and equipment–net	377,788	300,068	218,176
Other assets:			
Intangibles, at cost, less amortization	77,726	80,512	57,726
Television program rights, noncurrent	88,732	58,540	19,768
Deferred charges	15,142	16,085	10,118
Other	44,290	42,125	34,100
Total other assets	225,890	197,262	121,712
Total assets	$ 1,410,876	$ 1,274,325	$ 1,101,140

Note M: Program Amortization

Based on a Company study completed in the fourth quarter of 1980 of the relationships between program revenues and costs, amortization rates for prime-time programming were modified. In order to more closely match revenues and costs for programming during prime time, amortization rates on the original broadcast were reduced and the rates on subsequent broadcasts of a program were increased. This modification of amortization rates for prime-time programming increased net earnings by $8,928,000 or $.32 per share for the year 1980.

7.3 EDUCATIONAL DEVELOPMENT CORPORATION

Development costs; capitalization and amortization

The Educational Development Corporation (EDC) is a publisher engaged in the business of developing, producing, and marketing materials and systems for use by elementary and secondary schools. Substantially all sales are made to schools, which are usually state or local government agencies. Listed on the NASDAQ stock exchange (Ticker = EDUC).

Study EDC's 19X1–19X2 Balance Sheets, 19X1–19X2 Statements of Income (Loss), and relevant portions of Notes 1 and 4 to the 19X2 financial statements in order to answer the following questions.

1. Provide journal entries to explain the increase in the account Other Assets from $33,742 in 19X1 to $398,462 in 19X2.

2. Use information in Part 1, as well as in the financial statements, to estimate approximately when in 19X1–19X2 the acquisition actually occurred.

3. Calculate 19X2 net income (loss) before provision (credit) for income taxes and extraordinary items, assuming that EDC had adopted the following accounting policies for product acquisition costs. Each case should be treated independently. Assume the accounting method for tax purposes remains unchanged as the accounting policy is changed.

   a. Amortization of product development costs is computed on a sum-of-year's-digits method using an estimated useful life of five years.

   b. Amortization of product development costs is computed on an effective-interest basis. Assume that the acquisition price of the testing program is the present value of an annuity of 40 equal quarterly installments discounted at 3 percent per quarter. Each installment is received at the end of the quarter. In other words, the economic life of the testing program is twice the period over which the program is now being depreciated.

4. Evaluate the effects on present and future reported net income of EDC's existing accounting policy with respect to product acquisition costs.

EDUCATIONAL DEVELOPMENT CORPORATION
Balance Sheets

	February 29 19X2	February 28 19X1
ASSETS		
Current assets		
Cash	$ 89,163	$ 29,427
Time certificates of deposit	950,000	1,600,000
Refundable income taxes	113,652	42,000
Accounts receivable (less allowances for doubtful accounts and returns: 19X2, $50,000; 19X1, $116,707)	937,409	973,584
Notes receivable	7,289	187,050
Inventories	1,450,349	1,041,206
Prepaid expenses	56,027	134,688
Deferred income tax benefits	243,731	14,841
Total current assets	3,847,620	4,022,796
Notes receivable	166,550	273,839
Property, plant and equipment, at cost (less accumulated depreciation: 19X2, $568,985; 19X1, $460,382)	1,002,698	962,368
Other assets (Note 4)	398,462	33,742
	$ 5,415,330	$ 5,292,745
LIABILITIES AND SHAREHOLDERS' EQUITY		
Current liabilities		
Current maturities of long-term debt	$ 34,773	$ 16,760
Accounts payable	362,372	294,799
Accrued salaries and bonuses	44,246	42,284
Accrued test scoring	352,652	305,139
Income taxes payable	219,774	131,385
Other liabilities and accruals	66,998	68,982
Total current liabilities	1,080,815	859,349
Long-term debt (less current maturities)	272,197	205,821
Shareholders' equity		
Common stock, par value of $.20 per share (authorized 3,000,000 shares; issued 2,104,120 shares)	420,824	420,824
Capital in excess of par value	4,308,321	4,308,321
Retained earnings	18,843	152,581
	4,747,988	4,881,726
Less common shares held in treasury at cost (19X2–420,422 shares, 19X1–394,970 shares)	685,670	654,151
Total shareholders' equity	4,062,318	4,227,575
	$ 5,415,330	$ 5,292,745

Certain reclassifications of the figures as of February 28, 19X1, not affecting net income, have been made to conform with the presentation for the current year.

EDUCATIONAL DEVELOPMENT CORPORATION
Statements of Income (Loss)

	Year ended	
	February 29 19X2	February 28 19X1
Revenues		
Sales and royalties	$ 4,533,855	$ 4,639,196
Interest and other income	212,984	212,839
	4,746,839	4,852,035
Costs and expenses		
Publication costs	1,672,911	1,495,987
Research and development costs	657,594	443,847
Marketing expense	2,188,610	1,882,600
General and administrative expense	490,417	429,280
Interest expense	20,045	18,120
	$5,029,577	$4,269,834
Income (Loss) before provision (credit) for income taxes and extraordinary item	(282,738)	582,201
Provision (Credit) for income taxes	(118,540)	285,000
Income (Loss) before extraordinary item	(164,198)	297,201
Extraordinary item – Realization of tax benefit not previously recorded	30,460	-
Net income (Loss)	$ (133,738)	$ 297,201
Earnings (Loss) per share		
Income (Loss) before extraordinary item	$ (0.10)	$ 0.17
Extraordinary item	.02	-
Net income (Loss)	(0.08)	0.17
Average common shares and common share equivalents outstanding	1,696,177	1,759,277

EDUCATIONAL DEVELOPMENT CORPORATION
Notes to the Financial Statements
Years Ended February 29, 19X2 and February 28, 19X1

1. Summary of Significant Accounting Policies

Product acquisition costs – Amortization is computed on the straight-line method using an estimated useful life of five years.

4. Other Assets:

Other assets at February 29, 19X2 and February 28, 19X1 consist of the following:

	19X2	19X1
Product acquisition costs (less accumulated amortization of $60,003)	$ 340,017	-
Other	58,445	33,742
	$ 398,462	$ 33,742

Product acquisition costs are outlays to acquire title to a testing program the Company has marketed in the past under an agreement with the author wherein the Company paid royalties to the author as sales were made.

7.4 LOCKHEED CORPORATION I

*Deferral of nonrecurring production costs,
recognition of expenses, and deferred revenues*

Lockheed Corporation researches, develops, and produces missiles and space satellite systems, communications and other electronic systems, high performance and cargo transport aircraft, and marine systems and information. Listed on the New York Stock Exchange (Ticker = LK).

Refer to the assets section of Lockheed's December 31, 1972 and December 30, 1973 Consolidated Balance Sheets and Statement of Earnings and Retained Earnings for fiscal 1972–1973. An excerpt from Note 2 pertaining to the TriStar is given also.

1. For each year December 31, 1972 and December 30, 1973, state how much of the cost of Inventories relate to the TriStar Jet Transport.

2. For each year December 31, 1972 and December 30, 1973, give the aggregate journal entries associated with the TriStar deliveries and the General and administrative costs. Assume General and administrative costs are paid in cash.

3. Comment on Lockheed's accounting treatment of costs and expenses associated with the TriStar program as described in Note 2 and whether this treatment is consistent with generally accepted accounting principles relating to cost recovery and expense recognition.

Based on an earlier case by Robert K. Jaedicke.

103

Lockheed Corporation
Consolidated Balance Sheet 1972–1973
(Assets Only)

	December 30 1973	December 31 1972
Current Assets		
Cash (including $7,288,000 restricted at December 30, 1973)	$ 60,664,000	$ 88,964,000
Short term securities	15,449,000	
Accounts receivable—U.S. Government	121,272,000	139,211,000
Other accounts receivable	48,755,000	35,692,000
Inventories (including TriStar Inventories of $1,160,000,000 at Dec. 30, 1973 & $959,000,000 at Dec. 31, 1972) (Note 2)	1,291,806,000	1,065,755,000
Prepaid expenses and deposits	25,257,000	31,537,000
Total current assets	1,563,203,000	1,361,159,000
Investments		
at lower of cost or estimated realizable value	1,727,000	1,447,000
Property, Plant and Equipment		
at cost, partially pledged as security for long term debt (Note 5):		
Land	29,708,000	24,918,000
Buildings, structures, and leasehold improvements	282,565,000	271,745,000
Machinery and equipment	395,558,000	364,947,000
	707,831,000	661,610,000
Less		
Accumulated depreciation and amortization	429,149,000	393,823,000
	278,682,000	267,787,000
Other Noncurrent Assets		
(net of allowance for doubtful notes receivable of $3,200,000 at December 30, 1973)	10,913,000	1,833,000
Total Assets	$ 1,854,525,000	$ 1,632,226,000

Note 2: L-1011 TriStar Program

All of the development costs and the normal production cost on the TriStar Jet Transport have been included in inventory except for General and Administrative expenses which are charged to Income in the year incurred. These G & A expenses amounted to $70 million in 1973 and $81 million in 1972. Customer advances are accounted for as liabilities until the aircraft to which they relate have been delivered. Since the cumulative development costs to date have been substantial, it is estimated that 300 aircraft will have to be delivered to make the total program profitable. Since 56 aircraft have been delivered to date (all during 1972 and 1973), the Company does not expect that a final determination of recoverability of Inventoried Cost can be made until a later date. Zero gross profit was recorded on the $730 million of sales in 1973 and $302 million of sales in 1972 (for deliveries in those years) and no gross profit will be recorded on deliveries until uncertainties are reduced. The customer advances applicable to deliveries were about $180 million for deliveries in 1973 and $90 million for 1972 deliveries.

LOCKHEED CORPORATION
CONSOLIDATED EARNINGS AND RETAINED EARNINGS 1972–1973

	DECEMBER 30 1973	DECEMBER 31 1972
Sales (Note 2)	$ 2,756,791,000	$ 2,472,732,000
less costs and expenses (Note 2)	2,674,686,000	2,404,235,000
Program profits*	82,105,000	68,497,000
add interest and other income	6,845,000	6,698,000
	88,950,000	75,195,000
less interest expense	69,329,000	47,461,000
Earnings before income taxes and extraordinary gain	19,621,000	27,734,000
less provision for income taxes	5,540,000	14,700,000
Earnings before extraordinary gain (Note 2)	14,081,000	13,034,000
Add gain on disposition of land **and** idle facilities, less applicable deferred federal income tax of $2,520,000 in 1973 and $2,930,000 in 1972	2,731,000	3,177,000
Net earnings for the year based on the assumptions of a 300 airplane TriStar program (Note 2)	$ 16,812,000	$ 16,211,000
Retained earnings at beginning of year	176,015,000	159,804,000
Retained earnings at end of year (Note 2)	$ 192,827,000	$ 176,015,000
Earnings per share of capital stock based on the assumption of a 300 airplane TriStar program:		
Earnings before extraordinary gain	$ 1.24	$ 1.15
Gain on disposition of land and idle facilities	0.24	0.28
Net earnings	$ 1.48	$ 1.43

* TriStar and Other Program profit or (loss), expressed in millions:

	1973			1972		
	TriStar	Other	Total	TriStar	Other	Total
Sales	$ 730	$ 2,027	$ 2,757	$ 302	$ 2,171	$ 2,473
Costs and expenses	800	1,875	2,675	383	2,021	2,404
Program profit (loss)	(70)	152	82	(81)	150	69

7.5 LOCKHEED CORPORATION II

Reclassification of TriStar nonrecurring production costs

Lockheed Corporation researches, develops, and produces missiles and space satellite systems, communications and other electronic systems, high performance and cargo transport aircraft, and marine systems and information. Listed on the New York Stock Exchange (Ticker = LK). This cases uses data from the Lockheed I case.

Study the assets section of the December 28, 1975 and December 29, 1974 (Reclassified) Consolidated Balance Sheet and an excerpt from Note 2 referring to the L-1011 TriStar program. The December 29, 1974 statement of assets prior to reclassification is also provided in the Consolidated Balance Sheet of 1973–1974. (The 1973 statement of assets prior to reclassification accompanies the Lockheed I case.)

Use the information referenced above to answer the following questions:

1. Provide a journal entry dated January 1974 which reflects the write-down of inventories made in the 1973–1974 Consolidated Balance Sheet regarding 1973 comparative data.

2. Provide a journal entry dated January 1975 to record the reclassification made in the 1974–1975 Balance Sheet regarding the 1974 data.

3. Give the journal entries made (a) September 30, 1975 and (b) December 28, 1975 to record the reduction in the carrying amount of "initial planning and tooling costs and of prior year's unrecovered start-up costs of delivered aircraft."

LOCKHEED CORPORATION
Consolidated Balance Sheet
ASSETS ONLY

Dollars in millions	DECEMBER 28 1975	DECEMBER 29 1974
		(Reclassified Note 2)
CURRENT ASSETS		
Cash and equivalents	$ 52.7	$ 96.8
Restricted cash	5.6	25.4
Accounts receivable	209.8	174.9
Inventories (including TriStar inventories of $204.3 at Dec. 28, 1975 and $185.3 at Dec. 29, 1974) (Note 2)	387.5	342.7
Future tax benefits (including $18.7 of deferred tax charges in 1975)	61.7	39.7
Prepaid expenses and deposits	49.1	48.4
Total current assets	766.4	727.9
PROPERTY, PLANT, AND EQUIPMENT, AT COST		
Land	29.6	29.7
Buildings, structures, and leasehold improvements	288.4	282.0
Machinery and equipment	414.6	397.4
	732.6	709.1
Less accumulated depreciation and amortization	476.6	451.2
Net property, plant, and equipment	256.0	257.9
NONCURRENT ASSETS AND DEFERRED CHARGES		
Future tax benefit, long-term portion	9.1	64.6
TriStar initial planning and tooling and unrecovered production start-up costs (Note 2)	502.5	549.8
Other noncurrent assets (net of allowance of $4.2 for doubtful notes receivable)	39.4	33.9
	$ 1,573.4	$ 1,634.1

Note 2: L-1011 TriStar program

Sales prices of TriStar aircraft and spare parts delivered during the first three quarters of 1975 exceeded their production costs by $34.8 million and, since this gross profit was not recognized in earnings, it served to reduce the carrying amount of initial planning and tooling costs and of prior years' unrecovered production start-up costs of delivered aircraft. Although management believes gross profit on future TriStar deliveries will be sufficient to recover the remainder of such costs, estimates of the extent and timing of their recovery have become less reliable because of the increased uncertainties referred to above. In recognition thereof, the Company changed its method of accounting for the TriStar, commencing with the fourth quarter of 1975, to amortize such costs to earnings ratably through 1985 ($12.5 million in the fourth quarter of 1975), so long as studies continue to indicate they are recoverable. If future assessments indicate that any such amortized costs would not be recoverable, the Company would be required to charge to earnings immediately the portion of any such costs determined to be nonrecoverable.

LOCKHEED CORPORATION
Consolidated Balance Sheet
ASSETS ONLY

Dollars in millions	DECEMBER 29 1974	DECEMBER 30 1973
		(Restated Note 2)
CURRENT ASSETS		
Cash and equivalents (including $25.4 restricted at December 29, 1974)	$ 122.2	$ 76.1
Accounts receivable—U.S. government	129.8	121.3
Other accounts receivable	45.1	48.7
Inventories (including TriStar inventories of $735.1 at December 29, 1974 and $702.8 at December 30, 1973)	892.5	834.6
Current portion of future tax benefit	39.7	
Prepaid expenses and deposits	48.4	25.3
Total current assets	$ 1,277.7	$ 1,106.0
PROPERTY, PLANT, AND EQUIPMENT, AT COST		
Land	29.7	29.7
Buildings, structures, and leasehold improvements	282.0	282.5
Machinery and equipment	397.4	395.6
	709.1	707.8
Less accumulated depreciation and amortization	451.2	429.1
Net property, plant, and equipment	257.9	278.7
FUTURE TAX BENEFIT		
Long-term portion	64.6	104.3
OTHER NONCURRENT ASSETS		
(Net of allowance of $4.2 at December 29, 1974 and $3.2 at December 30, 1973 for doubtful notes receivable)	33.9	12.6
	$ 1,634.1	$ 1,501.6

7.6 LOCKHEED CORPORATION III

Abandonment of TriStar program

Lockheed Corporation researches, develops, and produces missiles and space satellite systems, communications and other electronic systems, high performance and cargo transport aircraft, and marine systems and information. Listed on the New York Stock Exchange (Ticker = LK). The data from the Lockheed I and II cases is useful though not necessary to analyze this case.

On May 31, 1981, the *Wall Street Journal* reported that "$265 million in unamortized start-up costs remain for the program, about half the total production cost of $550 million to $560 million originally established." Also, *Business Week*, December 21, 1981, reported:

> The company's net worth, following the $400 million writeoff, now drops to only $100 million. That is relatively unimportant because it is a paper writeoff; the money was spent a decade ago. More significant is that the TriStar's death throes will cost Lockheed $200 million or more in cash over the next year or so because of low production rates.

Study Lockheed's 1979–1980 Consolidated Statement of Earnings, 1979–1980 Consolidated Balance Sheet, and the notes on the L-1011 TriStar program, inventories, deferred charges, and operating results from the 1980 statements.

Use the information referenced above to answer the following questions.

1. Assess the effect on current profits and financial position (assets only) if Lockheed were to completely abandon the L-1011 TriStar program (except for current orders that should be filled sometime in 1984). More specifically, recast the December 31, 1980 financial statements (assets only) as if the TriStar program had been terminated on that date. Assume that the amounts available as unamortized costs would have no effect on present or future tax liabilities.

2. Assume that you hold 500 shares of Lockheed's common stock. If you knew privately in early December 1981 that Lockheed was about to abandon its TriStar program, would you buy more of the stock or sell your existing holdings? Note: Such a transaction would be considered illegal if based on "insider information."

LOCKHEED CORPORATION
Consolidated Statement of Earnings

	YEAR ENDED	
Dollars in millions except per-share data	DECEMBER 28 1980	DECEMBER 30 1979
Sales	$ 5,395.7	$ 4,057.6
Costs and expenses	5,252.2	3,935.0
Program profits*	143.5	122.6
Other income (deductions)—net	(0.1)	6.6
Interest expense	(106.1)	(72.1)
Earnings from continuing operations before income taxes	37.3	57.1
Provision for income taxes	9.7	20.6
Earnings from continuing operations	27.6	36.5
Extraordinary tax benefits from carryforward of operating losses and foreign tax credits		20.0
Net earnings	27.6	56.5
Preferred stock dividend requirement and provision for redemption value	(5.2)	(5.8)
Net earnings applicable to Common Stock	22.4	50.7
Earnings per share of Common Stock:		
Primary:		
Continuing operations	$ 1.53	$ 2.16
Net earnings	1.53	3.56
Fully diluted:		
Continuing operations	1.50	2.01
Net earnings	1.50	3.22

* See note on L-1011 TriStar Program.

LOCKHEED CORPORATION: Consolidated Balance Sheet
(ASSETS ONLY)

Dollars in millions	DECEMBER 28 1980	DECEMBER 30 1979
Current assets:		
Cash	$ 44.2	$ 70.5
Accounts receivable	518.5	435.0
Inventories	1,031.6	798.5
Deferred tax charges	32.8	27.5
Prepaid expenses	55.5	71.5
Total current assets	1,682.6	1,403.0
Property, plant, and equipment, at cost:		
Land	24.7	24.6
Buildings, structures, and leasehold improvements	380.7	349.2
Machinery and equipment	639.6	533.3
	1,045.0	907.1
Less accumulated depreciation and amortization	618.4	574.7
Net property, plant, and equipment	426.6	332.4
Noncurrent assets and deferred charges:		
TriStar initial planning and tooling and unrecovered production start-up costs	280.2	335.8
Investment–Lockheed Finance Corporation	42.2	25.5
Other noncurrent assets	10.9	16.2
	333.3	377.5
	$ 2,442.5	$ 2,112.9

NOTE ON L-1011 TRISTAR PROGRAM

The Consolidated Financial Statements include significant inventories and deferred charges related to the L-1011 TriStar program as discussed below:

Inventories—L-1011 TriStar inventories are stated at the lower of the production cost of aircraft in the process of manufacture or estimated net realizable value. Estimated net realizable value is based on projections of costs to complete, selling prices, and other factors, such as production rates. Therefore, such realizable value cannot be determined with precision and is subject to revision as later information affecting such projections becomes available.

L-1011 TriStar inventories, substantially all of which are covered by firm orders, were as follows (in millions of dollars):

LOCKHEED CORPORATION: Inventories—1979–1980

Dollars in millions	DECEMBER 28 1980	DECEMBER 30 1979
Work in process	$ 736	$ 637
Materials and spare parts	168	107
Advances to subcontractors	98	71
Gross inventories	1,002	815
Less customer advances	367	327
Net inventories	$ 635	$ 488

LOCKHEED CORPORATION: Notes to the financial statements

Deferred Charges and Related Uncertainties—Deferred initial planning and tooling costs on the basic L-1011 and Dash 500 TriStar models and unrecovered production start-up costs related to the basic L-1011 TriStar model are stated at cost net of amortization. The cost is being amortized through 1985 on a straight-line basis.

Management believes that production and deliveries of L-1011 TriStars will extend at least into the late 1980s and that, based on currently projected sales and manufacturing costs, the gross profit on future L-1011 TriStar deliveries will be sufficient to recover the unamortized planning and tooling and unrecovered start-up costs as of December 28, 1980. Such recovery, however, is dependent upon the number of aircraft ultimately sold, continuity and rate of production, and actual selling prices and costs. While projected sales and manufacturing costs take into account factors such as expected sales price level increases and anticipated production costs, all such factors are subject to variations, and many of them are beyond Lockheed's control. Consequently, these factors cannot be quantified with precision, and these estimates are subject to periodic revisions. If future assessments indicate that any such unamortized costs would not be recoverable, Lockheed would be required to charge to earnings immediately any such costs determined to be unrecoverable.

Operating Results—The following summarizes L-1011 TriStar operating results, which include sales of aircraft, spare parts, and other related services, and in 1979, the sale of used aircraft (in millions of dollars):

Lockheed TriStar operating results

Dollars in millions	DECEMBER 28 1980	DECEMBER 30 1979	DECEMBER 31 1978
Net sales	$ 950.9	$ 526.3	$ 294.3
Cost of sales	1,005.3	637.0	276.7
Standby production costs			12.7
Amortization of deferred charges	55.6	54.2	50.0
Development costs	8.6	20.0	16.7
General and administrative expenses	80.8	71.4	57.0
	1,150.3	782.6	413.1
Program loss	$ (199.4)	$ (188.4)	$ (118.8)

Included in cost of sales are provisions for excess production costs, both incurred and anticipated, of $80 million in 1980 and $67 million in 1979.

8

Debt

8.1 DOW JONES & COMPANY, INC. II

Present value calculations and long-term debt

Dow Jones & Company, Inc. is a leading publisher of business news and information and community newspapers. The *Wall Street Journal*, the company's best known publication, is the largest daily newspaper in the United States, with a daily circulation of nearly 2 million copies. Listed on the New York Stock Exchange (Ticker = DJ). This case should be viewed independently of the Dow Jones & Company I case.

The following note on long-term debt states the individual amounts due, the interest rates, the timing of future repayments of principal, and other information. Use that information, together with the assumptions, to answer the questions that follow.

Note 6. Long-term debt

In thousands	19X1	19X0
Commercial paper, 9.80% at December 31, 19X1	$ 117,695	$ 271,888
Floating rate demand industrial development revenue bonds, 7.10% at December 31, 19X1, maturing 20Y2	14,500	14,500
Notes payable, 9 1/4% due November 1, 19X5	99,425	99,275
Notes payable, Associated Press, 7 3/4%	58,500	58,500
	$ 290,120	$ 444,163

Payments on long-term debt are due as follows: $30,000,000 in 19X3, $35,318,000 in 19X4, $134,743,000 in 19X5, $33,013,000 in 19X6, and $57,046,000 thereafter. On November 1, 19X0, the company sold $100 million of 9-1/4 percent notes due November 1, 19X5. The notes are general unsecured obligations of the company and may not be redeemed prior to maturity. The notes payable to Associated Press are owed by subsidiary Telerate, Inc. in equal annual payments of $5,318,000 commencing in 19X4.

1. Compute the principal repayments associated with each long-term debt amount and, for each year, reconcile those amounts with the total of the long-term debt payments.

2. Compute the interest payment associated with each long-term debt amount for each year.

3. Determine the present value of the outstanding debt obligation as of December 31, 19X1.

4. Prepare journal entries to record the bond interest amortization on the 9-1/4 percent Note payable for years 19X0 and 19X1.

   Use the following assumptions in answering the preceding questions.

   a. Principal and interest payments are made only once a year on December 31, including the payments stated as due on November 1.

   b. Long-term debt amounts are stated at face value, except for the 9-1/4 percent notes payable due November 1, 19X5, which are stated at face value less unamortized bond discount.

   c. Principal payments after 19X6 are made at December 31, 19X7. This assumption means that the present value calculation in Part 3 will be an upper bound.

   d. Investors apply a discount rate of 10 percent per annum in assessing the present value of the long-term debt of Dow Jones.

8.2 MATTEL, INC.

*Analysis of footnote on debt and market
vs. book value of debt*

Mattel manufactures and markets toys, primarily the "Barbie" fashion dolls and accessories. Mattel also produces "Hot Wheels" toy vehicles and accessories and "See and Say" preschool educational toys. Listed on the New York Stock Exchange (Ticker = MAT).

Study the note on Long-Term Liabilities and Credit Lines from the liabilities section of the 1992 Consolidated Statement of Financial Position.

1. Show that the scheduled maturities of long-term loan for the 1993 fiscal year amount to $9,643,000. Assume that the 1993 principal payment associated with the 6.75 percent note secured by land and building amounts to $76,000.

2. Given the scheduled maturities and stated interest rates, calculate the amount of interest payable each year for years 1994 through 2009. Assume that Mattel makes interest and principal payments at the end of each year; bank term loans are based on prime (assume 10 percent) plus 0.75 percent; and that principal on the 6.75 percent note secured by land and building amounts is paid in equal amounts for years 1994-1998. Except as otherwise stated in the Note on Long-term Debt, assume the amortization of principal amounts are on a straight-line basis, rather than the effective interest basis.

3. Calculate the present value of the long-term debt, using the interest and principal schedule derived in part 2 and a discount rate of 12 percent per annum.

4. Interpret (in words) the difference between your answer to part 3 and the balance sheet value of long-term debt as shown in the note. Comment about whether investors and creditors should be informed of such differences.

MATTEL, INC.
Note on Long-term debt

Long-term liabilities and credit lines

Long-term loans consist of the following:

(In thousands)	1992	1991
Bank term loans, payable fiscal 1994–2000	$ 73,400	$ 73,434
9.5% secured term loan, payable $6,667 in fiscal 1993, balance in fiscal 1994	10,000	16,667
10% Malaysian term loan secured by land and building, payable fiscal 1995 through 2001	1,964	
6.75% note secured by land and building, due through fiscal 1998	847	918
Unsecured debt of Western 9.625% notes, payable $1,300 annually through fiscal 2005, balance in 2006	18,700	20,000
9.5% notes, payable $1,400 annually fiscal 1996–2008, balance in fiscal 2009	20,000	20,000
8.625% note, payable $600 annually through fiscal 1996, balance in fiscal 1997	7,000	7,600
5.75% note, payable $1,000 in fiscal 1993	1,000	2,000
	132,911	140,619
Less: Current portion	9,643	9,638
	$ 123,268	$ 130,981

8.3 THE FIRESTONE TIRE & RUBBER COMPANY II

Contingent liabilities, actual liabilities, phasing-out operations, tire recall

The Firestone Tire & Rubber Company's principal business is the development, production, and marketing of tires for all types of vehicles both in the United States and abroad. Firestone also produces and markets thousands of other products, including rims and wheels for trucks, tractors, and earth moving equipment; synthetic and natural rubber; polyurethane foam; vinyl resins and sheeting; metal and industrial rubber products; synthetic fibers; textiles and chemicals. Prior to 1987, listed on the New York Stock Exchange (Ticker = D.FER). This case should be viewed independently of the Firestone Tire & Rubber Company I case.

Study Firestone's Statements of Income for 1978–1979; Balance Sheets for 1978–1979; Note 14, Provision for Phase-out of Facilities; Note 15, Provision for Tire Recall and Related Costs; and Note 16, Contingent Liabilities, to the 1979 financial report. The Report of Independent Certified Public Accountants is also included. Tax effects should be ignored in answering the following questions.

1. a. Provide a journal entry dated April 1978 that would record the $110 million charge against income to cover costs of terminating bias tire production in various U.S. and non–U.S. facilities.

   b. Provide a journal entry dated October 1978 that would record the $234 million charge against income representing management's estimate of the cost of fulfilling the company's obligations under the National Highway Traffic Safety Administration (NHTSA) agreement and program for cash refunds.

2. a. Provide journal entries to explain all changes in the Provision for Phase-out of Facilities account during 1979. Assume that "Amounts Charged Thereto" were paid in cash on December 31, 1979.

   b. Provide journal entries to explain all changes in the Provision for Tire Recall and Related Costs account during 1979. Assume that "Amounts Charged Thereto" were paid in cash on December 31, 1979.

3. a. Describe management's views with respect to the potential liability that may result from the litigation pending in the various state and federal courts.

b. Comment on the nature of the assurance that the independent certified public accounting firm gives stockholders and investors regarding the fairness of the financial statements.

THE FIRESTONE TIRE & RUBBER COMPANY AND CONSOLIDATED SUBSIDIARIES

Statements of Income

For the Years Ended October 31
Dollars in millions, except per share amounts

	1979	1978
Net sales	$ 5,284.2	$ 4,878.1
Cost of goods sold	4,325.1	3,958.7
Selling, administrative and general expenses	709.3	669.5
Interest and debt expense	104.1	100.6
Other income, net	(24.2)	(23.0)
Provision for phase-out of facilities (Note 14)	42.6	110.0
Provision for (credit from) tire recall and related costs (Note 15)	(46.9)	234.0
	5,110.0	5,049.8
Income (loss) before income taxes, minority interest and extraordinary credit	174.2	(171.7)
Domestic and foreign income taxes (Notes 14 and 15)	86.2	(27.2)
Minority interests in income of subsidiary companies	10.3	3.8
Income (loss before extraordinary credit)	77.7	(148.3)
Extraordinary credit – tax carryforwards	35.2	-
Net income (loss)	$ 112.9	$ (148.3)
Per share of common stock*		
Income (loss) before extraordinary credit	$ 1.35	$ (2.58)
Extraordinary credit	.61	-
Net income (loss)	$ 1.96	$ (2.58)

*Based on average number of shares outstanding during the year.

Balance Sheets

Assets (Dollars in millions)	October 31 1979	October 31 1978
Current assets		
Cash	$ 27.8	$ 26.7
Time deposits and short-term investments	63.8	130.5
	91.6	157.2
Accounts and notes receivable, less allowance for doubtful accounts: 1979–$8.8; 1978–$9.8	864.6	959.8
Raw materials and supplies	244.1	213.3
Work in process	82.6	73.2
Finished goods	527.9	531.6
	854.6	818.1
Prepaid expenses	15.0	13.0
Total current assets	1,825.8	1,948.1
Properties, plants, and equipment, at cost		
Land and improvements	127.2	122.5
Buildings and building fixtures	668.5	637.3
Machinery and equipment	2,196.2	2,077.7
	2,991.9	2,837.5
Less accumulated depreciation	1,496.1	1,392.6
	1,495.8	1,444.9
Other assets		
Investments, at cost or equity	100.1	55.2
Miscellaneous assets	23.3	25.6
Deferred charges	12.1	12.6
	135.5	93.4
Total assets	$ 3,457.1	$ 3,486.4

THE FIRESTONE TIRE & RUBBER COMPANY AND CONSOLIDATED SUBSIDIARIES

Balance Sheets

Liabilities and Stockholders' Equity (Dollars in millions)	October 31	
	1979	1978
Current liabilities		
Short-term loans	$ 216.6	$ 215.5
Accounts payable, principally trade	301.9	300.8
Accrued compensation	165.2	141.3
Domestic and foreign taxes	128.6	128.0
Accrued liability for phase-out of facilities (Note 14)	70.1	14.2
Accrued liability for tire recall and related costs (Note 15)	56.4	227.2
Long-term debt due within one year	18.0	14.2
Other accrued liabilities	129.2	114.4
Total current liabilities	1,086.0	1,155.6
Accrued liability for phase-out of facilities–non-current (Note 14)	16.2	53.4
Long-term capital lease obligations	62.9	68.0
Deferred income taxes	123.6	94.8
Minority interests in subsidiary companies	89.6	90.7
Commitments and contingent liabilities (Note 16)		
Stockholders' equity		
Serial preferred stock (cumulative), $1 par value, voting, authorized 10,000,000 shares, none issued		
Common stock, without par value, authorized 120,000,000 shares, shares issued: 1979 and 1978–60,090,127	62.6	62.6
Additional paid-in capital	194.6	194.7
Reinvested earnings	1,267.2	1,210.5
	1,524.4	1,467.8
Less common stock in treasury	58.6	60.0
Total stockholders' equity	1,465.8	1,407.8
Total liabilities and stockholders' equity	$ 3,457.1	$ 3,486.4

Notes to the Financial Statements

14. *Provision for phase-out of facilities*

In April 1978, a charge of $110 million ($73 million after income taxes) was made against income to cover costs of terminating bias passenger tire production in Akron, Ohio, and another domestic location and all tire production at plants in Calgary, Canada, and Switzerland. Costs of terminating bias passenger tire production in Los Angeles, California, announced in August, 1979, were included in the April, 1978 provision. In October, 1979, based on experience to date and anticipated future charges, the 1978 provision was reduced by $32.5 million ($19.1 million after income taxes).

In October 1979, a charge of $75.1 million ($56.0 million after income taxes) was made against income to cover costs of discontinuing certain other foreign operations, including operating losses during the phase-out period. The charge includes the disposal of Australian facilities for manufacture and sale of tires and industrial products and the discontinuation of certain production and marketing operations in Europe.

Accordingly, the amount accrued and charged to income in 1979 for phase-out of facilities, net of the reduction in the 1978 provision, was $42.6 million ($36.9 million after income taxes). The activity in the accrued liability for phase-out of facilities for 1979 and 1978, follows:

	1979	1978
Accrued liability at beginning of year	$ 67.6	$ -
Amount accrued during the year	42.6	110.0
Amounts charged thereto	(23.9)	(42.4)
Accrued liability at end of year	$ 86.3	$ 67.6

15. *Provision for tire recall and related costs*

In October, 1978, a provision for tire recall of $234.0 million ($147.4 million after income taxes) was charged against income. The provision represented management's estimate of the cost of fulfilling the Company's obligations under the agreement with the National Highway Traffic Safety Administration and the Company's program of cash refunds to those customers who had received an adjustment on tires that would otherwise have been subject to recall and free replacement.

In October, 1979, based on experience to date and anticipated future charges, the 1978 provision was reduced. Management also determined that the provision should be broadened to include $30.8 million of other related costs which were not considered for inclusion in the original provision. The net effect of the above was to reduce the provision by $46.9 million, for which no provision for income taxes was required because of the use of 1978 foreign tax credits of $20.8 million.

It should be recognized that the number of tires still to be returned and the other costs yet to be incurred may vary from management's estimates. Any additional adjustments required by such variance will be reflected in income in the future.

The activity in the accrued liability for tire recall and related costs for 1979 and 1978, follows:

	1979	1978
Accrued liability at beginning of year	$ 227.2	$ –
Amount accrued (reversed) during the year	(46.9)	234.0
Amounts charged thereto	(123.9)	(6.8)
Accrued liability at end of year	$ 56.4	$ 227.2

16. *Contingent liabilities*

Twelve purported consumer commercial class actions (one of which consolidates five previous actions) are presently pending against the Company in various state and federal courts. An additional case is pending which is not denominated as a class action but requests relief on behalf of all those similarly situated. In the purported class actions, the named plaintiffs are requesting, on behalf of claimed classes of consumers, six national in scope, five state-wide, and one city-wide, various forms of injunctive and monetary relief, including punitive damages, as a result of the Company's having manufactured and sold allegedly defective Steel Belted Radial 500 and other steel belted radial passenger tires.

The complaints in these cases define the classes of persons sought to be represented to include very broad and heterogeneous memberships with various kinds of potential claims under the National Traffic and Motor Vehicle Safety Act of 1966, the Magnuson-Moss Act, and under state warranty, consumer protection and other laws.

In all of the twelve actions the complaints pray for actual or compensatory damages such as recovery of the purchase price of the tires, or damages for injury to person or property, in amounts ranging from amounts to be determined at trial to over $2 billion. Ten of the complaints request punitive damages ranging to as much as $300 million on behalf of the class sought to be represented. Many of the complaints also include requests for equitable relief in the form of rescission of tire purchase transactions, recall and free replacement of the tires (see Note 15 for information with respect to tire recall), and other types of relief.

In addition to the class actions, there are several thousand individual claims pending against the Company for damages allegedly connected with steel belted radial passenger tires. Several hundred of these claims are the subject of pending litigation and in approximately two hundred cases the compensatory damages sought for wrongful death, personal injuries, or property damage are substantial. Punitive damages are sought in many of the cases.

The Company is also a defendant in approximately one hundred lawsuits that seek damages for personal injuries, wrongful death, or property damage arising from alleged malfunctions of multi-piece truck wheel components manufactured by the Company. Many of these cases seek substantial compensatory as well as punitive damages. Additionally, various other product liability lawsuits and other suits and claims are pending against the Company.

The Company is a defendant in a purported class action which seeks, among other things, recovery for losses by stockholders who purchased the Company's common stock between December 1975 and July 1978 by reason of the decline in market price for such stock alleged to result from the Company's alleged failure to make proper disclosure of, among other things, the steel belted radial passenger tire situation.

In March 1979, the United States brought an action seeking recovery against the Company in the amount of approximately $62 million by reason of alleged illegal gold trading activity in Switzerland.

Following a federal grand jury investigation into the Company's income taxes, the Company entered into a plea agreement in July 1979 under which the Company pleaded guilty to two counts charging the inclusion in its taxable income for 1972 and 1973 amounts that had been generated in prior years; the court imposed a total fine of ten thousand dollars on the Company by reason of its plea. A civil tax audit by the Internal Revenue Service is currently in progress covering some of the same matters investigated by the grand jury as well as other matters. The government may assess substantial tax, interest and penalties in connection with the matters under investigation.

The Securities and Exchange Commission is conducting an investigation of the adequacy of the Company's disclosures in earlier years concerning the Steel Belted Radial 500 tire, and the Company is included in an industry-wide investigation by the National Highway Traffic Safety Administration regarding truck multipiece wheels and rims.

The Company has various other contingent liabilities, some of which are for substantial amounts, arising out of suits, investigations and claims related to other aspects of the conduct of its business and based upon various legal theories.

Increased uncertainties have developed during the past year with regard to some of the contingencies identified in this note. Because of the existing uncertainties, the eventual outcome of these contingencies cannot be predicted, and the ultimate liability with respect to them cannot be reasonably estimated. Since the minimum potential liability for a substantial portion of the claims and suits described in this note cannot be reasonably estimated, no liability for them has been recorded in the financial statements. Management believes, however, that the disposition of these contingencies could well be very costly. Although the Company's management, including its General Counsel, believes it is unlikely that the ultimate outcome of these contingencies will have a material adverse effect on the Company's consolidated financial position, such a consequence is possible if substantial punitive or other damages are awarded in one or more of the cases involved.

Report of Independent Certified Public Accountants

To the Stockholders and Board of Directors,
The Firestone Tire & Rubber Company:

We have examined the balance sheets of the Firestone Tire & Rubber Company and consolidated subsidiaries at October 31, 1979 and 1978, and the related statements of income, stockholders' equity, and changes in financial position for the years then ended. Our examinations were made in accordance with generally accepted auditing standards and, accordingly, included such tests of the accounting records and such other auditing procedures as we considered necessary in the circumstances.

As set forth in Note 16 to the financial statements, the Company is a party to various legal and other actions. These actions claim substantial amounts as a result of alleged tire defects and other matters. The ultimate liability resulting from these matters cannot be reasonably estimated. In our report dated December 18, 1978, our opinion on the financial statements for the year ended October 31, 1978, was unqualified. However, due to the increased uncertainties that developed during the year ended October 31, 1979, with respect to these matters, our present opinion on the financial statements for the year ended October 31, 1978, as presented herein, is different from that expressed in our previous report.

In our opinion, subject to the effects on the financial statements of adjustments that might have been required had the outcome of the matters referred to in the preceding paragraph been known, the financial statements referred to above present fairly the financial position of The Firestone Tire & Rubber Company and consolidated subsidiaries at October 31, 1979 and 1978, and the results of their operations and the changes in their financial position for the years then ended, in conformity with generally accepted accounting principles applied on a consistent basis.

Coopers & Lybrand

Cleveland, Ohio
December 12, 1979

8.4 UNION CARBIDE CORPORATION

Disclosure of contingent liabilities

Union Carbide is one of the ten largest U.S. manufacturers and distributors of chemicals and related products with operations worldwide. Listed on the New York Stock Exchange (Ticker = UK).

On December 3, 1984, the international news media reported that a lethal cloud of methyl isocyanate had leaked from an underground storage tank at a processing plant in Bhopal, India, spreading over a 10 mile area of the sleeping city, killing over 1,750 people and injuring thousands more. The plant was owned by Union Carbide India Limited, a 50.9 percent subsidiary of the Union Carbide Corporation.

Stemming from this accident were numerous class action suits against Union Carbide and in two instances against the Chairman of the corporation alleging, among other things, personal injuries or wrongful death from exposure to the gas. In addition, several class action suits were filed on behalf of investors alleging gross negligence, waste, mismanagement, and breach of fiduciary duty. The initial aggregate amount of the claims against Carbide totaled about $50 billion, $20 billion of which was filed by the government of India.

To protect itself against claims in general for wrongful operation or accident, Union Carbide at the time had estimated worldwide insurance coverage of approximately $200 million. However, though the amount is small relative to the billion dollar claims, the question also arises as to whether the insurance coverage would be applicable to the Bhopal kinds of claims, especially if there could be shown serious misconduct on the part of Carbide's management.

1. Study the relevant excerpts from Carbide's December 31, 1984 and December 31, 1985 annual reports to stockholders and various reports in the *Wall Street Journal*. Summarize the accounting treatment of the anticipated effects of the disaster and comment whether you believe that the company's accounting and disclosure for this event is in accordance with generally accepted accounting and reporting principles. Comment also on the presentation in the 1984 auditor's report. As of the end of fiscal 1987, approximately how much had Carbide booked as expenses relating to the disaster?

2. The table below reports the volume, price, and returns for Carbide's stock, the return on the Standard & Poor's 400 industrial index, and the return on a Standard & Poor's index of U.S. chemical companies from 20 weekdays before the Bhopal disaster to 20 weekdays after. Use the stock market's immediate assessment of the effects of the tragedy to estimate what the probable economic consequences were at the time. Assess also the extent to which the disaster affected the U.S chemical industry generally. The return variables are calculated as the percentage daily change in price or level of the index. For example, the return on Union Carbide for day t = [Price (t) - Price (t-1)] ÷ Price (t-1). The "day of event" column shows the day relative to December 3, 1984. Carbide had approximately 211.4 million shares outstanding at the time of the accident (after a January 1986 three-for-one stock split). It had approximately 70.5 million shares outstanding prior to the Janaury 1986 stock split.

3. Absent FASB and SEC regulations, comment on what objectives and criteria Carbide's management should consider to determine the amount of information and disclosure to be provided by the financial reporting process.

4. Optional: Multiple regression analysis

    Estimate the following regression relation between Union Carbide's stock returns and the returns for the chemical industry and economy more generally using the daily price data given in the question:

$$R_t(\text{Carb}) = a + b_1 R_t(\text{S\&P}) + b_2 R_t(\text{Chem}) + b_3 D_{1t} + e_t$$

    where:

$R_t(\text{Carb})$ = return for day t for Union Carbide from November 5, 1984 to December 31, 1984;

$Rt(\text{S\&P})$ = return for day t for S&P 400 stock index from November 5, 1984 to December 31, 1984;

$Rt(\text{Chem})$ = return for day t for S&P chemical stock index from November 5, 1984 to December 31, 1984;

$D1t$ = dummy variable = 1 for days December 3 through 7, 1984, zero elsewhere; and

e_t = serially uncorrelated random error, assumed.

UNION CARBIDE CORPORATION
Annual Report 1984

Note 5: Extraordinary Charge Relating to Accident at Bhopal, India

As a result of the accident at the Union Carbide India Limited facility in Bhopal, India, 1984 net income included an extraordinary charge of $18 million (after applicable taxes of $14 million), or $0.25 per share. The charge covers operating, distribution, and administrative costs incurred and anticipated relating to the incident.

Note 17: Commitments and Contingencies

Numerous lawsuits have been brought against the Corporation and/or Union Carbide India Limited (UCIL), and in two instances the Chairman of the Corporation, in United States District Courts and in state courts in the United States and in Indian courts alleging, among other things, personal injuries or wrongful death from exposure to a release of gas at UCIL's Bhopal, India plant in December 1984. The Corporation owns 50.9% of the stock of UCIL. Some of these actions are purported class actions in which plaintiffs claim to represent large numbers of claimants alleged to have been killed or injured as a result of such exposure.

Generally, these actions seek compensatory and punitive damages, either in unspecified amounts or in varying amounts ranging up to billions of dollars. Certain of the actions also seek injunctive relief including, among other things, restraints on operation of the UCIL plant ...on production of certain chemicals by the Corporation.

In addition, three purported stockholder derivative actions on behalf of the Corporation, and four purported class actions on behalf of purchasers of the Corporation's securities, have been commenced in United States Courts naming the Corporation and officers and directors of the Corporation in connection with matters directly or indirectly relating to the Bhopal accident.... Among other things, the derivative actions allege gross negligence, waste, mismanagement and breach of fiduciary duties in that the individual defendants knew of, or should have known of, and failed to remedy alleged deficiencies in the plant. It is claimed that the Corporation is faced with large liabilities, as a result of which recovery is sought against the officers and directors for the benefit of the Corporation. Among other things, the class actions allege that the defendants, including the Corporation, violated Federal securities laws in that they failed to disclose the existence of alleged deficiencies at the plant and alleged business risks and potential liabilities to which the company was exposed, and that there had been a decrease in the price of the stock as a result of such alleged liabilities. Unspecified damages are sought with respect to shares purchased in the open market during various periods beginning in 1981 and 1982 and continuing into December 1984, and unspecified damages or rescission are sought with respect to shares purchased between December 13, 1981 and December 4, 1984, inclusive, under the Corporation Dividend Reinvestment and Stock Purchase Plan.

While it is impossible at this time to determine with certainty the outcome of any of the lawsuits described above, in the opinion of management, based in part on the advice of counsel, they will not have a material adverse effect on the consolidated financial position of the Corporation. In the opinion of management, based in part on the advice of counsel, no charge or accrual is required for any liabilities or any impairment of assets that may result from lawsuits described above relating to the Bhopal plant....Should any losses be sustained in connection with any of the matters referred to above, in excess of provisions therefore, they will be charged to income in the future.

REPORT OF THE INDEPENDENT CERTIFIED PUBLIC ACCOUNTANTS
MAIN HURDMAN

To the Stockholders and Board of Directors of Union Carbide Corporation

We have examined the consolidated balance sheet of Union Carbide Corporation and subsidiaries at December 31, 1984 and 1983, and the consolidated statements of income and retained earnings and of changes in financial position for the years ended December 31, 1984, 1983, and 1982. Our examinations were made in accordance with generally accepted auditing standards and, accordingly, included such tests of the accounting records and such other auditing procedures as we considered necessary in the circumstances.

Numerous lawsuits have been brought against Union Carbide Corporation and/or its 50.9% owned subsidiary, Union Carbide India Ltd. (UCIL), in connection with an escape of methyl isocyanate at UCIL's Bhopal, India plant in December 1984. These lawsuits are described in Note 17 of Notes to the financial statements.

In our opinion, the consolidated statements identified in the first paragraph present fairly the financial position of Union Carbide Corporation and subsidiaries at December 31, 1984 and 1983 and the results of operations and the changes in financial position for the years ended December 31, 1984, 1983, and 1982, in conformity with generally accepted accounting principles applied on a consistent basis.

Stamford, Connecticut   *Main Hurdman*
February 19, 1985   Certified Public Accountants

UNION CARBIDE CORPORATION
Annual Report 1985

Note 11: Other Expense (Income)

The following is an analysis of *Other expense (income):*

Millions of dollars	1985	1984	1983
Investment income	$ (42)	$ (45)	$ (35)
Foreign currency adjustments	(3)	(17)	(49)
Net discount expense of sales of customer obligations	18	23	20
Special litigation costs	185*	-	-
Costs relating to tender offer	58	-	-
Sales and disposals of businesses	(63)	(30)	(27)
Other	20	(8)	(29)
	$ 173	$ (77)	$ (120)

*Represents accruals to cover reserves for litigation contingencies, including product liability, patents, trade regulation, and the Bhopal suits.

Note 19: Commitments and Contingencies

Numerous lawsuits have been brought against the Corporation and/or Union Carbide India Limited (UCIL) (50.9 percent of the stock of which is owned by the Corporation), and in certain instances the Chairman of the Corporation of Union Carbide Eastern, Inc. (a wholly-owned subsidiary of the Corporation) in Federal and state courts in the United States and in Indian courts alleging, among other things, personal injuries, wrongful death, property damage, and economic losses from the release of gas at UCIL's Bhopal, India plant in December 1984....

While it is impossible at this time to determine with certainty the outcome of any of the lawsuits described above, management believes that adequate provisions have been made for probable losses with respect thereto and that such ultimate outcome, after provisions therefor, will not have a material adverse effect on the consolidated financial position of the Corporation. Should any losses be sustained in connection with any of the matters referred to above, in excess of provisions therefor, they will be charged to income in the future.

Wall Street Journal, November 2, 1987

Union Carbide Corp. and the Indian Government appeared near a settlement in their bitter legal wrangling over compensation of victims of the 1984 Bhopal poison gas disaster. Sources close to both sides indicated that the settlement is likely to call for Carbide to pay the victims between $500 million and $600 million. The Indian government had sued for $3 billion in compensation. Last year, Carbide offered to pay $350 million. "They can afford to weather the storm of that kind of settlement," says Fred Siemer, an analyst with Lynch, Jones & Ryan. Mr. Siemer estimates that Carbide has $200 million in insurance along with $85 million to $100 million of a $185 million charge against earnings the company took in the fourth quarter of 1985.

Wall Street Journal, January 13, 1988

Union Carbide Corp. says it plans an $85 million pretax charge against [1987] fourth quarter earnings for possible litigation costs, primarily related to the Bhopal disaster. Carbide took a litigation-contingency charge of $185 million before taxes in 1985. The company didn't disclose the after-tax or per-share effect of that charge. But the spokesman said that Carbide's 1985 tax rate was 25% and that it had 104 million shares outstanding [after a stock repurchase], indicating that the charge reduced profit $138.8 million, or $1.33 per share. The charges reflect reserves for litigation expenses but not possible damage awards.

UNION CARBIDE CORPORATION
Trading volume and share prices for period November 5 to December 31, 1984

Date	Volume of shares (presplit)	Day around event	Carbide's stock price	S&P 400 index % return	Chemical indy. index % return	Carbide's % stock return
11/5/84	136,800	-20	49.500	0.00670	0.00454	0.02062
11/6/84	154,700	-19	49.750	0.01114	0.00452	0.00505
11/7/84	231,700	-18	50.375	-0.00778	0.00340	0.01256
11/8/84	188,500	-17	51.125	-0.00263	-0.01117	0.01489
11/9/84	221,200	-16	50.875	-0.00686	-0.00394	-0.00489
11/12/84	181,400	-15	50.375	-0.00085	-0.00395	-0.00983
11/13/84	84,300	-14	50.750	-0.00878	-0.00397	0.00744
11/14/84	135,700	-13	50.750	0.00075	0.00347	0.00000
11/15/84	139,800	-12	50.250	-0.00097	-0.00921	-0.00985
11/16/84	101,500	-11	49.750	-0.01165	-0.00291	-0.00995
11/19/84	87,400	-10	49.375	-0.00586	-0.00291	-0.00754
11/20/84	158,600	-9	49.375	0.00688	-0.00292	0.00000
11/21/84	132,500	-8	50.000	0.00108	0.00352	0.01266
11/22/84	Holiday	-7				
11/23/84	68,300	-6	50.500	0.01376	0.00025	0.01000
11/26/84	75,900	-5	50.125	-0.00909	0.00025	-0.00743
11/27/84	439,700	-4	50.375	0.00469	0.00025	0.00499
11/28/84	138,700	-3	49.625	-0.00854	0.00351	-0.01489
11/29/84	178,700	-2	49.375	-0.00709	-0.01529	-0.00504
11/30/84	150,400	-1	48.875	-0.00224	-0.00599	-0.01013
12/3/84	356,000	0	46.500	-0.00448	-0.00602	-0.04859
12/4/84	2,018,000	1	45.875	0.00373	-0.00606	-0.01344
12/5/84	2,210,000	2	44.500	-0.00848	0.00362	-0.02997
12/6/84	6,686,000	3	38.750	0.00403	-0.01386	-0.12921
12/7/84	3,641,000	4	36.875	-0.00297	-0.00520	-0.04839
12/10/84	4,603,000	5	35.250	0.00331	-0.00523	-0.04407
12/11/84	2,102,000	6	35.250	0.00143	-0.00525	0.00000
12/12/84	1,738,000	7	35.375	-0.00346	0.00372	0.00355
12/13/84	1,106,000	8	37.000	-0.00611	0.00650	0.04594
12/14/84	1,788,000	9	36.250	0.00526	0.00507	-0.02027
12/17/84	1,476,400	10	34.000	0.00490	0.00504	-0.06207
12/18/84	1,537,000	11	35.750	0.02708	0.00502	0.05147
12/19/84	699,900	12	35.375	-0.00641	0.00362	-0.01049
12/20/84	1,069,700	13	36.750	-0.00419	-0.00621	0.03887
12/21/84	492,900	14	37.000	-0.00399	-0.00131	0.00680
12/24/84	460,900	15	38.125	0.00823	-0.00131	0.03041
12/25/84	Holiday	16				
12/26/84	405,700	17	37.625	-0.00167	0.00365	-0.01311
12/27/84	519,600	18	38.000	-0.00506	-0.00070	0.00997
12/28/84	258,700	19	37.375	0.00319	0.00147	-0.01645
12/31/84	492,400	20	36.750	0.00469	0.00147	-0.01672

8.5 LEISURE+TECHNOLOGY, INC.

Exchange of debentures and preference stock

Leisure+Technology is a developer of planned adult and retirement communities and has sold over 15,000 homes since it began operations in 1957. Listed as an over-the-counter security (Ticker = D.LCF).

Notes 6 and 7 below, extracted from the Company's March 31, 19X3 annual report, describe the company's exchange of convertible subordinated debentures for preference stock and convertible senior debentures. As of the end of fiscal years March 31, 19X2 and 19X3, the balances for the convertible subordinated debentures were:

	19X2	19X3
Convertible, subordinated debentures: net of unamortized discount (Notes 6 and 7)	$ 4,674,000	$ 4,785,000

1. Prepare journal entries dated March 31, 19X1 and April 15, 19X1 to record the exchange of the old (6-3/4 percent) subordinated debentures for the new (14-5/8 percent) senior debentures. The entries should include amounts to record the issuance of Class A preference stock. The unamortized discount relating to the old debentures and the cash costs of the exchange offer totaled $322,200 in fiscal 19X1 (cash paid March 31, 19X1) and $10,040 in fiscal 19X2 (cash paid April 15, 19X2).

2. Provide a journal entry (or entries) that would account for the change in the balance sheet amount of the convertible subordinated debentures from March 31, 19X1 to March 31, 19X2. Explain how the amount was derived based on the information in Note 6.

3. a. Calculate the present value at August 2, 19X1 of $1,000 of the 6-3/4 percent convertible debentures due August 1, 19X16. Assume a discount factor of 16 percent per annum and that cash interest payments only are made each August 1st and February 1st. Note that the August 2, 19X1 date is used to simplify the calculations. The actual date of issuance was March 10, 19X1. Also, for simplicity, ignore the preference stock and convertibility/redemption provisions in the present value valuation process.

b. Given the calculation in (a), or using other information in the case, comment on the likely interest rate used by investors to determine the market value per $1,000 on August 2, 19X1 of the (new) 14-5/8 percent convertible senior debenture. Ignore the preference stock and convertibility/redemption provisions in the present value valuation process.

4. Comment on the economic and accounting interpretation of the $3,163,000 extraordinary credit.

LEISURE+TECHNOLOGY, INC.
Note 6—Debenture exchange and extraordinary credit

In an Exchange Offer dated March 10, 19X1, the Company offered the exchange $600 principal of 14-5/8 percent Convertible Senior Subordinated Debentures ("New Debentures") due March 9, 19X10, plus one share of Class A Preference Stock for each $1,000 principal amount of the Company's 6-3/4 percent Subordinated Debentures ("Old Debentures") due August 1, 19X16.

During the initial period of the Exchange Offer, which ended on March 31, 19X1, $7,095,000 of the Old Debentures were tendered in exchange for $4,257,000 of the New Debentures and 7,095,000 Class A preference shares, resulting in the reduction of the principal amount of long-term obligations of $2,838,000. The New Debentures were issued at a discount of $931,000. The discount is being amortized on a straight-line basis over the term of the new debentures as additional interest. This exchange resulted in an extraordinary gain of $3,163,000 in fiscal 19X1.

The Exchange Offer was extended beyond the initial period to April 15, 19X1. During this extension, an additional $499,000 of the Old Debentures were tendered in exchange for $299,000 of the New Debentures and 499 Class A preference shares. This resulted in an extraordinary gain of $234,000 in fiscal 19X2.

The gain represents the principal amount of the Old Debentures tendered over the fair market value of the New Debentures and has been reduced by unamortized debt issuance expense relating the Old Debentures, the costs of the Exchange Offer, and the aggregate par value of the Class A preference shares issued. The Company has been advised by tax counsel that the Exchange offer should constitute a tax-free exchange. The Class A Preference Stock has a par value of $40, a liquidation value of $400, and is convertible into three shares of common stock at any time prior to December 1, 19X12.

LEISURE+TECHNOLOGY, INC.
Note 7—Convertible Subordinated Debentures

At March 31, 19X3, the Company had two issues of convertible subordinated debentures outstanding:

14-5/8 percent Convertible Senior Subordinated Debentures

The outstanding debentures at March 31, 19X3 are convertible at any time prior to maturity (March 9, 19X10) into a maximum of 628,414 common shares of the Company (conversion price of $7.25 per share). Under the indenture, the Company is not required to provide a sinking fund. The debentures may be redeemed at the option of the Company after April 1, 19X3 at prices ranging from 103 percent to 100 percent of the principal amount, together with accrued interest.

6-3/4 percent Convertible Senior Subordinated Debentures

The outstanding debentures at March 31, 19X3 are convertible at any time prior to maturity (August 1, 19X16) into a maximum of 41,792 common shares of the Company (conversion price of $24.00 per share). Under the indenture, the Company is required to provide, through a sinking fund, in each of the fiscal years 19X3 to 19X16 an amount sufficient for the full retirement of such debentures at maturity. The Company has retired or exchanged debentures in amounts necessary to satisfy the sinking fund requirements through fiscal 19X14 (refer to Note 6 for additional information with regard to the exchange of those debentures). The debentures may be redeemed at the option of the Company at any time; the current redemption price is 102.84 percent of the principal amount together with accrued interest.

A schedule of outstanding debentures at March 31 is as follows:

	19X2	19X3
Outstanding principal balance--		
14-5/8% debentures	$ 4,556,000	$ 4,556,000
6-3/4% debentures	1,003,000	1,003,000
	5,559,000	5,559,000
Less unamortized discount pertaining to the		
14-5/8% debentures	885,000	774,000
	$ 4,674,000	$ 4,785,000

THE JAMES H. MEYER CORPORATION

Bond issuance, bond redemption,
debt for equity swap, defeasance

Part A: Issuance, conversion, redemption

The Meyer Corporation sold $10 million of ten-year, 12 percent convertible bonds on September 30, Year 1, for $9,064,000 plus interest for three months. Bond issue costs of $123,400 were incurred and recorded in a separate ledger account. No value was assigned to the conversion feature. Interest is payable semiannually on June 30 and December 31. Issuance costs and bond discounts (premiums) are amortized on a straight line basis.

The bonds were callable after June 30, Year 6, and until June 30, Year 8 at $104 (per $100 face value); thereafter until maturity they were callable at $102; they were convertible into $10.00 par value common stock as follows:

1. Until June 30, Year 6, at the rate of six shares for each $1,000 bond;

2. From July 1, Year 6, to June 30, Year 9, at five shares for each $1,000 bond;

3. After June 30, Year 9, at the rate of four shares for each $1,000 bond.

The bonds, dated July 1, Year 1, mature on June 30, Year 11. Meyer prepares adjusting entries monthly and closes its books yearly on December 31. Bond discount and issue costs are amortized on a straight line basis over the life of the bond from the date of sale.

The following transactions occurred:

July 1, Year 7: $2 million of bonds converted to $10 par value common stock;

Jan 1, Year 9: $1 million of bonds acquired in the open market at 98 were extinguished; and

June 30, Year 9: The remaining $7 million of bonds were called for redemption.

In order to obtain the necessary funds for redemption and business expansion, Meyer issued $2 million of 10 percent Series A bonds and $10 million

10 percent Series B bonds; both at par or face amount. These bonds were dated and sold on May 31, Year 9, and were due on May 31, Year 29. Total bond issue costs of $140,060 were paid at the time of issuance. Prepare journal entries on

a. July 1, Year 7;

b. January 1, Year 9; and

c. June 30, Year 9.

Include supporting computations as part of the journal entry explanations.

In answering (c) make separate entries for (1) accrual of interest and related amortization of issue costs, (2) the payment of interest, (3) the redemption of $7 million of 12 percent convertible bonds, and (4) the issuance of $12 million of 10 percent series A and B bonds and payment of bond issue costs.

Part B: Debt-equity swap, defeasance

Assume that the Meyer Corporation decided to "clean up" its Year-10 balance sheet and on December 31, Year 10 completed the following transactions.

a. Debt-equity swap: Issued 40,000 shares of $10 par value stock with fair market value of $42.50 per share to the investment banking firm of Sullivan and Sullivan in a debt-equity swap. The investment banker acquired 100 percent of the Series A bonds from several institutional investors for $1,682,000 (inclusive of his fees and commissions of $150,000);

b. Defeasance: Acquired 12 percent U.S. Treasury Bills due May 31, Year 29, with interest payable December 31 and June 30, at par, and transferred (by way of defeasance) sufficient Treasury Bonds to an irrevocable trust for servicing of the Series B bonds. The present value of the trustee's fees during the remaining period of the Series B bonds was estimated to be $300,000. The trust is able to borrow short term at 12 percent if necessary.

1. Prepare journal entries in Meyer's books to record the debt-equity swap and the defeasance transactions. Assume both occurred on December 31, Year 10.

2. What does Meyer Corporation probably mean by the phrase "cleaning up its balance sheet," and how might the firm benefit economically by this series of actions? Based on the financial effects of the journal entries in (1), comment on differences between a debt-equity swap and a defeasance transaction.

9

Income Taxes

9.1 MOORE MCCORMACK RESOURCES

Income taxes and investment tax credits

Moore McCormack Resources is a natural resources company, involved in exploration, production, and transportation. The company's primary markets are the construction, energy, and steel industries. Listed on the New York Stock Exchange (Ticker = D.MIF).

Attached are the company's 1981–1982 Consolidated Statement of Income, liabilities section of the balance sheet, and Notes 5 and 6 on income taxes and the sale of tax benefits, respectively.

1. Identify the following:

   a. Method of accounting for timing differences in income taxes.

   b. Method of accounting for the investment tax credits claimed as reductions in taxes currently payable.

   c. Amount of 1982 taxes currently payable or refund due.

   d. Amount of 1982 tax expense (credit) subtracted (added) in deriving Net Income of $6,648,000.

   e. Cumulative impact (on retained earnings) as of December 31, 1982 of switching from the deferral method of accounting for income taxes to the flow-through method of accounting for income taxes.

   f. Amount by which 1982 net income after taxes increased (decreased) as a result of the sale of tax benefits in accordance with the Economic Recovery Tax Act of 1981. (Ignore any impact on discontinued operations.)

2. a. Provide a journal entry to record the $29,811,000 amount shown in Note 5. Assume that the amount relates *only* to unutilized investment tax credits.

   b. Had Moore McCormack not been allowed to make the journal entry in 2a (and assuming that the amount relates solely to unutilized investment tax credits), restate 1982 net income after taxes.

   c. Justify the entry in 2a in both accounting and economic terms.

MOORE MCCORMACK RESOURCES
Consolidated Statement of Income

For the years ended December 31,	1982	1981
Sales and revenues	$ 405,064,000	$ 552,462,000
Costs and expenses	(316,615,000)	(422,049,000)
Administrative, general and selling expenses	(46,189,000)	(43,400,000)
Interest income	3,907,000	7,955,000
Interest expense	(42,461,000)	(38,225,000)
Income from continuing operations before income taxes	3,706,000	56,743,000
Income taxes	4,119,000	(20,248,000)
Income from continuing operations	7,825,000	36,495,000
Discontinued operations		
Income from discontinued operations, net of income taxes	1,542,000	14,898,000
Loss on disposal of discontinued operations, net of income taxes	(2,719,000)	-
Net income	$ 6,648,000	$ 51,393,000

For the years ended December 31,	1982	1981
LIABILITIES:		
Current liabilities		
Accounts payable	$ 34,041,000	$ 52,315,000
Accrued liabilities	36,475,000	34,031,000
Long-term debt due within one year	7,443,000	3,410,000
Income taxes payable	1,012,000	3,718,000
	78,971,000	93,474,000
Deferred income taxes	93,632,000	90,908,000
Other liabilities	$ 6,801,000	$ 7,198,000

5. Income Taxes
(Dollars in thousands)

For the years ended December 31,	1982	1981	1980
Continuing operations			
Currently receivable	$ (6,347)	$ (154)	$ (6,758)
Deferred:			
Capitalized interest and development costs	16,938	10,548	11,398
Excess of tax over book depreciation	8,623	5,303	5,813
Sale of tax benefits (Note 6)	5,994	8,938	-
Unutilized investment credit and tax losses	(29,811)	(2,553)	2,656
Other, net	484	(1,834)	480
Total deferred	2,228	20,402	20,347
Total tax provision (credit), continuing operations	(4,119)	20,248	13,589
Discontinued operations			
Currently payable	5,862	4,773	10,686
Deferred	1,434	879	(1,610)
Loss on disposal: Deferred	(1,798)	-	-
Total tax provision	$ 1,379	$ 25,900	$ 22,665

6. Sale of Tax Benefits

In 1982 and 1981, the company sold tax benefits (investment tax credits and depreciation deductions) under the leasing provisions of the Economic Recovery Tax Act of 1981. The effect of these transactions was to increase net income by $2,037,000 (net sales proceeds of $13,031,000, less income taxes of $10,994,000, including $5,000,000 reduction of investment credits) in 1982, and by $5,500,000 (net sales proceeds of $19,430,000, less income taxes of $13,930,000, including $5,000,000 recapture of investment credits) in 1981. The company also sold tax benefits on cargo liners in 1982 which are included in *Discontinued operations*.

9.2 WESTINGHOUSE ELECTRIC CORPORATION II

Income tax effects of gains and losses,
impact on earnings per share, Treasury stock

Westinghouse Corporation sells and services electronic equipment and components for the generation, transmission, distribution, utilization, and control of electricity. The company also operates broadcasting and cable television stations, develops land, distributes beverage products, and operates transport refrigeration. Listed on the New York Stock Exchange (Ticker = WX). This case should be viewed independently of the Westinghouse Electric Corporation I case.

In its December 31, 19X2 annual report, Westinghouse reported a "healthy" 26 percent increase in earnings per share from $3.52 in 19X1 to $4.42 in 19X2. Although the company's stock price rose steadily during 19X2 and responded favorably to the 19X2 earnings announcement, a major shareholder/investor asks you to comment on the impact of several items which might have been glossed over by the financial marketplace. The shareholder gives you the following excerpts from the company's financial statements and footnotes.

1. Refer to the information on income taxes (Note 3), acquisition, divestitures, and business restructuring (Note 17), and liabilities (Notes 11 and 13).

   a. Provide a journal entry dated June 19X2 to record the pretax effects of the major business restructuring.

   b. Provide a journal entry dated June 19X2 to record the deferred tax consequences of the major business restructuring. Provide a rationale for the accounting treatment of the deferred taxes associated with the restructuring.

2. State which method (or methods) of accounting the company uses to account for investment tax credits, and use the information in Note 3 on income taxes to provide journal entries dated December 31, 19X2 to record the following.

   a. Investment tax credit amounts of $23.1 million credited to 19X2 income tax expense.

   b. Investment tax credits deferred at the end of fiscal year 19X2 of $54 million. Assume these credits relate to assets purchased on the last day of 19X2.

3. Refer to Note 17 on acquisition, divestitures, and business restructuring.

   a. Provide a journal entry to record the cash received and the pretax gain associated with the 19X2 sale of the Group W Cable Company.

   b. Comment on whether the financial information presented suggests that the company actually paid or expects to pay taxes on the pretax gain associated with the sale. Discuss the possible interaction between the accounting and reporting effects of the business restructuring and the gain on sale. A precise, numerical answer is not possible.

4. Refer to the information on Average Shares of Common Stock and Treasury Stock activity in Note 14. Estimate how much (in dollars and cents) of the increase in primary earnings per share was the result of shares purchased by the company under its stock repurchase program. In other words, estimate what would have been the change in fiscal 19X2 primary earnings per share had no treasury shares been purchased under the stock repurchase program) during fiscal 19X2. Assume that all Treasury stock activity for 19X2 took place on January 1, 19X2.

WESTINGHOUSE ELECTRIC CORPORATION
NOTE 3: INCOME TAXES

Income taxes

(In millions)	19X2	19X1	19X0
Current:			
Federal	$ 100.7	$ 54.3	$ (16.0)
State	45.5	32.7	13.3
Foreign	47.4	44.9	42.6
Deferred:			
Federal	(34.3)	51.2	73.9
State	(17.7)	-	4.3
Foreign	(12.6)	5.5	4.5
Income taxes	$ 129.0	$ 188.6	$ 122.6

Under the Tax Reform Act, investment tax credit was repealed retroactive to January 1, 19X2, except for investment tax credit on certain property under a contract that was binding on December 31, 19X1. Income tax expense for financial reporting was reduced by investment tax credits of $23.1 million in 19X2, $48.0 million in 19X1, and $45.7 million in 19X0. In addition, investment tax credits of $54 million were deferred at the end of 19X2 by the financial service subsidiary and remain to be amortized.

Deferred taxes result from timing differences in the recognition of revenue and expense for tax and financial statement purposes. The sources of these differences and the tax effect of each are shown in the following table.

Westinghouse Electric Corporation
INCOME TAXES DEFERRED

(In millions)	19X2	19X1	19X0
Investment and research tax credits	$ 145.0	$ 11.5	$ (50.5)
Leasing transactions	65.5	49.3	35.9
Depreciation	59.1	101.1	77.0
Disposal of asset previously written down	29.3	-	-
Inventory valuation methods	12.6	2.1	16.7
Sale-leaseback of facilities	0.2	(18.7)	
Provision for estimated credit losses	(18.9)	-	-
Long-term contracts in process	(25.1)	0.2	4.0
Pension deduction less than pension expense	(40.8)	-	(18.7)
Major business restructuring program	(225.8)	-	-
Federal tax on undistributed earnings		(26.9)	(2.2)
Miscellaneous	(65.7)	(61.9)	20.5
Income taxes deferred	$ (64.6)	$ 56.7	$ 82.7

NOTE 11: OTHER CURRENT LIABILITIES

	19X2	19X1	19X0

Other current liabilities (In millions)

	19X2	19X1	19X0
Major business restructuring program	$ 343.8	-	-

NOTE 13: OTHER NONCURRENT LIABILITIES

	19X2	19X1	19X0

Other noncurrent liabilities (In millions)

	19X2	19X1	19X0
Major business restructuring program	$ 140.5	-	-

NOTE 14: COMMON AND PREFERRED STOCK

The following average shares were used for the computation of primary and fully diluted earnings per share,

	19X2	19X1	19X0
Primary	152,331,187	172,488,375	177,301,873
Fully diluted	157,325,433	179,157,479	180,085,369

In 19X0 the Company initiated a common stock repurchase program under which 25 million shares were purchased at an average price of $43.15 per share. Upon this program's completion in July 19X2, another stock repurchase program was initiated, and an additional 10 million shares were purchased at an average price of $56.60 per share.

	19X2	19X1	19X0
Shares in treasury at January 1	26,841,833	5,648,587	5,131,430
Shares purchased under stock repurchase programs	13,555,700	21,444,300	-
Other shares purchased	1,301,300	1,888,000	2,009,966
Shares issued	(1,050,806)	(2,139,054)	(1,492,809)
Shares in treasury at December 31	40,648,027	26,841,833	5,648,587

NOTE 17: ACQUISITION, DIVESTITURES, AND BUSINESS RESTRUCTURING

In June 19X2, the Corporation completed the sale of the stock of its Cable W Group subsidiary to a consortium of cable television operators for cash proceeds of approximately $1.7 billion and realized a pretax gain of $651.2 million. The transaction included all of the Corporation's remaining cable television properties except for its interest in a limited partnership which operates two franchises in Chicago.

Also in June 19X2, a provision totaling $790 million was recorded to provide for all the costs and expenses associated with the Corporation's major business restructuring program and for certain other unusual items. The restructuring program consists primarily of product-line relocations, the closedown or sale of certain businesses and facilities, and the writedown of inventories, fixed assets, goodwill and other assets to recognize the impairment of value resulting from the restructuring activities. As of December 31, 19X2, asset writedowns and other charges to the restructuring liability totaled $306 million. The after-tax impact of the gain from the sale of Cable W Group offset the after-tax impact of the provision for restructuring because of the different income tax rates associated with these transactions.

9.3 POTLATCH CORPORATION

Impact of interest on net earnings;
income tax accounting

Potlatch is an integrated forest products company with more than 1 million acres of timberland in Arkansas, Idaho, and Minnesota. Facilities convert wood fiber into two main lines of products: solid wood items (lumber plywood, oriented strand board, particleboard, and wood specialties) and bleached fiber products (bleached kraft pulp and paperboard, printing and business papers, packaging, and household tissue products). Listed on the New York Stock Exchange (Ticker = PCH).

On February 10, 1982, the *Wall Street Journal* reported:

> For much of what good news is found in some companies' fourth quarter annual reports, the credit goes to the sale of tax credits. Potlatch Corp., for example, reported a 114% surge in quarterly net to $30.6 million from $14.2 million a year earlier. Included in the latest figure was a $19.2 million gain on tax credit sales. Without that gain, profit of the forest products company would have dropped 20%.

Study Potlatch's Note 6 on taxes, Note 14 on capitalization of interest, and its 1979–1981 Statements of Earnings and Retained Earnings. Analyze Potlatch's earnings trend from 1979 to 1981, paying particular attention to the effects of accounting rules for reporting (1) income tax payments and related benefits and (2) interest expense. Are the income statements comparative? Did Potlatch really enjoy an increase in earnings in 1981?

148

POTLATCH CORPORATION
SUMMARY OF PRINCIPAL ACCOUNTING POLICIES
(Dollars in thousands–except per-share amounts)

Note 6: Taxes on Income

The company's federal income tax returns have been examined for all years through 1976. Certain assessments including interest have been paid for 1971 and 1972. During 1980, these assessments were successfully litigated; however, the court's decision has been appealed by the government. The amounts paid are included in "Receivables." Settlements have been reached for the years 1973 through 1976. At December 31, 1981, the company had investment tax and other credit carryforwards of approximately $8,800 (expiring in 1996) available as credits against future federal income taxes. There are no available credit carryforwards for financial statement purposes at December 31, 1981.

The provision for taxes on income is divided between current and deferred portions as follows:

December 31	1981	1980	1979
Current federal income tax	$ –	$ (6,762)	$ 11,028
Current state income tax	499	1,997	5,256
Total current	499	(4,765)	16,284
Deferred income tax on:			
Difference in timber market values over cost, included in inventories	(797)	799	(546)
Difference between tax and financial depreciation	13,882	13,112	10,045
Difference between tax and financial accounting for insurance	(913)	331	(1,617)
Difference between tax and financial accounting for capitalized interest	7,762	4,973	–
Difference between tax and financial accounting for sale of depreciation tax benefits	14,491	–	–
All other timing differences	(1,278)	(2,082)	(1,319)
Net earnings	$ 33,646	$ 12,368	$ 22,847

The 1981 provision for taxes on income represents an effective rate of 36.8 percent (20.2 percent in 1980 and 24.3 percent in 1979) of financial income before taxes, and is less than the amount which would normally be expected by applying the statutory federal income tax rate of 46 percent to such income. The reasons for the difference are as follows:

December 31	1981	1980	1979
Computed "expected" tax expense	$ 42,067	$ 28,673	$ 43,165
Benefits from income taxed as capital gains	–	–	(10,580)
Investment tax credit	(7,910)	(8,267)	(13,814)
Energy tax credit	(2,117)	(3,142)	(2,061)
State and local taxes, net of federal income tax benefit	269	1,134	2,862
Reversal of prior year's overaccruals of federal income taxes	–	(6,000)	–
All other items	1,337	(30)	3,275
Provision for taxes on income	$ 33,646	$ 12,368	$ 22,847

Deferred income taxes of $102,686 and $69,854 at December 31, 1981 and 1980, respectively, resulted principally from deducting depreciation allowances for federal tax purposes in amounts greater than the allowances determined using the straight-line method for financial reporting purposes. Depreciation for tax purposes reflects use of Internal Revenue Service guidelines and permissible accelerated depreciation of certain assets. Included in the balance sheet caption "Prepaid expenses" are the tax effects of other timing differences in the amount of $10,587 and $10,827 at December 31, 1981 and 1980, respectively.

Note 14: Capitalization of Interest

Effective January 1, 1980, the company changed its method of accounting for interest costs to comply with Financial Accounting Standards Board Statement No. 34, "Capitalization of Interest Cost," which requires the capitalization of interest on certain assets during construction. The company previously followed the policy of expensing such interest costs as incurred.

Interest expense for the years ended December 31, 1981 and 1980, does not include $17,307 and $10,850, respectively, of interest charges which have been capitalized. Interest expense for 1979 has not been restated as the Statement does not require retroactive application.

POTLATCH CORPORATION
STATEMENTS OF EARNINGS AND RETAINED EARNINGS
(Dollars in thousands–except per-share amounts)

Earnings:

Years Ended December 31	1981	1980	1979
Net sales	$ 880,493	$ 818,301	$ 808,213
Costs and expenses:			
Depreciation, amortization and cost of fee timber harvested	54,640	44,984	40,454
Materials, labor and other operating expenses	700,389	652,784	611,415
Selling, administrative and general expenses	52,315	54,276	52,501
	807,344	752,044	704,370
Earnings from operations	73,149	66,257	103,843
Interest expense (Note 14)	(19,100)	(17,756)	(22,348)
Interest income	4,688	7,743	12,631
Other income (expense), net	32,713	4,875	(268)
Earnings before taxes on income	91,450	61,119	93,858
Provision for taxes on income (Note 6)	33,646	12,368	(22,847)
Net earnings	$ 57,804	$ 48,751	$ 71,011

	1981	1980	1979
Net earnings per common share	$ 3.25	$ 3.21	$ 4.69

Retained Earnings:

Years Ended December 31	1981	1980	1979
Balance at beginning of year	$ 411,479	$ 383,074	$ 330,248
Net earnings	57,804	48,751	71,011
Dividends:			
Common ($1.42 per share in 1981; $1.34 per share in 1980; $1.20 per share in 1979)	(21,690)	(20,346)	(18,185)
Preferred ($12.375 per share)	(8,223)	–	–
Balance at end of year	$ 439,370	$ 411,479	$ 383,074

9.4 BOISE CASCADE CORPORATION

*Measurement and disclosure of proceeds
from sale of depreciation tax benefits*

Boise Cascade is an integrated forests products company engaged principally in the manufacture, distribution, and sale of paper, packaging and office products, wood products, and building materials. In addition, the company has one of the industry's more extensive timber bases on which it grows and harvests timber to support these operations. Its timberlands and manufacturing facilities are located primarily in the United States and Canada. Listed on the New York Stock Exchange (Ticker = BCC).

Study the excerpts from Notes 1 and 2 to the 1981 financial statements of the Boise Cascade Corporation.

1. Provide a journal entry to record Boise's sale of depreciation tax benefits for approximately $60 million. Distinguish between the before-tax and after-tax effects of this transaction. Approximately how much tax is owing by Boise as a result of this $60 million transaction?

2. a. How much 1981 federal U.S. income tax is Boise likely to pay in 1982? State this amount as a percentage of Boise's domestic (U.S.) 1981 earnings before tax of $92,160,000. Foreign pretax earnings for 1981 were $92,580,000.

   b. Would this percentage alter significantly in future years if Boise could no longer sell its depreciation tax benefits to other companies? Explain.

3. a. What would you expect to be the stock market's reaction to the disclosure of the sale of depreciation tax benefits by Boise?

   b. As a financial vice-president of Boise, what strategy for reporting the effects of tax benefit sales would be in the best interest of Boise's stockholders?

1. Summary of Significant Accounting Policies

   Other Income. "Other income, net" in the Statements of Income includes the sale of depreciation tax benefits, foreign exchange gains and losses, interest income, equity in earnings of joint ventures, gains and losses on the sale of property and other miscellaneous income and expense items.

   Sale of Tax Benefits. Following the passage of the Economic Recovery Tax Act of 1981, the Company sold certain depreciation tax benefits for approximately $60,000,000. In accordance with the tentative decision of the Financial Accounting Standards Board, referenced in its recent announcement, the net proceeds of $31,100,000 after taxes, or $1.17 per common share, were included in income.

2. Income Taxes

   The Company provides income taxes for all items included in the Statements of Income, regardless of when such items are reported for tax purposes and when the taxes are actually paid. Investment tax credits are recognized currently as a reduction of income tax expense. Approximately $67,115,000 of investment tax credits recognized in current and prior years is available to reduce income taxes expected to be paid in future years. The Company expects to utilize these credits prior to their statutory expiration. The Company uses the progress expenditure method for taking investment tax credits on projects which will be under construction for more than two years.

Income tax expense includes the following: (In thousands)	Year Ended December 31		
	1981	1980	1979
Current income taxes			
Federal	$ 3,552	$ 5,740	$ 22,764
State	4,101	7,480	8,116
Foreign	35,710	26,800	1,413
	43,363	40,020	32,293
Deferred income taxes			
Federal	11,542	(27,599)	10,182
State	3,072	1,107	2,582
Foreign	6,683	11,632	2,043
	21,297	(14,860)	14,807
Total income tax expense	$ 64,660	$ 25,160	$ 47,100

A reconciliation of the theoretical tax expense. Assuming all income had been taxed at the statutory U.S. Federal income tax rate, and the Company's actual tax expense is as follows:

| | Years Ended December 31 | | | | | |
| | 1981 | | 1980 | | 1979 | |
	Amount	Percentage of Pretax Income	Amount	Percentage of Pretax Income	Amount	Percentage of Pretax Income
(In thousands, except percentages)						
Theoretical tax expense	$ 84,980	46.0%	$ 73,876	46.0%	$101,738	46.0%
Resulting from Increases (decreases) in taxes						
Income taxed at the capital gains rate	(24,273)	(13.1)	(23,725)	(14.8)	(22,568)	(10.2)
U.S. investment tax credits	(19,420)	(10.5)	(44,339)	(27.6)	(38,519)	(17.4)
Tax on foreign dividends, net of foreign tax credits	10,761	5.8	10,460	6.5	1,242	.6
Foreign income taxed at less than theoretical tax rate	(1,571)	(.9)	(2,470)	(1.5)	(3,077)	(1.4)
State tax	3,874	2.1	4,640	2.9	5,777	2.6
Minimum tax on preference items	4,403	2.4	4,755	3.0	1,889	.8
Other	5,906	3.2	1,963	1.2	618	.3
Actual tax expense	$ 64,660	35.0%	$ 25,160	15.7%	$ 47,100	21.3%

The deferred income tax provision (benefit) results from timing differences in recognition of revenue and expense for tax and financial reporting purposes. The nature of these differences and the tax effect of each are as follows:

| | Year Ended December 31 | | |
Income tax expense includes the following:	1981	1980	1979
(In thousands)			
Sale of depreciation tax benefits (Note 1)	$ 28,906	$ -	$ -
Investment tax credits carried forward	(15,626)	(28,334)	(14,797)
Deferred expense, net of amortization	15,128	8,573	8,310
Book depreciation less than tax depreciation	8,066	19,024	24,672
Provision for pensions not funded	(4,619)	(16,866)	-
Foreign exchange loss	(4,249)	-	-
Decrease (increase) in tax basis of inventories resulting from timber capital gains	(1,093)	202	53
Other	(5,216)	2,541	(3,431)
Deferred income tax provision (benefit)	$ 21,297	$ (14,860)	$ 14,807

9.5   SOFTDRINKCO, INC.

Accounting for the purchase of tax benefits

This case covers the accounting entries for a purchase of tax benefits through an asset purchase and leaseback transaction. Under such a transaction, SoftdrinkCo purchases the tax-advantaged assets for a price that includes the purchased future tax benefits. SoftdrinkCo then leases the asset back to the seller. The transaction is arranged such that SoftdrinkCo's lease income receipts are equal to the payments to be made on the money borrowed to finance the asset purchase. The purchased benefits are recorded initially as assets by SoftdrinkCo and subsequently amortized as the tax benefits are realized by the company. The value of the tax benefits is derived as a present value analysis of the future tax benefits. Numerous assumptions are specified below.

Use the information below, which has been excerpted from SoftdrinkCo's 19X1 annual financial statements, to answer the following questions.

1. Assume that the leases discussed in Notes 1 and 6 are signed on December 31, 19X1. Determine the purchase price of the equipment for tax purposes assuming: (a) a 10 percent tax credit is available, (b) SoftdrinkCo's tax rate is a flat 40 percent, (c) a 15 percent first-year ACRS (accelerated cost recovery system) depreciation tax benefit is available, and (d) the first year tax benefit is equal to the sum of "realized benefit on investment in tax leases" (Statement of Cash Flows) and "income tax refund due in 19X2" (Note 6).

2. What journal entries did SoftdrinkCo make on December 31, 19X1 relating to tax leases? Assume all tax leases were signed on that date.

3. Assuming the 19X2 refund referred to in Note 6 takes place on January 1, 19X2, what is the required journal entry for that refund?

4. Verify that SoftdrinkCo expects additional tax benefits in 19X2 of $87,951,000.

5. Assume the following: that (a) the second-year depreciation is available to SoftdrinkCo equal to 22 percent of the purchase price of equipment under tax leases; (b) the lease is for a single piece of equipment; (c) the rental payments and loan payments are equal to each other and are made annually

---

Based on materials provided by Mark A. Wolfson.

on December 31st; and (d) the "loan" amount is the difference between the purchase price of the equipment and the tax benefits purchased. Given the expected new 19X2 tax benefit of $87,951,000, and assuming a 20 percent discount rate, what is the approximate term (length) of the lease between SoftdrinkCo and the seller of the tax benefits?

6. Assume that all the tax benefits are realized on December 31 each year, except for the first year when $75,986,000 was realized on December 31, 19X1 and $149,712,000 was realized on January 1, 19X2. Assume ACRS depreciation for years 3-5 is 21 percent per annum. Calculate the present value of the tax benefits to SoftdrinkCo at the date the contract is signed, assuming a 20 percent discount rate and a 40 percent tax rate. Use the following format for a schedule of the various payments, benefits, and other calculations.

End of period	Depre- ciation	% Interest rate	Interest on loan	Principal outstanding	Income from lease	P. V. of loan	Inv. tax credit	Tax deduction	Tax benefit of deductions	P. V. of benefits
1	2	3	4	5	6	7	8	9	10	11

The columns are:

1. December 31 or (date derived in part 5)
2. Depreciation on the asset subject to the sale and leaseback transaction
3. Interest rate applied to ACRS depreciation on asset
4. Interest expense on loan
5. Remaining principle on loan
6. Rental income from leasing of the asset
7. Present value of loan
8. Investment tax credit (first year only)
9. Tax deduction (depreciation + interest - lease rental income)
10. Total tax benefit, including investment tax credit
11. Present value of total tax benefits.

SOFTDRINKCO., INC.

Note 1: Explanation of tax leases:

The investment in tax leases represents the unamortized cost of tax leases purchased under the safe harbor leasing provisions of the Economic Recovery Tax Act of 1981. The investment is reduced as tax credits and tax savings from accelerated depreciation deductions equal to the purchase cost are realized. These tax benefits are not included in SoftdrinkCo's tax provision (see Note 6). The remaining unamortized cost is amortized by an interest method over the periods during which the company has the use of the additional temporary tax savings. The income accrued effectively offsets the incremental interest costs incurred in connection with the funding of the initial investment and results in no effect on net income in 19X1.

Note 6: Income tax expense:

(Dollars in thousands)	19X1	19X0
Current provision: U.S.	$ 147,403	$ 132,947
Current provision: Foreign	41,224	45,334
Deferred income taxes	22,400	22,800
Total provision	$ 211,027	$ 201,081

The provision for U.S. income taxes *excludes* tax benefits in 19X1 of $225,698,000 from tax lease transactions (see Note 1). Of this amount, $149,712,000 represents an income tax refund in 19X2, which is included in Current Portion of Investment in Tax Leases.

Selected information from December 31 financial statements:

(Dollars in thousands)	19X1	19X0
Balance Sheet		
CURRENT ASSETS		
Current portion of investment in tax leases	$ 237,663	0
LONG TERM RECEIVABLES AND INVESTMENTS		
Investment in tax leases	53,630	0
Statement of Cash Flows		
FINANCIAL RESOURCES PROVIDED		
Realized benefit on investment in tax leases	$ 75,986	0
FINANCIAL RESOURCES APPLIED		
Investment in tax leases	367,279	0

9.6 CITICORP

Allowance for loan losses and tax benefits

Citicorp is the largest money center bank in the United States. In 1988, the bank had a U.S. network of over 700 bank offices in 37 states and served more than 18.5 million U.S. households and businesses. The bank also conducts extensive banking business in 39 foreign countries. Listed on the New York Stock Exchange (Ticker = CCI).

In recent years—notably 1987—many of the larger money center banks suffered unusually large losses primarily due to nonperforming loans to Latin American and other countries. Prior to the Tax Reform Act of 1986, banks could compute their bad debt deductions for tax purposes based on a reasonable addition to the loan loss reserve account to provide for the possibility that some loans might become uncollectable (called the reserve method). Since cumulative estimated loan losses generally ran ahead of cumulative actual loan writeoffs, banks were able to defer the payment of taxes on income. For example, Citicorp's Consolidated Statements of Operations for fiscal years 1988 and 1987 report expense amounts for the Provision for Credit Losses of $1,330 and $4,410 million, respectively. These amounts also represent increases in the loan loss allowance account in the Consolidated Balance Sheet to estimate future possible credit losses on outstanding loans at balance sheet date. The December 31, 1988 and 1987 balances in the loan loss allowance account were $3,248 and $3,528 million, respectively.

The Tax Reform Act of 1986 set forth provisions designed to phase out the reserve method of calculating bad debt deductions beginning in January 1987. This meant that future tax deferrals due to the reserve method would not be forthcoming. Also, for large banks such as Citicorp, the Tax Reform Act of 1986 ruled that the prior tax benefits of the reserve method taken in 1986 and earlier would be subject to recapture. Thus, large banks would potentially be required to pay back the prior benefits. (The Act specified schedules that would recapture the benefits over years 1987–1990.) However, the Act also specified that large banks (e.g., Citicorp) that would otherwise be subject to a recapture of the tax benefits may elect to suspend recapture during any recapture year if it qualified as a troubled bank. A bank was considered "troubled" if the ratio of nonperforming loans to equity capital exceeded a certain percentage.

The overall result, then, is that the tax benefits of the 1987 and later loan loss transactions (mostly future benefits) are limited to the extent that they can be recognized in the financial statements. However, if recognizable in the future, then such unrecognized tax benefits should be disclosed since the recognition of such benefits reduces future tax expense, thus increasing future reported net income.

This case attempts to reconstruct the accounting treatment and certain tax effects of Citicorp's 1987 and 1988 additions to the allowance for loan losses account. Particular attention is paid to the treatment of recognized and unrecognized tax benefits for financial reporting purposes. Relevant excerpts from the 1988 and 1987 financial statements are provided.

1. Provide two entries dated December 31, 1988 and 1987, respectively, to record the increases in the Allowance for possible credit losses. Assume that all entries to that account are recorded at the end of the year. Ignore any tax effects.

2. a. Calculate the maximum recognizable tax benefit (deferral) in each year that such *increases* in the allowance account would have generated for Citicorp had the Tax Reform Act of 1986 *not* phased out the reserve method of calculating tax deductions for bad debts after 1986. Use a tax rate of 34% and 40% for 1988 and 1987, respectively, and round numbers to the nearest million.

   b. Use the management discussion on income taxes from the 1988 annual report and Note 15 from the 1987 financial statements to determine how much of the 1987 tax benefits calculated in 2a appear to have been recognized in the determination of 1987 reported income as a result of the 1987 Provision for credit losses. If necessary, assume that benefits recognized for reporting purposes are also recognized for tax purposes.

   c. Use the management discussion on income taxes from the 1988 annual report and Note 15 from the 1988 financial statements to determine how much of the 1988 maximum tax benefits calculated in 2a appear to have been recognized in the determination of 1988 reported income as a result of the credit loss provision. If necessary, assume that benefits recognized for reporting purposes are also recognized for tax purposes.

3. Identify from the management discussion in the 1988 statements the amount of unrecognized tax benefits available to reduce Citicorp's future taxes as of December 31, 1988. Use these data and other information in the notes to estimate the *1987 recognizable tax benefits* presumably due to the effects of the 1987 increase in the provision for credit losses. If necessary, assume that benefits recognized for reporting purposes are also recognized for tax purposes. Assume also that both unrecognized tax benefits as of January 1, 1987 and recognizable tax benefits for 1988 amounted to zero.

MANAGEMENT DISCUSSION ON INCOME TAXES

Income tax expense for 1988 was $1,009 million, compared with $894 million in 1987 and $617 million in 1986. Recognizable income tax benefits attributable to the 1987 addition to the loan loss allowance for possible credit losses were $160 million in 1988 and $259 million in 1987. The $160 million of carryforward tax benefits recognized for financial statement purposes in 1988 are reported as an extraordinary item and are not included in 1988 income tax expense. Remaining unrecognized income tax benefits of approximately $700 million are available to reduce income taxes that would otherwise be provided in Citicorp's financial statements in future years.

NOTE 15 ON INCOME TAXES

In millions of dollars	1988	1987	1986
Provision for taxes on income	$ 1,009	$ 894	$ 617
Income tax benefits related to foreign currency translation reported in stockholders' equity	(13)	(43)	(94)
	996	851	523
Extraordinary item			
Carryforward tax benefits	(160)	-	-
Total income tax expense	$ 836	$ 851	$ 523

COMPONENTS OF DEFERRED TAXES

In millions of dollars	1988	1987	1986
Lease financing transactions	$ 112	$ 95	$ 130
Effects of changes in tax rates on leveraged lease portfolios	-	-	(55)
Credit loss deduction	53	(1,172)	(204)
Interest income	11	(35)	(20)
Domestic taxes on overseas income	77	(43)	(21)
Pension settlement	-	149	-
Mortgage pass-through sales	28	34	51
Deferred tax benefits not recognized	-	1,038	-
Other	68	(177)	(97)
Total (included in total income tax expense)	$ 349	$ (111)	$ (216)

NOTE 15 ON INCOME TAXES

In millions of dollars	1987	1986	1985
Provision for taxes on income	$ 898	$ 642	$ 718
Income tax benefits related to foreign currency translation reported in stockholders' equity	(43)	(94)	(46)
Total income tax expense	$ 855	$ 548	$ 672

COMPONENTS OF DEFERRED TAXES

In millions of dollars	1987	1986	1985
Lease financing transactions	$ 121	$ 130	$ 105
Effects of changes in tax rates on leveraged lease portfolios	-	(55)	(19)
Credit loss deduction	(1,241)	(204)	(55)
Interest income	(104)	(20)	(29)
Domestic taxes on overseas income	21	(21)	9
Pension settlement	149	-	-
Mortgage pass-through sales	48	51	20
Deferred tax benefits not recognized	1,022	-	-
Other	(77)	(75)	(18)
Total (included in total income tax expense)	$ (61)	$ (194)	$ 13

10

Leases

10.1 K MART CORPORATION

Capital vs. operating leases, present value

K Mart Corporation is the second-largest retail merchandiser in sales volume in the United States. The company engages principally in the distribution of a wide range of products through the operation of a chain of department stores (K mart), variety stores (Kresge), and limited-line discount stores (Jupiter). Listed on the New York Stock Exchange (Ticker = KM).

Study the liabilities and shareholders' equity section of the fiscal 19X1–19X2 Consolidated Balance Sheets and the notes to the statements about leases.

1. For capital leases only, prepare journal entries to record the fiscal 19X2 lease rental payment, 19X2 amortization (depreciation) expense on leased property, and 19X2 interest expense relating to lease obligations. Use minimum lease payments excluding executory costs.

2. Whereas K Mart recognizes interest and amortization relating to capital leases as expenses for financial reporting purposes, the U.S. taxing authorities normally allow only the capital lease payments to be expensed for income taxes. This difference in the timing of lease expenses for tax and financial reporting purposes requires an adjustment to the company's deferred tax liability. Assuming a 35 percent tax rate, provide a journal entry dated January 28, 19X2 that would recognize the change in deferred tax liability relating to the timing of capital lease expenses in fiscal 19X2.

3. State by how much fiscal 19X2 and fiscal 19X1 net earnings would have been affected if all K Mart leases had been accounted for as operating leases. Use the information in the footnote on deferred income taxes relating to capital leases, as shown below:

The provision for income taxes consists of:

(Dollars in millions)	19X2	19X1	19X0
Current	$ 400	$ 195	$ 318
Deferred			
Excess of tax over book depreciation	46	51	45
LIFO inventory	(4)	44	6
Lease capitalization	(7)	(8)	(9)
Other	23	3	(28)
Total income tax expense	$ 458	$ 285	$ 332

The amounts shown in the balance sheets for deferred income taxes result principally from the difference between financial statement and income tax depreciation, reduced by the effect of accounting for certain leases as capital leases.

4. Identify the amounts stated as the present value of the minimum lease payments under capital leases as of February 29, 19X1 and February 28, 19X2. Assuming all lease payments and new acquisitions of leased assets took place on February 28, 19X2 and that the company sold two retail chains during fiscal year ended January 28, 19X2 with net capital lease obligations of $63 million, estimate the value of the *new* capital lease obligations incurred during 19X2.

5. Assume the minimum capital lease payments are made at the end of each year and that amounts in "Later years" and Estimated executory costs are made equally over 20 years beginning at the end of fiscal 19X8. Estimate a *single* average rate of interest implicit in the future payments that comprise the capital lease obligation (net of executory costs) as of February 28, 19X2.

K MART CORPORATION
Consolidated Balance Sheets
Fiscal year ended February 28

(Dollars in millions)	19X2	19X1
Liabilities and shareholders' equity*		
Current liabilities		
Long-term debt due within one year	$ 4	$ 15
Capital lease obligations due within one year	79	76
Notes payable	296	127
Accounts payable	2,207	1,908
Accrued payrolls and other liabilities	560	548
Taxes other than income taxes	223	218
Income taxes	162	198
Total current liabilities	3,531	3,090
Capital lease obligations	1,600	1,713
Long-term debt	1,011	1,456
Other long-term liabilities	315	345
Deferred income taxes	182	114
Shareholders' equity	3,939	3,273
	$ 10,578	$ 9,991

*See also accompanying notes to consolidated financial statements.

Leases
(Dollars in millions)

Description of leasing arrangements

The company conducts operations primarily in leased facilities. K mart store leases are generally for terms of 25 years with multiple five-year renewal options which allow the company the option to extend the life of the lease up to 50 years beyond the initial non-cancellable term. The majority of special retail units are leased, generally for terms varying from 5 to 25 years with varying renewal options. Certain leases provide for additional rental payments based on a percent of sales in excess of a specified base and for the payment by the lessee of executory costs (taxes, maintenance, and insurance). Also, selling space has been sublet to other retailers in certain of the company's leased facilities.

Lease commitments:
Future minimum lease payments with respect to capital and operating leases are:

(millions)	Minimum lease payments Capital	Operating
19X3	$ 330	$ 333
19X4	326	325
19X5	319	314
19X6	315	303
19X7	312	288
Later years	3,310	2,644
Total minimum lease payments	4,912	4,207
less minimum sublease payments	-	(273)
Net minimum lease payments	$ 4,912	$ 3,934
less		
Estimated executory costs	(1,448)	
Amount representing interest	(1,785)	
Obligations under capital leases of which $79 million is due within one year	$ 1,679	

Rental expense:
A summary of operating lease rental expense and short-term rentals follows:

(Dollars in millions)	Fiscal year ended February 28 (29) 19X2	19X1	19X0
Minimum rentals	$ 332	$ 302	$ 253
Percentage rentals	54	52	47
less-sublease rentals	(47)	(46)	(37)
Total	339	308	263

Reconciliation of capital lease information:

The impact of recording amortization and interest expense versus rent expense on capital leases is as follows:

(Dollars in millions)	Fiscal year ended February 28 (29)		
	19X2	19X1	19X0
Amortization of capital lease property	$ 97	$ 98	$ 97
Interest expense related to obligations under capital leases	178	181	184
Amounts charged to earnings	275	279	281
Related minimum lease payments net of executory costs	(254)	(255)	(255)
Excess of amounts charged over related minimum lease payments	$ 21	$ 24	$ 26

Related minimum lease payments above exclude executory costs for 19X2, 19X1, and 19X0 of $80 million, $79 million, and $79 million, respectively.

10.2 AMERICAN BRANDS, INC.

Long-term lease commitments and present values

In their 19X3 Annual Report to stockholders, American Brands, a tobacco products and financial services company, reported the following information regarding future lease payments under capital and operating leases. The company reported long-term debt for 19X3 of $693,215,000 and common stockholders' equity of $2,540,870,000.

Assume an interest (discount) rate of 10 percent that the *capital* lease obligation will be fully amortized at the end of 20 years; that the *operating* lease obligation will be fully amortized at the end of 15 years; that the minimum lease payments are made annually on December 31; and that all capital and operating lease payments made after 19X8 are of equal amounts.

Use the information in the note on Lease commitments to answer the following questions:

1. With regard to the capital lease obligations, calculate as of December 31, 19X3 the "amount representing interest," shown as "a" in the note, and the "total minimum lease payments" (undiscounted), shown as "b" in the note. The amount shown as "?" can be derived only after amounts "a" and "b" have been calculated.

2. With regard to the operating lease obligations, calculate as of December 31, 19X3 the present value of the minimum lease payments and the amount representing interest.

3. Provide a journal entry that would record the 19X4 operating lease *payment* (assumed made at the end of that year) on the basis that the company accounted for all operating leases as capital leases.

4. As of December 31, 19X3, state (a) the amount of long-term debt that the company *presently* records under lease obligations and (b) the amount of long-term debt it would record if operating leases were capitalized as of that date. Given the assumptions above, what is the impact of capitalizing *all* lease obligations on the company's December 31, 19X3 long-term debt to stockholders' equity ratio?

Lease commitments

Future minimum lease payments under capital leases together with present value of net minimum lease payments as of December 31, 19X3 are as follows:

(Dollars in thousands)	
19X4	$ 2,323
19X5	2,128
19X6	1,846
19X7	1,459
19X8	1,385
Remainder	?
Total minimum lease payments	b
Less amount representing interest	a
Present value of net minimum lease payments	$ 16,635

Future minimum rental payments under noncancelable operating leases as of December 31, 19X3 are as follows:

(Dollars in thousands)	
19X4	$ 38,312
19X5	35,910
19X6	32,201
19X7	29,186
19X8	27,280
Remainder	290,092
Total minimum lease payments	$ 452,981

10.3 COLT INDUSTRIES INCORPORATED

Present value of long-term debt, capital leases

Colt Industries manufactures and markets automotive carburetors, air pumps, and oil seals; small engine accessories and aerospace landing gear; fuel control systems and machinery diesel engines; and transformers, compressors, pipe and tubing, magnets, firearms, and shock mitigation systems. Listed prior to 1989 on the New York Stock Exchange (Ticker = D.CWF).

Study the excerpts from Colt's Consolidated Balance Sheet for 19X2–19X3, Consolidated Statement of Earnings for 19X2–19X3, and Notes 1 and 2 to the 19X3 financial statements.

1. Identify and state assets recorded under capital leases in 19X2 and 19X3 and liabilities recorded under capital lease obligations in 19X2 and 19X3. Also, explain the difference between the asset and liability value for capital leases.

2. The 19X3 Consolidated Statement of Cash Flows states that long-term debt provided cash proceeds of $1,386,912 during the year. Estimate cash paid to decrease the principal amounts owing on long-term debt during 19X3. Include amounts paid to reduce capital lease obligations.

3. a. Calculate the weighted average rate of interest on Colt's long-term debt as of December 31, 19X3. Assume that the expected prime rate will remain constant at 10 percent and Colt chooses "option i" of the loan agreement for the Term loan and that Revolving credit facilities are charged at the prime rate less 0.5 percent. Use the rates given in the Note 2 for the other components of long-term debt.

   b. Assume that long-term debt, including capital lease obligations, will be paid off in accordance with Note 2, which describes the minimum payments on long-term debt, and that the remaining annual payments of principal will be spread equally over 15 years, beginning 19X9. Use the weighted average rate of interest calculated in (a) for all 20 years beginning 19X4.

   Calculate the present value of Colt's long-term debt using a discount factor of 10 percent per annum. To answer this question, construct a table with the following columns: year, principal payment, interest expense, total cash payment, discount factor, present value of payment. Assume that Colt makes its lease payments at the end of each year.

c. Calculate by how much would the company be better (or worse) off if the prime rate were to decrease suddenly to 7.5 percent per annum as of January 1, 19X4.

4. The footnote on long-term debt states various restrictions and conditions on the company's financial operations and position. Examine whether Colt would appear to be in compliance with the requirements that, as of the end of 19X3, the interest coverage and current ratios be less that 1.3:1 and 1.6:1, respectively. State a rationale that underlies the 19X3 debt ratio of senior debt to subordinated debt, net earnings, proceeds of common stock, etc., required to decline from 2.7 to 1:1 within seven years from balance sheet date.

COLT INDUSTRIES INCORPORATED
Consolidated Balance Sheet
December 31

ASSETS

(In thousands)	19X3	19X2
Total current assets	$ 533,599	$ 695,537
Total assets	1,145,018	1,250,544
Current liabilities	325,157	285,959
Shareholders' equity	$ (1,077,837)	$ 414,304

COLT INDUSTRIES INCORPORATED
Consolidated Statement of Earnings
For the years ended December 31

(In thousands)	19X3	19X2
SALES	$ 1,616,267	$ 1,579,325
Total costs and expenses	1,406,375	1,346,878
Earnings from continuing operations before interest and taxes	209,892	232,447
Interest expense	73,061	14,331
Interest income	17,083	8,724
EARNINGS FROM CONTINUING OPERATIONS BEFORE INCOME TAXES	$ 153,914	$ 226,840
Provision for income taxes	64,644	97,540
Earnings from continuing operations	89,270	129,300
Discontinued operations		8,733
NET EARNINGS	$ 89,270	$ 138,033

Note 1: Summary of accounting policies

At December 31, 19X3 and 19X2, the company had the following assets recorded under capital leases:

(In thousands)	19X3	19X2
Land and improvements	902	902
Buildings and equipment	16,972	16,671
Machinery and equipment	13,124	13,286
Leasehold improvements	1,028	1,028
	32,026	31,887
Less—Accumulated depreciation and amortization	14,209	12,944
	$ 17,817	$ 18,943

Note 2: Long-term debt

(In thousands)		19X3	19X2
Term loan facility due 19X4–19Y1	$	695,000	-
Revolving credit facility		110,000	-
10.125% notes due 19Y2		150,000	$ 150,000
11.25% notes due 19Z2		150,000	150,000
12.5% senior subordinated debentures due 19Y4–19Y8		550,000	-
Capital lease obligations—8.9%		25,013	26,151
8.875% notes payable to insurance company repaid in 19X3		-	9,000
Other due 19X4–19Y1, at 5.8%		10,699	11,752
		1,690,712	346,903
less—Amounts due within one year		47,592	4,489
	$	1,643,120	$ 342,414

a. Interest on the term loan facility is calculated, at the option of the company, at either (i) prime rate plus a margin which is initially 1.5%, (ii) London interbank rate plus a margin which initially is 2.5%, (iii) certificate of deposit rate plus a margin which initially is 2.625%.

b. The term loan and revolving credit facilities contain various restrictions and conditions. The most restrictive of these require that the ratio of earnings before interest and taxes to interest expense be at least 1.3 to 1 for any period of four consecutive quarters ending in 19X4. This ratio increases annually in increments to 2 to 1 in 19X9; and for any two consecutive quarters it must be at least 1 to 1. The ratio of current assets to current liabilities must be at least 1.6 to 1; and the ratio of senior debt to the sum of subordinated debt, net earnings after recapitalization, and aggregate sale proceeds of common stock after the recapitalization (less certain amounts) must not exceed a maximum of 2.7 to 1 in 19X3, decreasing in annual increments to 1 to 1 in 19Y0. The company is in compliance with the financial covenants.

c. The amounts payable under capital lease obligations are as follows:

(In thousands)	
19X4	$ 3,567
19X5	3,545
19X6	3,455
19X7	3,126
19X8	2,186
Remainder	59,721
Total minimum lease payments	75,600
Less--amount representing interest	50,587
Total minimum lease payments at present value, in long-term debt	$ 25,013

d. Minimum payments on long-term debt, including capital lease obligations, due within five years from December 31, 19X3 are as follows:

(In thousands)	
19X4	$ 47,592
19X5	52,677
19X6	52,656
19X7	102,200
19X8	$ 101,710

11

Employee Benefits

11.1 GENERAL MOTORS CORPORATION II

Pension accounting, impact of change in accounting estimate, present value

General Motors Corporation is the largest automotive manufacturer in the United States and one of the largest corporations in the world. Listed on the New York Stock Exchange (Ticker = GM). This case should be viewed independently of the General Motors I case.

Study the Note on Pension Program from General Motors' 19X2 annual report. This note describes the company's pension program, the amount of pension expense (included as part of Other income), and the effects of a change in an accounting estimate associated with pension expense. General Motors reported net income (loss) after income taxes as $(15.0) million, $(983.6) million, and $2,674.4 million for years 19X0, 19X1, and 19X2, respectively.

General Motor's pension plan is no different from that of other firms in that it provides benefits for retired employees. Contributions to the fund each year depend on the expected future retirement payments to be made to present employees—an obligation of the company. Pension costs are expensed periodically to update the expected future obligation of the company. Such periodic expenses depend, in part, on the interest rate used to discount future employee benefits and the rate of return assumed to be earned by the pension fund assets. Many companies assume equal the rates for discounting and pension fund returns.

1. Suppose a company expenses this year a lump sum pension benefit to be paid at the end of 20 years (Year 20). Provide a journal entry as of Year 0 to record the expected future payment of $100,000 if the company expects a rate of return on fund assets of (a) 6 percent and (b) 7 percent, compounded annually.

2. The pension expense amounts reported by General Motors are assumed to represent the actuarial value of pension obligations arising from employee services for the years 19X1 and 19X2. To simplify the analysis, assume that instead of receiving a series of pension payments upon retirement, employees receives a lump sum amount, F (the assumed actuarial value of retirement benefits at retirement date).

   Use the present value (PV) formula $PV = F(1+R)^{-N}$, which can be written in logarithmic form as $\ln PV = \ln F - N \ln(1+R)$, to estimate the average future time period (N) that General Motors uses to determine its future payment (F). Use information about General Motors derived from the footnote. R is the assumed rate of return on plan assets (also equal to the discount rate).

All amounts should be viewed as estimates and averages since General Motors provides benefits for a spectrum of employees retiring at different dates.

3. Using your estimate of N in part 2, determine what the pension expense would have been if General Motors had switched to the 7 percent discount rate in 19X1. You need to calculate first the future payment (F) associated with the 19X1 pension expense of $1,922.1 million. Given a 35 percent tax rate, determine the effect on 19X1 net income (loss) after taxes.

4. Determine the impact on net income after taxes (assume a 35 percent tax rate) if the rate of return increases from 6 percent to (a) 8 percent and (b) 10 percent.

5. General Motors' audit report states that the results of operations are in conformity with generally accepted accounting principles *applied on a consistent basis* (emphasis added). Comment as to whether the audit report should alert investors and others to the change in measurement assumption regarding pension expense.

GENERAL MOTORS CORPORATION
NOTE: PENSION PROGRAM

(Dollars in millions)	19X2	19X1	19X0
Other income	$ 427.9	$ 392.1	$ 507.0
Interest	123.6	81.7	72.2
Income deductions	(183.8)	(125.1)	(18.9)
Net	$ 367.7	$ 348.7	$ 560.3

Total pension expense of the Corporation and its consolidated subsidiaries amounted to $1,493.8 million in 19X2, $1,922.1 million in 19X1, and $1,571.5 million in 19X0. For purposes of determining pension expense, the Corporation uses a variety of assumed rates of return on pension funds in accordance with local practice and regulations. Those rates approximated 6 percent in 19X1 and 19X0. In 19X2, the assumed rate in determining retirement plan costs in the United States and Canada was increased to 7 percent. The Corporation's independent actuary recommended this change, and other changes in actuarial assumptions after taking into account the experience of the plans and reasonable expectations. The total effect of these changes was to reduce retirement plan costs for 19X2 by $411.1 million and accordingly increase net income by $205.6 million ($0.69 per share). The following table compares accumulated plan benefits and plan net assets for the Corporation's defined benefit plans in the United States and Canada as of October 1 (generally, the plans' anniversary date) of both 19X2 and 19X1.

(Dollars in millions)	19X2	19X1
ACTUARIAL PRESENT VALUE OF ACCUMULATED BENEFIT OBLIGATION		
Vested	$ 16,228.5	$ 17,438.5
Nonvested	1,890.3	2,234.1
Total	$ 18,118.8	$ 19,672.6
MARKET VALUE OF PLAN ASSETS		
Held by trustees	$ 10,795.1	$ 10,584.6
Held by insurance companies	3,049.4	2,769.2
Total	$ 13,844.5	$ 13,353.8

The assumed rates of return used in determining the actuarial present value of accumulated plan benefits (shown in the table above) were based on those published by the Pension Benefit Guaranty Corporation, a public corporation established under the Employee Retirement Security Act (ERISA). Such rates averaged approximately 10 percent for 19X2 and 8.25 percent for 19X1.

11.2   GSA CORPORATION

Pension disclosures under Statement 87

The GSA Corporation adopted FASB Statement No. 87, *Employers' Accounting for Pensions,* for the year ended December 31, 19X1 and provided the following disclosures in the footnotes to the December 31, 19X1 financial statements.

Actuarial present value of benefit obligation (dollars in millions)	
Vested benefits	$ 1,100
Nonvested benefits	150
Accumulated benefit obligation	1,250
Projected benefit obligation	1,900
Plan assets at fair value	1,150
Excess of projected benefit obligation over plan assets	750
Unrecognized prior service cost	480
Unrecognized net obligation at initial application, January 1, 19X1	270
Accrued/prepaid pension cost, before additional minimum liability	0
Net minimum liability on balance sheet	$ 100
Intangible pension asset on balance sheet	$ 100

Assume that the unrecognized prior service cost and unrecognized net obligation at initial application will be amortized on a straight-line basis over eleven years beginning January 1, 19X1; service cost for 19X2 amounts to $60 million; and the assumed and actual return on pension assets and discount factor is 10%.

At the end of the year, the company plans to contribute cash to the plan exactly equal to the pension expense to be shown in the 19X2 Statement of Income. No changes will be made in the pension formula; the distribution of employee pension benefits will remain constant.

Based on an example in Accounting News Briefs, Arthur Andersen & Co., January 1986.

Based on the preceding information, answer the following questions.

1. Provide a journal entry to record the 19X2 pension expense under Statement 87. Identify the components of that expense.

2. Provide a journal entry to make any adjustments to the minimum pension liability and intangible asset that would be shown in the 19X2 balance sheet.

3. Repeat parts 1 and 2, except that assume that at the end of 19X2, the company contributes $30 million more to the plan than the expense calculated in part 1.

4. Provide a journal entry that would convert the December 31, 19X1 balance sheet to show the economic or fair value of the plan assets and the projected benefit obligation.

5. Comment on how GSA's financial statements would differ if the corporation had remained on the old accounting standard (APB Opinion No. 8, *Accounting for the Cost of Pension Plans.*). A numerical answer is not necessary.

6. Write a press report to be released to the Dow Jones news service at the same time that preliminary earnings of $5.60 a share, up from $5.40 in 19X0, are to be released that explains the adoption of Statement 87 and the new numbers that appear in the balance sheet. Make any assumptions you wish, but use no more than *150* words.

11.3 PHILIP MORRIS COMPANIES, INC.

Pension plan accounting and disclosures under Statement 87

Philip Morris is a diversified, consumer food and related products company, with operations in tobacco (Philip Morris), food (General Foods, Oscar Mayer), beer (Miller Brewing), and other areas (e.g., Mission Viejo Realty). Listed on the New York Stock Exchange (Ticker = MO).

The company adopted FASB Statement No. 87, *Employers' Accounting for Pensions*, as of January 1, 19X2. For the years ended December 31, 19X3 and 19X2, the company reported net income before taxes of $3.348 and $2.811 million, respectively. Pension expense for 19X1 and 19X0 was reported under the old accounting standard (APB Opinion No. 8, *Accounting for the Cost of Pension Plans*) as $74 and $73 million, respectively.

Refer to the attached footnotes on Pension Plans taken from the 19X2 and 19X3 financial reports. Make the following assumptions in answering the questions below:

a. Pension funding (i.e., cash payments to the pension fund) for 19X2 and 19X3 amounted to $62 and $7 million, respectively.

b. The (off-balance sheet) account "Unrecognized net loss from experience differences and assumption changes" contains adjustments that change the pension asset account, projected benefit obligation account, as well as amounts that amortize those adjustments in order that they may be included in pension expense. However, the net gain upon adoption of Statement 87 and amortization of that net gain are included in separate accounts.

c. No pension settlements or curtailments occurred during the year.

1. For both years, show the journal entries in Philip Morris' books to record pension expense and pension funding.

2. Identify the amounts of projected benefit obligation as of January 1, 19X2, December 31, 19X2, and December 31, 19X3 and prepare a table for *each* year (19X2 and 19X3) that shows all the adjustments to the various off-balance sheet, unrecognized items, and reconciles to the prepaid account. Note: Not every cell in the table need be filled.

	Beginning amount	Pension expense	Pension funding	Other adjustments	Ending amount
Plan assets	X	X	X	X	X
Projected benefit obligation	X	X	X	X	X
Difference	X	X	X	X	X
Unrecognized net loss (gain)	X	X	X	X	X
Unrecognized net asset (obligation) at 1/1/19X2 adoption	X	X	X	X	X
Prepaid (accrued) pension cost	X	X	X	X	X

3. Does Philip Morris recognize a pension liability in its financial statements? Explain.

PHILIP MORRIS COMPANIES, INC.
Note to 19X2 financial statements

Pension Plans

Effective January 1, 19X2, the company adopted Statement of Financial Accounting Standards No. 87, *Employers' Accounting for Pensions* ("SFAS 87"), for its U.S. pension plans. Pension cost and related disclosures for non-U.S. plans in 19X2 and for all plans in 19X1 and 19X0 were determined under the provisions of the previous accounting principles.

U.S. Plans

The company and its subsidiaries sponsor noncontributory defined benefit pension plans covering substantially all of their employees. The plans generally provide retirement benefits for salaried employees based on years of service rendered and compensation during the last years of employment. Retirement benefits for hourly employees generally are a flat amount for each year of service rendered. The company funds these plans in amounts consistent with the funding requirements of Federal law and regulations.

Net pension cost for 19X2 included the following components (in millions):

Service cost–benefits earned during the year	$ 88
Interest cost on projected benefit obligation	172
Return on Assets—actual	(436)
—deferred gain	211
Amortization on net gain at January 1, 19X2	(28)
Net pension cost	$ 7

The adoption of SFAS 87 decreased 19X2 pension cost by approximately $76 million. Pension cost for 19X1 and 19X0 was $74 million and $73 million, respectively. The funded status of the plans at December 31 and January 1, 19X2 was as follows (in millions):

	December 31	January 1
Actuarial present value of accumulated benefit obligation		
—vested	$ 1,758	$ 1,430
—nonvested	94	71
	1,852	1,501
Benefits attributable to projected salaries	551	454
	2,403	1,955
Plan assets at fair value	2,917	2,519
Excess of assets over projected benefit obligation	514	564
Unrecognized net gain at December 31 and January 1, 19X2	(401)	(429)
Unrecognized net loss from experience differences and assumption changes	77	-
Prepaid pension cost	$ 190	$ 135

The projected benefit obligation at December 31 and January 1, 19X2 was determined using assumed discount rates of 7-3/4 percent and 9 percent and assumed compensation increases of 6-3/4 percent and 8 percent, respectively. The assumed long-term rate of return on plan assets was 9 percent at both dates. Plan assets consist principally of common stocks and fixed income securities.

The company sponsors a deferred profit-sharing plan covering certain salaried, nonunion and union employees. Contributions and cost are determined as a percentage of consolidated pre-tax earnings, as defined by the plan. Subsidiaries of the company also maintain other defined contribution plans. Amounts charged to expense for defined contribution plans totaled $99 million, $77 million and $53 million in 19X2, 19X1 and 19X0, respectively.

PHILIP MORRIS COMPANIES, INC.
Note to 19X3 financial statements

Pension Plans

Effective January 1, 19X2, the company adopted Statement of Financial Accounting Standards No. 87, *Employers' Accounting for Pensions* ("SFAS 87"), for its U.S. pension plans. Pension cost and related disclosures for non-U.S. plans in 19X3 and 19X2 and for all plans in 19X1 were determined under the provisions of the previous accounting principles.

U.S. Plans

The company and its subsidiaries sponsor noncontributory defined benefit pension plans covering substantially all employees. The plans generally provide retirement benefits for salaried employees based on years of service and compensation during the last years of employment. Retirement benefits for hourly employees generally are a flat dollar amount for each year of service. The company funds these plans in amounts consistent with the funding requirements of Federal law and regulations. Net pension cost included the following components:

(In millions)	19X3	19X2
Service cost–benefits earned during the year	$ 93	$ 88
Interest cost on projected benefit obligation	190	172
Return on Assets		
—actual	(148)	(436)
—deferred gain (loss)	(94)	211
Amortization on net gain upon adoption of SFAS 87	(28)	(28)
Net pension cost	$ 13	$ 7

The adoption of SFAS 87 decreased 19X2 pension cost by approximately $76 million. Pension cost for 19X1 was $74 million. The funded status of the plans at December 31 was as follows:

(In millions)	19X3	19X2
Actuarial present value of accumulated benefit obligation		
—vested	$ 1,756	$ 1,758
—nonvested	104	94
	1,860	1,852
Benefits attributable to projected salaries	561	551
	2,421	2,403
Plan assets at fair value	2,936	2,917
Excess of assets over projected benefit obligation	515	514
Unrecognized net gain upon adoption of SFAS 87 (January 1, 19X2)	(373)	(401)
Unrecognized net loss from experience differences and assumption changes	42	77
Prepaid pension cost	$ 184	$ 190

The projected benefit obligation at December 31, 19X3 and 19X2 was determined using assumed discount rates of 8-1/2 percent and 7-3/4 percent and assumed compensation increases of 7-1/2 percent and 6-3/4 percent, respectively. The assumed long-term rate of return on plan assets was 9 percent at both dates. Plan assets consist principally of common stocks and fixed income securities.

The company sponsors a deferred profit-sharing plan covering certain salaried, nonunion and union employees. Contributions and cost are determined as a percentage of consolidated pretax earnings, as defined by the plan. Subsidiaries of the company also maintain other defined contribution plans. Amounts charged to expense for defined contribution plans totaled $118 million, $99 million and $77 million in 19X3, 19X2 and 19X1, respectively.

11.4 THE LTV CORPORATION

Postemployment health and other benefits

The LTV Corporation operates in four basic industries, primarily through its subsidiaries LTV Steel, LTV Steel Tubular Products, LTV Aerospace and Defense, and LTV Energy Products. On July 17, 19X0, the Company and substantially all of its subsidiaries filed petitions for reorganization under Chapter 11 of the Federal Bankruptcy Code. LTV's results for 19X2 include special charges that relate to the Chapter 11 filing. Additionally, the Company changed its method of accounting for postemployment benefits, other than pensions. Listed on the New York Stock Exchange (Ticker = LTV).

Study the 19X1–19X2 Consolidated Statement of Operations, the Note on Postemployment Health Care and Life Insurance, and the balances on Deferrals and Noncurrent liabilities shown in the 19X1–19X2 Consolidated Balance Sheet. Use this information to answer the following questions.

1. Describe the company's new and old methods of accounting for employee health and life insurance benefits. In general terms, and in light of the FASB's pronouncements on defined benefit pensions, evaluate whether LTV's new method would represent an acceptable method of accounting. Note: In February 1989, the FASB issued an Exposure Draft on this topic, *Employers' Accounting Par Postretirement Benefits Other than Pensions*.

2. Provide journal entries that would record all entries to the liability account Employee benefits that would have occurred during fiscal year 19X2. Be sure to recognize the current portion of the Employee benefit liability as well as any amounts that may have been offset against or included in with the opening and closing liability balances reported in the Consolidated Balance Sheet. State whether the accounts listed are assets, liabilities, expenses, revenues, and so forth.

3. State what the effect on retained earnings as of December 31, 19X1 and 19X1 net income would have been if the change had been made as of January 1, 19X1 (and not January 1 19X2).

THE LTV CORPORATION AND SUBSIDIARIES
Consolidated Statement of Operations
Year Ended December 31
(In millions, except per share data)

	19X2	19X1
NET SALES	$ 7,324.7	$ 7,581.8
OPERATING COSTS AND EXPENSES:		
Cost of products sold	6,299.3	6,448.2
Depreciation and amortization	242.0	250.4
Selling, general, and administrative expenses	367.9	355.5
Special charges, net	1,346.2	
Interest and debt discount expense	7.5	28.2
Interest expense (income)	(63.4)	(44.2)
Other expense (income), net	(39.4)	(8.0)
Chapter 11 administrative expenses	30.0	29.0
Total	$ 8,190.1	$ 7,059.1
INCOME (LOSS) BEFORE INCOME TAXES AND CUMULATIVE EFFECT OF ACCOUNTING CHANGE	(865.4)	522.7
Income tax provision	$ 25.2	$ 20.1
INCOME (LOSS) BEFORE CUMULATIVE EFFECT OF ACCOUNTING CHANGE	(890.6)	502.6
Cumulative effect of accounting change	(2,263.0)	-
NET INCOME (LOSS)	$ (3,153.6)	$ 502.6

Earnings (loss) per share:		
Primary:		
Income (loss) before cumulative effect of accounting change	$ (8.97)	$ 4.24
Cumulative effect of accounting change	(21.97)	
NET INCOME (LOSS)	$ (30.94)	$ 4.24
Proforma amounts assuming the change made in 19X2 in the Company's method of accounting for post employment benefits other than pensions had been applied retroactively:		
NET INCOME (LOSS)	$ (890.6)	$ 395.7
Earnings (loss) per share, primary	$ (8.97)	$ 3.30

POSTEMPLOYMENT HEALTH CARE AND LIFE INSURANCE

Effective January 1, 19X2, the company changed its method of accounting for postemployment health care and life insurance benefits (including to a lesser extent, long-term disability benefits), to a method which accrues these benefits over the period in which active employees become eligible for such postemployment benefits. Previously, such costs were generally expensed as incurred by retirees. The company believes the new accrual method is preferable because it recognizes retiree health care and life insurance benefits, especially current benefit plans, on an accrual basis as earned by the employees during their active service.

At January 1, 19X2, the actuarial present value of the accumulated benefit obligation for retiree health care and life insurance benefits was $2,263 million. Of this amount, $89 million had been recorded previously in conjunction with idlings or shutdowns of facilities. Of the total liability, retirees account for $1,635 million and active employees account for $728 million, of which approximately $230 million is for active employees who are currently eligible for such benefits. The accumulated benefit obligation was determined using the credit method, an assumed health care cost trend rate of 17% in 19X2 and 14% in 19X3, declining to 6.8% in the year 2002 and thereafter over the projected payout period of the benefits, and an assumed discount rate of 8.5%. The weighted average health care cost trend rate over the projected payout period used is 9.0%. At December 31, 19X2, the projected recorded liability for such postemployment benefits was $2,492 million, $124 million of which is included in current liabilities as accrued compensation and benefits.

This change resulted in an additional noncash expense in 19X2 of $2,395 million ($23.26 per fully diluted share), including a charge as of January 1, 19X2 of $2,263 million (net of a related tax benefit of $11 million) for the cumulative effect adjustment. The cumulative effect adjustment recognizes the unfunded present value of the accumulated benefit obligation for retirees and an obligation for the prior services of current active employees. In addition to the one-time cumulative effect adjustment, the expense includes an incremental effect for 19X2 of $132 million as a result of having adopted this new method. Excluding the cumulative effect adjustment, the total expense recorded in 19X2 under this new method was $239 million, consisting of $196 million in interest on the accumulated benefit obligation and $43 million for the current service costs of benefits earned by active employees during the period. Proforma amounts for the years ended December 31, 19X2 and 19X1 are shown in the Consolidated Statement of Operations. Because LTV is operating under Chapter 11, it was determined that the aggregate liability for the cumulative effect adjustment at January 1, 19X2 should recognize all of the pre Chapter 11 effects of actuarial gains and losses and any plan amendments to these benefits.

The effect on the present value of the accumulated benefit obligation at January 1, 19X2 of a change in each year of one percent upwards or downwards in the health care cost trend rates used would result in an increase of $310 million or a decrease of $256 million in the obligation respectively. Correspondingly, such a change each year of one percent upwards or downwards in the health care cost trend rates would result in an increase or decrease in expense of $38 million or $30 million, respectively.

THE LTV CORPORATION AND SUBSIDIARIES
Consolidated Balance Sheet
Year Ended December 31
(In millions, except per share data)

Liabilities & Shareholders' Equity	19X2	19X1
CURRENT LIABILITIES		
Accounts payable	$ 420.1	$ 418.9
Accrued employee compensation and benefits	455.1	384.6
Other accrued liabilities	246.2	253.4
Income taxes	8.9	22.4
Current maturities of long-term debt	3.3	5.0
Total current liabilities	$ 1,133.6	$ 1,084.3
LONG-TERM DEBT (CAPITAL LEASE OBLIGATIONS)	18.5	25.2
DEFERRALS AND NONCURRENT LIABILITIES		
Employee benefits (primarily post employment in 19X2)	2,662.4	34.2
Noncurrent plant rationalization	509.3	227.2
Other	87.2	81.5
Total deferrals and noncurrent liabilities	$ 3,258.9	$ 342.9
TOTAL LIABILITIES	$ 4,411.0	$ 1,452.4

11.5 GOODYEAR TIRE & RUBBER COMPANY III

*Pension plan accounting and disclosures,
effects of settlement and curtailment*

Goodyear's principal business is the development, manufacture, distribution, and sale of tires throughout the world. In addition to being the world's largest producer of tires, Goodyear is a diversified company which manufactures a broad spectrum of rubber, chemical, and plastic products. The company also has oil and gas drilling operations in California and Louisiana. Listed on the New York Stock Exchange (Ticker symbol = GT). This case should be viewed independently of the Goodyear Tire & Rubber Company I & II cases.

Study the Note on Pensions extracted from Goodyear's 19X2 annual report. The company's net income after taxes for 19X2 and 19X1 was $124.1 million and $412.4 million, respectively. For reporting purposes, Goodyear adopted FASB Statement No. 87, *Employer's Accounting for Pensions,* and FASB Statement No. 88, *Employers' Accounting for Settlements and Curtailments of Defined Benefit Pension Plans and for Termination Benefits*, for its domestic pension plans as of January 1, 19X2.

1. If Statement 87 had not been adopted, what would Goodyear have reported as consolidated 19X2 net income after taxes? Assume a 40 percent tax rate in your calculations.

2. Provide journal entries to record the 19X2 pension expense and the funding associated with the domestic plan. Assume that the funding amount for 19X2 was $50 million cash.

3. Estimate domestic pension expense for 19X3 assuming the plan assets and projected benefit obligation levels continue throughout the year. Assume that the service cost benefits increase at the same rate as the rate of increase in compensation levels; that the discount rate and rate of return on assets stay at the expected levels for 19X2; and that all unrecognized amounts are being amortized over ten years beginning January 1, 19X2.

4. Prepare a reconciliation of Plan Assets, Projected Benefit Obligation, unrecognized items, and Prepaid and Deferred Pension Cost as of December 31, 19X3. Assume that 19X3 change in the prepaid pension asset/liability account is equal to the net pension expense calculated in part 3. Use the suggested format below.

5. Provide a journal entry that would have recorded the pre-tax gain on the pension settlement, i.e., the purchase of an annuity contract from a major

insurance company. Assume that the gain will have the effect of reducing future pension funding. How much would the company's after-tax profit have been had they not taken the gain into income?

6. If the settlement had taken place on December 31, 19X2, what would the domestic pension plan projected benefit obligation and plan assets amounts have been on January 1, 19X2? Assume that (1) the annuities purchased by the pension plan during the third quarter of 19X2 had a present value of $914.7 million as of December 31, 19X2; (2) the special retirement costs reduced the pension plan assets by $29.8 million and that the curtailment costs increased the pension liability by $10.9 million as of December 31, 19X2 (i.e., the same amount as the recorded costs and losses); (3) the discount rate of 9 percent is applied to the beginning of year balance; and (4) the unrecognized net asset at January 1, 19X2 is being amortized over a ten-year period, beginning January 1, 19X2.

GOODYEAR TIRE & RUBBER COMPANY
PENSIONS

The Company and its subsidiaries provide substantially all domestic and foreign employees with pension benefits.

In 19X2 the Company adopted SFAS No. 87 for all domestic and certain foreign plans. Pension cost for these plans for 19X2, and related disclosures as of December 31, 19X2, are determined under the provisions of SFAS No. 87. Pension cost and related disclosures for 19X1 and 19X0 were determined using the previous accounting principles.

Domestic and foreign plans under SFAS No. 87

The principal domestic plans provide benefits based on length of service. The principal domestic plans covering salaried employees also include voluntary employee contributions. The voluntary contributory benefit is based on the amount contributed by an employee or compensation in the final 120 months of service, whichever is greater. Other plans provide benefits similar to the principal domestic plans.

The Company's funding policy is consistent with the funding requirements of Federal laws and regulations. Plan assets are invested primarily in common stocks, fixed income securities, and real estate.

Net periodic pension credit from continuing operations follows:

In millions	19X2
Service cost-benefits earned during the period	$ 30.3
Interest cost on projected benefit obligation	132.9
Actual return on assets	(359.5)
Net amortization and deferrals	193.8
Net periodic pension credit	(2.5)

The following table sets forth the principal plan's funded status and amounts recognized in the Company's Consolidated Balance Sheet at December 31, 19X2. At this date, assets exceeded accumulated benefits for these plans. This table includes amounts for discontinued operations.

In millions	19X2
Actuarial present value of benefit obligations:	
Vested benefit obligation	$ (996.5)
Accumulated benefit obligation	(1,113.6)
Projected benefit obligation	(1,226.7)
Plan assets	1,656.5
Plan assets in excess of projected benefit obligation	429.8
Unrecognized net gain	(10.7)
Prior service cost not yet recognized in net periodic pension cost	0.8
Unrecognized net asset at January 1, 19X2	(69.6)
Prepaid and deferred pension cost recognized in the Consolidated Balance Sheet	350.3
Assumptions for the principal domestic plans are:	
Discount rate	9.0%
Rate of increase in compensation levels	5.5%
Expected long-term rate of return on assets	9.0%

Pension settlement and curtailment

In the third quarter of 19X2, the Company settled a significant portion of its liability for the principal domestic salary plan through the purchase of an annuity contract from a major insurance company. The result was a gain of $304.4 million ($152.0 million after tax or $1.39 per share), which was accounted for in accordance with Statement of Financial Accounting Standards No. 88 (SFAS No. 88), "Employers' Accounting for Settlements and Curtailments of Defined Benefit Pension Plans and Termination Benefits."

During the fourth quarter of 19X2, the Company offered certain employees special retirement incentives which will be paid from plan assets. The cost of this program was $29.8 million. In addition, the Company closed or sold certain locations which resulted in a net curtailment loss of $10.9 million. These amounts were calculated in accordance with SFAS No. 88 and have been charged against 19X2 income.

Consolidated basis

On a consolidated basis, net pension cost for 19X2 was $15.1 million. Pension cost for 19X2 is not directly comparable with 19X1 and 19X0 pension cost because of the significant changes in accounting for pension cost under SFAS No. 87. Pension cost would have been $40.3 million higher if the Company had not adopted SFAS No. 87. Pension costs for 19X1 and 19X0 were $56.5 million and $77.4 million, respectively.

The actuarial present value of the domestic plan's accumulated plan benefits was $2,005.2 million at December 31, 19X1. Of this amount, $1,857.3 million represented vested benefits. An assumed 8% rate of return on plan assets was used in determining the actuarial present value of plan benefits in 19X1. Net assets available for plan benefits was $2,191.5 million.

Suggested format for Part 4

Account	Begin 1/1/19X2	Other changes	Expense	Fund	Settle	Curtail	End 12/31/19X2
Plan assets	x	x	x	x	x	x	x
Projected benefit obligation	x	x	x	x	x	x	x
Plan assets minus PBO	x	x	x	x	x	x	x
Unrecognized net gain	x	x	x	x	x	x	x
Prior service cost	x	x	x	x	x	x	x
Unrecognized net asset at adoption 1/1/X2	x	x	x	x	x	x	x
Prepaid asset (accrued cost)	x	x	x	x	x	x	x

Note: Not every cell need be filled

12

Shareholders' Equity

12.1 CONAGRA, INC. II

*Transactions that affect stockholders' equity,
purchase of companies, gain/loss on sale*

ConAgra, Inc., conducts operations across the food chain in agriculture, grain, and food. ConAgra manufactures and markets agricultural chemicals, formula feeds and fertilizers, grain milling and merchandising, poultry products, prepared food, and seafood. Listed on the New York Stock Exchange (Ticker = CAG). This case should be viewed independently of the ConAgra, Inc. I case.

Study ConAgra's note on Business Combinations, Consolidated Statement of Common Stockholders' Equity, and relevant portions of the Statement of Cash Flow.

1. Prepare journal entries dated May 31, 19X2 that would record all transactions affecting common stockholders' equity during the year ended May 31, 19X2. Stockholders' equity increased from $640,169,000 to $722,504,000 during the period. Use the account name "Net assets" to describe the firm's assets and liabilities generally. Identify also those transactions that would appear in the company's Statement of Cash Flow.

2. Provide a journal entry that records and accounts for all businesses acquired and recorded as "purchase" transactions during fiscal year 19X2. Reconcile the total amount of cash indicated as paid in the note on Business Combinations with the amounts shown as uses of cash in the Statement of Cash Flow. Conjecture as to why a difference might arise if the amounts do not reconcile exactly.

3. Estimate the gain or loss on the disposition of property, plant, and equipment sold, scrapped, or otherwise retired during fiscal year 19X2.

CONSOLIDATED STATEMENT OF CONAGRA'S COMMON STOCKHOLDERS' EQUITY FOR THE YEAR ENDED MAY 31, 19X2

	Common Stock	Additional Paid-in Capital	Retained Earnings	Foreign Currency Translation Adjustment	Treasury Stock	Total CR(DR)
Balance, 6/1/19X1	$ 226,388	$ 86,483	$ 346,784	$ (2,301)	$ (17,185)	$ 640,169
Shares issued in connection with employee stock purchase plan	-	-	(7,522)	-	11,647	4,125
Shares issued in connection with incentive plans	-	196	(176)	-	3,670	3,690
Shares issued in connection with executive stock purchase plan	-	-	(4,674)	-	5,691	1,017
Conversion of preferred shares into common stock	408	490	-	-	-	898
Shares issued in connection with acquisition of Peavey Company	-	-	-	-	73	73
Purchase of Treasury shares	-	-	-	-	(27,947)	(27,947)
Two-for-one stock split-up, issued 33,516,608 shares	167,583	(87,004)	(80,579)	-	-	-
Foreign currency translation adjustment	-	-	-	1,640	-	1,640
Change in year-end of pooled companies	-	-	(6,465)	-	-	(6,465)
Cash dividends						
Preferred stock	-	-	(1,336)	-	-	(1,336)
Common stock	-	-	(37,591)	-	-	(37,591)
Dividends of pooled companies	-	-	(4,465)	-	-	(4,465)
Net income	-	-	148,726	-	-	148,726
Balance, 5/31/19X2	$ 394,379	$ 165	$ 352,672	$ (661)	$ (24,051)	$ 722,504

NOTE ON BUSINESS COMBINATIONS

During the year ended May 31, 19X2, the company acquired the following as purchases. In June 19X1, the company acquired the frozen food business of RJR Nabisco, Inc. for approximately $64 million in cash. The business produces a wide variety of frozen foods under the Morton, Patio, Chun King, and Award brands.

In December 19X1, the company acquired three Swiss companies, with operations in Canada and the United States, all for approximately $7 million in cash, net of $34 million excess cash withdrawn from the businesses. The Canadian operations market wheat, barley, and oats and trade domestic grains for export. The U.S. operations trade grain and grain by-products domestically and for export to Caribbean basin countries.

In December 19X1, the company acquired Dyno Merchandise Corp. and Unique Packaging, a sewing notions distributor for approximately $5 million in cash; and Howe, Inc., a fertilizer and agricultural chemical business, for approximately $6 million in cash.

Effective January 1, 19X2, the company acquired O'Donnell Usen Fisheries Corporation, with fishing, fish processing, and marketing operations in Canada and the United States, for approximately $16 million in cash and the assumption of approximately $19 million in long-term debt.

CONSOLIDATED STATEMENT OF CONAGRA'S CASH FLOW
FOR THE YEAR ENDED MAY 31, 19X2

Excerpts only

Uses of cash for investment activities:	(In thousands)
Increase in investment in unconsolidated subsidiaries	$ 35,968
Additions to property, plant, and equipment	126,273
Increase in trademarks	7,494
Purchase of businesses, less cash equivalents acquired of $52,297	
Property, plant, and equipment	51,951
Goodwill	14,619
Long-term liabilities assumed	(19,184)
Other assets acquired (net)	738
Uses of cash for financing activities:	
Repayment and current maturities of long-term debt	$ 52,312

12.2 NATIONAL TECHNICAL SYSTEMS, INC.

Accounting for stock split as stock dividend, computation of earnings per share

National Technical Systems is an integrated engineering services company, providing environmental testing, analytical engineering, qualification and design services for the defense, aerospace, and energy industries, and for government and state agencies. Listed on the NASDAQ exchange (Ticker = NTSC).

Study the company's 19X1–19X3 Consolidated Statement of Stockholders' Equity, excerpts from the 19X1–19X3 Consolidated Statement of Earnings, and Note 2 on stock splits to be effected in the form of stock dividends.

1. a. Calculate how many shares were outstanding as of April 10, 19X2, the date of record of the 66-2/3 percent stock split.

    b. Calculate the number of common shares outstanding after February 5, 19X3, assuming no other equity transactions took place between year end and that date.

2. As of January 31, 19X3, the company had granted 262,000 options to purchase common stock that were expected to provide cash proceeds of $382,000. Assume that the split shares could be purchased on the open market for $2.00 per share on the average. Derive the 19X3 primary earnings per share calculation stated as $0.34.

3. Use the information in the table on trading volume and stock prices during March and April of 19X2 to assess the apparent stock price impact of the April 10, 19X2 (first quarter fiscal year 19X3) stock split.

NATIONAL TECHNICAL SYSTEMS, INC.
Consolidated Statement of Stockholders' Equity
Years Ended January 31, 19X3, 19X2, and 19X1

	Common Stock Number of Shares (Note 2)	Amount	Additional Paid-in Capital	Retained Earnings	Total Stockholders' Equity
Balance at January 31, 19X0	844,000	$ 84,000	$ 1,018,000	$ 1,346,000	$ 2,448,000
Net earnings				567,000	567,000
Purchase and retirement of common shares	(106,000)	(10,000)	(311,000)	-	(321,000)
Balance at January 31, 19X1	738,000	74,000	707,000	1,913,000	2,694,000
Net earnings				379,000	379,000
Purchase and retirement of common shares	(6,000)	(1,000)	(18,000)	-	(19,000)
Balance at January 31, 19X2	732,000	73,000	689,000	2,292,000	3,054,000
Net earnings				707,000	707,000
Stock options exercised	33,000	3,000	56,000		59,000
Stock split effected in the form of a stock dividend	495,000	50,000	(50,000)	-	-
Balance at January 31, 19X3	1,260,000	$ 126,000	$ 695,000	$ 2,999,000	$ 3,820,000

Consolidated Statement of Earnings
Years Ended January 31, 19X3, 19X2, and 19X1

	19X3	19X2	19X1
Revenues	$18,175,000	$13,217,000	$11,929,000
Net earnings	707,000	379,000	567,000
Earnings per share after giving effect to the stock split			
Primary	$0.34	$0.19	$0.26
Fully diluted	0.33	0.19	0.26

NOTE 2:

On March 31, 19X2, the Board of Directors approved a stock split to be effected in the form of a 66-2/3 percent stock dividend of the Company's common stock to shareholders of record on April 10, 19X2 and paid on April 30, 19X2.

On December 14, 19X2, the Board of Directors approved a stock split to be effected in the form of a 60% stock dividend of the Company's common stock to shareholders of record on January 18, 19X3. The dividend is payable on February 5, 19X3. Net earnings per share in the consolidated financial statements have been restated to give effect to the stock splits.

NATIONAL TECHNICAL SYSTEMS
February 26, 19X2 to April 30, 19X2

Date	Volume of trading (00s)	Closing stock price	Date	Volume of trading (00s)	Closing stock price
2/26/19X2	1066	2.25	4/1/19X2	6399	2.50
2/27/19X2	1066	2.25	4/2/19X2	4266	2.58
3/2/19X2	10666	2.25	4/3/19X2	19733	2.88
3/3/19X2	0	2.25	4/6/19X2	8533	3.06
3/4/19X2	7999	2.31	4/7/19X2	533	3.19
3/5/19X2	2666	2.31	4/8/19X2	0	3.19
3/6/19X2	3733	2.50	4/9/19X2	0	3.19
3/9/19X2	0	2.50	4/10/19X2	0	3.19
3/10/19X2	1599	2.50	4/13/19X2	11199	3.56
3/11/19X2	0	2.50	4/14/19X2	18133	3.50
3/12/19X2	0	2.50	4/15/19X2	12266	3.75
3/13/19X2	0	2.50	4/16/19X2	2666	3.75
3/16/19X2	533	2.50	4/17/19X2	0	3.75
3/17/19X2	0	2.50	4/20/19X2	23999	3.81
3/18/19X2	533	2.50	4/21/19X2	10666	3.81
3/19/19X2	0	2.50	4/22/19X2	7999	3.75
3/20/19X2	0	2.50	4/23/19X2	1066	3.75
3/23/19X2	0	2.50	4/24/19X2	4799	3.75
3/24/19X2	0	2.50	4/27/19X2	533	3.75
3/25/19X2	3733	2.50	4/28/19X2	0	3.75
3/26/19X2	0	2.50	4/29/19X2	1066	3.75
3/27/19X2	0	2.50	4/30/19X2	0	3.75
3/30/19X2	1066	2.50			
3/31/19X2	0	2.50			

12.3 GENERAL DYNAMICS CORPORATION

Common shareholders' equity

General Dynamics operates in five principal business segments: government aerospace (F-16 fighter plane), submarines (Seawolf), land systems and tanks (M-1 tank), general aviation (Cessna), and mining. Listed on the New York Stock Exchange (Ticker = GD).

The table below, from the Consolidated Statement of Common Stockholders' Equity, summarizes the transactions that took place during years 19X0–19X2 affecting common stockholders' equity. The company reported earnings per share from continuing operations for 19X0–19X2 of $2.92, $5.30, and $8.08, respectively.

1. For the year ended December 31, 19X1, construct journal entries that would record the transactions that affected common stock, retained earnings, and Treasury stock. Assume the company uses the cost method to account for purchases of Treasury stock. Also, assume that the book value method is used to account for the conversion of preferred stock.

2. Estimate the impact on 19X2 net earnings per share of the increase in Treasury shares acquired as part of the stock purchase program from 3,499,885 shares in 19X1 to 10,130,746 shares in 19X2. Assume that the Treasury shares were all purchased on July 1, in both years.

3. Use the end-of-month stock price data to estimate the gain to the company as of December 31, 19X2 as a result of the stock purchases made during 19X1 and 19X2. Assume that all shares were purchased at the average purchase price. Provide a journal entry that would record the hypothetical sale of all Treasury stock at December 31, 19X2 to the general investing public at the market price at that date. Assume the company uses the cost method to account for Treasury stock purchases and sales.

CONSOLIDATED STATEMENT OF COMMON STOCKHOLDERS' EQUITY
Dollars in millions, except per share amounts

	Common stock		Ret. Earngs.	Treasury stock	
	Shares	Amount CR(DR)	CR(DR)	Shares	Amount DR(CR)
Balance, 1 January 19X0	55,442,100	$ 87.8	$ 1,020.0	1,829,220	$ 36.3
Net earnings			132.8		
Cash dividends			(41.1)		
Stock options exercised		(5.2)		(948,913)	(19.1)
Conversions of preferred stock				(3,006)	(0.1)
Shares acquired, at cost				174,355	4.5
Shares issued under incentive compensation plan		0.3		(98,917)	(2.0)
Balance, 31 December 19X0	55,442,100	82.9	1,111.7	952,739	19.6
Net earnings			286.6		
Cash dividends			(52.2)		
Stock options exercised		(3.9)		(433,334)	(15.0)
Conversions of preferred stock		(0.3)	(29.7)	(1,228,110)	(57.0)
Stock purchase program (average cost per share $54)				3,499,885	189.2
Other shares acquired, at cost				24,247	1.0
Shares issued under incentive compensation plan		1.4		(94,144)	(1.9)
Balance, 31 December 19X1	55,442,100	80.1	1,316.4	2,721,283	135.9
Net earnings			381.7		
Cash dividends			(48.3)		
Stock options exercised			(5.2)	(437,853)	(22.3)
Stock option plan contributions		0.9		(84,016)	(4.5)
Stock purchase program (average cost per share $55)				10,130,746	557.8
Other shares acquired, at cost				34,439	2.2
Shares issued under incentive compensation plan		(0.9)		(128,612)	(6.5)
Balance, 31 December 19X2	55,442,100	80.1	1,644.6	12,235,987	662.6

END-OF-MONTH STOCK PRICES: JANUARY 1, 19X2 TO DECEMBER 31, 19X3

1-Jan-19X2	$58.125	31-Jan-19X3	$76.500
31-Jan-19X2	52.875	28-Feb-19X3	79.250
29-Feb-19X2	48.000	31-Mar-19X3	73.000
31-Mar-19X2	45.625	30-Apr-19X3	66.625
30-Apr-19X2	50.000	31-May-19X3	71.750
31-May-19X2	45.000	30-Jun-19X3	74.375
30-Jun-19X2	52.500	31-Jul-19X3	76.000
31-Jul-19X2	53.000	31-Aug-19X3	77.750
31-Aug-19X2	64.500	30-Sep-19X3	69.625
30-Sep-19X2	60.000	31-Oct-19X3	62.375
31-Oct-19X2	64.250	30-Nov-19X3	68.375
30-Nov-19X2	65.875	31-Dec-19X3	68.750
31-Dec-19X2	69.500		

12.4 GIFFORD TECHNOLOGIES CORPORATION

Earnings per share

On April 25, 19X3, the following article appeared in the *Daily Financial Journal.*

"GTC GOOD NEWS NOT FULLY DILUTED"

The big question at GTC annual meeting Monday was just how the company fared in the first quarter ended March 31. Right at the start, Chairman Gary Walters had what sounded like good news: The company's sales were $1.474 billion, up from $1.362 billion in the same three-month period a year before. Net income was $48.3 million, up from $37.2 million in 19X2. And, Walters told the group, fully-diluted earnings per share were $1.14, up from $1 flat the first quarter the year before.

It all sounded fine. But Rick Chambers of San Francisco left to call his broker during the meeting and asked him how GTC stock was doing that afternoon in the New York market. Poorly, the broker told Chambers. Poorly, because the Dow Jones wire service had issued a report that morning that the company's earnings were down.

So when Chambers returned to the meeting, he had a question for Walters: "What's going on?"

Walters replied that GTC had issued a press release to Dow Jones late the previous Friday, but that "..the company cannot be responsible for what the news service says." Walters went over the earnings per share numbers again. The probable catch was that primary earnings per share had dropped by 2 cents to $1.39, relative to the same quarter last year.

"Dow Jones is reporting only the primary earnings per share, and that's what the market is seemingly reacting to," said Walters. He continued: "We reported both of them, primary and fully-diluted."

However, the press release made no mention of primary earnings per share until the fourth and final page where a cumbersome statistical chart was presented. Moreover, the late-Friday report to Dow Jones and the other wire services didn't include the chart. Thus no mention was made to the wire services of primary earnings per share at all. And a year earlier, the press and wire service material made no mention of fully-diluted earnings per share for the first quarter, supplying the public with only primary earnings per share.

Walters explained that the reason for emphasizing the fully diluted figures was because some 6,876,001 shares were issued in the first quarter as a result of a conversion of the company's $8 convertible preferred shares the company had issued earlier to acquire a successful, research-oriented company called GSA, Inc. (Some 1.1 million shares of the $8 preferred shares are still outstanding and can be converted into 4.8 million shares of common.)

The effect of the conversions was that the average common shares outstanding for the first quarter of this year was 34.6 million, up from 26.5 million a year before. And even though GTC's profits advanced by 15.8 percent, when the number of shares outstanding increases by 30.9 percent, that means lower primary earnings per share.

The stock showed a modest loss for the day. It closed down at $39.625 per share, down 37.5 cents from Friday's closing price, and down relative to a NYSE market.

The earnings per share presentation in the first quarter report was:

Per share of common stock	19X3	19X2
Primary earnings	$ 1.39*	$ 1.41*
Fully diluted earnings	$ 1.14	$ 1.00
Average number of shares outstanding	34,648,994	26,462,074

*During the three months ended March 31, 19X3, 6,876,001 shares of common stock were issued upon conversion of 1,547,296 shares of $8.00 preferred stock. Had these conversions, as well as conversions of these securities and conversions of 4.25 percent convertible subordinated debentures which occurred during 19X2, taken place on January 1, 19X2, primary earnings per share would have been $1.29 and $1.10, respectively, for the quarters ended March 31, 19X3 and 19X2.

Use the preceding information to answer the following questions. Make any reasonable assumptions you wish.

1. Explain why primary earnings per share dropped while fully-diluted earnings per share rose.

2. Refer to the footnote in the earnings per share presentation. Why are the proforma earnings per share figures lower than those presented in the statements?

3. Discuss possible reasons why the company placed more emphasis on fully diluted earnings per share.

4. What might account for the stock market's reaction to the quarterly earnings report? Should management rely on the efficiency of the market to reflect "correctly" all available information about the company's future prospects? What is the role of press releases and reports given to the wire services in reporting the results of operations?

5. Which of primary or fully-diluted earnings per share is a better measure of this company's performance? Does either method properly reflect the future potential dilution of common shares?

12.5 BENDIX CORPORATION

Earnings per share and common stock dividends

This case is designed to replicate the calculations for earnings per share from continuing operations used by Bendix Corporation to compute primary earnings per share for each of the years 19X1 to 19X3. The calculations to be made are based on Exhibit 11 submitted in conjunction with the Corporation's SEC Form 10-K report for the year ended September 30, 19X3. Later in 19X3, Bendix and Allied Corporation consummated a merger providing for Allied's acquisition of Bendix, financed by the conversion of each outstanding share of Bendix not owned by Allied into shares of Allied common stock plus fixed income securities.

In addition to the information below, taken directly from the company's financial statements, the following notes and assumptions should be used in developing an answer.

Notes and assumptions:

1. Both the Series A and Series B convertible preferred stock were issued at a time when the Aa corporate bond yield was more that 50 percent higher than the effective yield on the convertible preferred stock securities at the time of their issuance. Assume that FASB Statement No. 85, *Yield Test for Determining whether a Convertible Security Is a Common Stock Equivalent* (an Amendment of *APB Opinion No. 15*) applies.

2. The table that follows states the assumed prices at which options to purchase Common Stock were granted, the assumed average Common Stock values during each of those years, and assumed Common Stock price at September 30.

For the Years Ended September 30	19X3	19X2	19X1
# outstanding options at September 30	661,479	695,584	633,839
Average price of options granted during year to purchase Common Stock	$ 39.00	$ 42.00	$ 27.00
Average price of Common Stock during year	44.875	48.875	32.00
Price of Common Stock at September 30	50.00	50.00	40.00

3. The table below states the actual and assumed average dates on which the various transactions involving Common Stock and Series A and Series B convertible preferred stock took place.

Date	Transaction	Common stock # shares	Series A Pref. # shares	Series B Pref. # shares
10/1/19X0	Opening balance	22,411,141	293,502	
10/1/19X0	Conversion.	86,563	(42,084)	(440)
12/31/19X0	Stock options	117,415		92,573
3/31/19X1	Acquisitions	407,842		3,976,562
10/1/19X1	Opening balance	23,022,961	251,418	4,068,695
10/31/19X1	Conversion	126,463	(57,258)	(11,962)
2/27/19X2	Repurchase	(4,000,014)		
9/30/19X2	Stock options	219,570		58,290
10/1/19X2	Opening balance	19,368,980	194,160	4,115,023
3/31/19X3	Stock options	60,891		85,621
9/30/19X3	Conversion	2,002,954	(25,112)	(2,541,303)
9/30/19X3	Closing balance	21,432,825	169,048	1,659,341

Information from the financial statements:

BENDIX CORPORATION
Summary Income Statements
For the Years Ended September 30

(Dollars in millions, except per share amounts)	19X3	19X2	19X1
Net sales, royalties, and other operating income	$ 4,112.6	$ 4,425.4	$ 3,864.1
Income from continuing operations	137.8	204.5	134.2
Net income	132.8	452.8	191.6
Cash dividends declared (in millions)			
Series A Preferred Stock	0.5	0.5	0.7
Series B Preferred Stock	16.2	16.6	8.2
Common Stock	64.5	60.6	64.9
Income per share from continuing operations:			
A: Before major dispositions	$ 6.02	$ 7.03	$ 4.94
B: Total	6.02	8.35	5.38
(Loss) Income from discontinued operations			
(net of taxes)	(0.22)	10.14	2.30
Net income per share	$ 5.80	$ 18.49	$ 7.68

STOCK OPTION PLANS

Under the Corporation's stock option plans, certain employees have been granted options to purchase Common Stock at prices which represented 100 percent of the fair market value on the dates the options were granted, as adjusted for stock splits and and stock dividends. Options may be generally exercised over a period of ten years from the date of the grant. No option may be exercised earlier that one year from the date the option was granted, and generally options become exercisable in three equal annual installments beginning with the first anniversary of the date of the grant.

EARNINGS PER SHARE

Net income per share has been computed based upon the weighted average number of common and common stock equivalent shares outstanding. The Corporation's Series A $3 Cumulative Convertible Preferred Stock, Series B 9-3/4% Cumulative Convertible Preferred Stock (issued during March 19X1), and options on Common Stock and Series B Preferred Stock are classified as common stock equivalents and are therefore included in the weighted average number of common and common equivalent shares outstanding.

STOCKHOLDERS' EQUITY

Each share of the Series A $3 Cumulative Convertible Preferred Stock (Series A Preferred Stock) is convertible into 2.05 shares of Common Stock, subject to adjustments in certain events. The Series A Preferred Stock is entitled to $60 per share in liquidation and is redeemable, at the Corporation's option, at $63 per share at September 30, 19X3, decreasing by $1 per share annually at each June 30 through June 30, 19X6, and thereafter at $60 per share. Each share of the Series B 9-3/4% Cumulative Convertible Preferred Stock (Series B Preferred Stock) is convertible into 0.768 shares of Common Stock, subject to adjustment in certain events. The Series B Preferred Stock is entitled to $41.50 per share in liquidation and is redeemable, at the Corporation's option, beginning March 31, 19X6 at $43.52, decreasing by $0.40 per share annually each March 31 through March 31, 19X11, and thereafter at $41.50 per share.

On February 27, 19X2, the Corporation purchased through a tender offer approximately four million shares of its outstanding Common Stock at $64 per share. All such purchased shares have been cancelled and retired.

At September 30, 19X3, 3,762,432 shares of Common Stock were reserved for conversion of Series A and Series B Preferred Stock and for the Company's Stock Option, Incentive Compensation, Performance Incentive, and Stock Ownership plans, and 279,180 shares of Series B Preferred Stock were reserved for a subsidiary's employee stock option plan.

BENDIX CORPORATION
A summary of the stockholders' equity accounts is set forth below:

In millions, except for number of shares	Series A Preferred Stock shares	amount	Series B Preferred Stock shares	amount	Common Stock shares	amount	Addtnl. Capital amount	Retained Earnings amount
Balance, October 1, 19X0 as previously reported	293,502	$2.2			22,411,141	$112.1	$31	$894
Cumulative effect of accounting change for compensated absences								(14)
As restated								881
Net income								192
Cash dividends declared								
Series A preferred stock								(1)
Series B preferred stock								(8)
Common stock								(65)
Stock issued for acquired businesses			3,976,562	165.0	407,842	2.0	14	
Conversion of preferred stock	(42,084)	(0.3)	(440)		86,563	0.4	0	
Stock sold under stock option plans and related income tax benefits			92,573	3.9	117,415	0.6	2	
Balance, September 30, 19X1	251,418	1.9	4,068,695	168.9	23,022,961	115.1	47	998
Net income								453
Cash dividends declared								
Series A preferred stock								(1)
Series B preferred stock								(17)
Common stock								(61)
Stock purchase					(4,000,014)	(20.0)	(9)	(228)
Conversion of preferred stock	(57,258)	(0.4)	(11,962)	(0.5)	126,463	0.6	0	
Stock sold under stock option plans and related income tax benefits			58,290	2.4	219,570	1.1	5	
Balance, September 30, 19X2	194,160	1.5	4,115,023	170.8	19,368,980	96.8	43	1,144
Net income								133
Cash dividends declared								
Series A preferred stock								(1)
Series B preferred stock								(16)
Common stock								(65)
Conversion of preferred stock	(25,112)	(0.2)	(2,541,303)	(105.4)	2,002,954	10.0	96	
Stock sold under stock option plans and related income tax benefits			85,621	3.5	60,891	0.3	3	
Balance, September 30, 19X3	169,048	$1.3	1,659,341	$68.9	21,432,825	$107.1	$142	$1,195

13

Business Combinations

13.1 BLACK AND DECKER MANUFACTURING

Effect of consolidation on balance sheet

Study Note 2 from the Black and Decker Manufacturing Company's 19X4 annual report. The company's fiscal year ends on September 30. Net earnings for 19X4 were reported as $95,404,000. All numbers in the note are in thousands, except per share amounts.

1. Prepare a journal entry showing the effect on Black and Decker's Consolidated Balance Sheet (as of April 27, 19X4) of the acquisition of General Electric's housewares operations. The par value of the common stock issued in connection with the acquisition was $0.50 per share.

2. Would it have been possible to record this acquisition as a pooling of interests? State reasons.

3. Estimate the amount of goodwill that would have been charged as an expense in Black and Decker's year end 19X4 income statement.

4. From an analysis of the pro forma results of operations, does it appear that *Housewares* was a profitable or unprofitable operation during 19X4? Explain.

Note 2: *Acquisition of Housewares Operations*

On April 27, 19X4, the Company acquired substantially all of the assets and businesses of General Electric Company's Housewares operations. This acquisition includes operations in the United States, Canada, Mexico, Brazil and Singapore and brings to the Company a wide range of products which generally could be termed small household appliances, including food processing, beverage making, ovening, garment care and personal care products. The acquisition has been accounted for as a purchase transaction, and the consolidated statement of earnings for the year ended September 30, 19X4, includes the results of the Housewares operations from the purchase date.

The cost of the acquisition was financed by the payment of $108,800 in cash, long-term promissory notes with a discounted value of $42,153, and the issuance of three million shares of the Company's common stock with a fair value of $61,125, estimated in accordance with Accounting Principles Board Opinion No. 16. The excess of the total acquisition cost over the fair value of net assets acquired (goodwill) was $91,303 and is being amortized on a straight-line basis over twenty years.

The fair value assigned to assets acquired and liabilities assumed, excluding cash and marketable securities of $7,698, were as follows:

Accounts receivable	$ 8,048
Inventories	99,463
Property, plant and equipment	119,361
Goodwill	91,303
Other assets	52,160
Current liabilities	(116,358)
Other long-term liabilities	(49,597)
	$ 204,380

Other assets consist primarily of patents and trade-marks. Included in current liabilities and other long-term liabilities are amounts of $24,000 and $48,600, respectively, which represent brand transition, redundancy, relocation and plant closing costs incident to the acquisition.

Pro forma results of operations, assuming the acquisition occurred at the beginning of each period presented, are displayed in the following table. These pro forma results have been prepared for comparative purposes only and do not purport to be indicative of the results of operations which actually would have resulted had the combination been in effect on the dates indicated, or which may result in the future.

	19X4	19X3
Net Sales	$ 1,780,231	$ 1,634,044
Earnings from continuing operations	87,153	30,558
Net Earnings	87,153	46,558
Earnings per share:		
Continuing Operations	$ 1.72	$ .66
Discontinued Operations	-	.35
Total	$ 1.72	$ 1.01
Average Shares Outstanding	50,700	46,200

13.2 ALLEGHENY LUDLUM CORPORATION

Equity vs. cost accounting for affiliated companies

Allegheny Ludlum manufactures and markets specialized products worldwide for a diversity of industrial and consumer uses. The range of Allegheny's businesses includes consumer products, specialty metals, industrial specialties, safety and protection equipment, and railway products. Listed on the New York Stock Exchange (Ticker = ALS).

Study Allegheny's Consolidated Statements of Earnings for 19X0–19X2, the excerpts from Note 6 to the consolidated financial statements, and the section on financial review.

1. State Allegheny's Equity Earnings for the years 19X0–19X2. Comment as to how equity earnings are considered distinct from earnings from continuing operations (before equity earnings).

2. State dividends received by Allegheny from unconsolidated affiliated companies in 19X0–19X2.

3. Allegheny accounts for its investments in affiliated companies on the "equity basis." Restate Allegheny's Net Earnings as if they had been computed on the "cost basis" of accounting for the unconsolidated affiliated companies.

4. Excluding Earnings (loss) from discontinued operations, to what extent did Allegheny's profit position improve from 19X1 to 19X2? Comment as to whether the Proforma Summaries of Sales and Earnings as shown in the accompanying Financial Review provide a better picture of the change in earnings from 19X1 to 19X2.

ALLEGHENY LUDLUM CORPORATION
Consolidated Statements of Earnings
for the Years 19X2, 19X1, and 19X0

In thousands	19X2	19X1	19X0
Earnings from continuing operations			
before income taxes and equity earnings	$ 34,190	$ 41,085	$ 23,422
Income taxes	13,153	23,108	9,492
Earnings from continuing operations			
before equity earnings	21,037	17,977	13,930
Equity earnings	45,839	28,126	12,255
Earnings from continuing operations	66,876	46,103	26,185
Earnings (loss) from discontinued operations,			
net of applicable income taxes	(20,981)	25,424	7,189
Net earnings	45,895	71,527	33,374
Common shares issued	7,669,772	7,579,532	7,323,608

Note 6

At December 28, 19X2 the quoted market price of the 3,335,000 shares of Liquid Air's common stock owned by Allegheny aggregated $99,216,000 and Allegheny's carrying value thereof was $78,101,000. Allegheny's carrying value exceeded its proportionate share of Liquid Air's net assets by $10,116,000 at December 28, 19X2 and $10,466,000 at December 30, 19X1.

Wilkinson Match Limited
Condensed Consolidated Balance Sheets

In thousands	September 30 19X2	March 31 19X1
ASSETS		
Current assets	$ 277,248	$ 330,068
Property, plant, and equipment	147,183	115,851
Other assets	24,910	14,683
	449,341	460,602
LIABILITIES AND SHAREHOLDERS' EQUITY		
Current liabilities	$ 167,787	$ 190,192
Long-term debt	53,535	85,618
Deferred income taxes and other long-term liabilities	29,420	6,625
Minority interests	29,559	31,894
Shareholders' equity	169,040	146,273
	449,341	460,602

Wilkinson's September 30, 19X2 balance sheet is consolidated in
  Allegheny's December 28, 19X2 balance sheet.

ALLEGHENY LUDLUM CORPORATION
Wilkinson Match Limited
Condensed Consolidated Summaries of Earnings

In thousands	Year ended September 30 19X2	Six months ended September 30 19X1	Year ended March 31 19X1
Net sales	$ 611,765	$ 280,174	$ 556,383
Earnings before minority interest	20,100	4,886	15,922
Minority interests	3,945	1,066	2,050
Net earnings	16,155	3,820	13,872
Equity earnings recognized by Allegheny after giving effect to dividend requirements on Wilkinson's preference stock	$ 7,079	$ 1,669	$ 6,105

The condensed financial statements of Wilkinson were translated by Allegheny into U.S. dollars and adjusted to reflect Allegheny's cost bases (at a 44.4% ownership level prior to September 30, 19X2 and 100% ownership effective on such date) in Wilkinson's net assets pursuant to Accounting Principles Board Opinion No. 16 and United States generally accepted accounting principles.

Wilkinson's consolidated balance sheets as of September 30, 19X2 and March 31, 19X1 and summaries of earnings for the years ended September 30, 19X2 and March 31, 19X1 and the six months ended September 30, 19X1, before translation and the adjustments described above, were examined by auditors other than Allegheny's independent public accountants.

The excess of Allegheny's proportionate share of Wilkinson's net assets over Allegheny's investment therein, aggregating $11,398,000 at December 28, 19X2 and $12,740,000 at December 30, 19X1, has been applied as an adjustment to appropriate noncurrent assets of Wilkinson.

Dividends received by Allegheny from all of its unconsolidated affiliated companies aggregated $7,771,000 in 19X2, $31,799,000 in 19X1 and $1,196,000 in 19X0. Allegheny's consolidated retained earnings as of December 28, 19X2 and December 30, 19X1 includes undistributed earnings of unconsolidated affiliated companies of $67,754,000 and $45,142,000, respectively.

Financial Review

Because of the accounting treatment afforded major corporate transactions completed in 19X2, the consolidated statement of earnings for 19X2, shown elsewhere in this report, does not reflect the level of sales and earnings of the Corporation as we entered 19X3.

Allegheny Ludlum Steel, which was owned for all of last year but sold at year-end, was treated as a discontinued operation. As a result, its sales and earnings for the year 19X2 were excluded from the results of Allegheny's continuing operations.

Full ownership of Wilkinson Match Limited was achieved in October 19X2. However, because Wilkinson is reflected in the Corporation's results on a three month delayed basis, Allegheny's earnings statement includes only the equity earnings from the 44.4 percent interest for twelve months ended September 30, 19X2.

In order to portray the Corporation as it exists today, pro forma summaries of sales and earnings for 19X2 and 19X1 are shown on this page. Wilkinson is reflected as though it were wholly-owned for both years, as is Schenuit Industries, Inc., a much smaller but dynamic enterprise acquired in mid-19X2. Operations of Allegheny Ludlum Steel are excluded from the summaries for both 19X1 and 19X2; the steel company is treated as though it had been sold at the end of 19X0.

ALLEGHENY LUDLUM CORPORATION
Proforma Summaries of Sales and Earnings

In millions except per share amounts	19X2	19X1
Net sales	$ 1,591.1	$ 1,516.6
Earnings from continuing operations before		
minority interests and equity earnings	41.2	35.0
Minority interests	(4.0)	(2.6)
Equity earnings	38.8	22.5
Earnings from continuing operations	76.0	54.9
Earnings (loss) from discontinued operations	(3.8)	$6.4
Net earnings	72.2	61.3
Earnings per share of Common Stock:		
Primary:		
Continuing operations	$ 8.28	$ 5.04
Net earnings	7.76	5.91
Fully diluted:		
Continuing operations	6.74	4.15
Net earnings	6.34	4.77

13.3 NATIONAL DISTILLERS AND CHEMICAL CORPORATION

Unconsolidated equity investments, purchase accounting

National Distillers and Chemical Corporation (NDCC) engages in the production and marketing of petrochemicals, alcoholic beverages, wines and brandy, metal products, and insurance. NDCC's associated companies produce and market natural gas liquids, polyethylene, titanium, and chemical raw materials. Listed on the NASDAQ exchange (Ticker = D.NQZ). Dollar amounts in thousands, except per share data.

Study the 19X1 Consolidated Statement of Cash Flow and the excerpts from the notes to the financial statements.

1. Identify the amounts reported as Investments in Associated Companies for years 19X2 and 19X3 and state whether those amounts are accounted for on the equity or cost basis.

2. State how NDCC's reported net income would change if NDCC's share of dividends received from Associated companies suddenly doubled from $34,910,000 to twice that amount.

3. Ignoring tax effects, calculate how NDCC's 19X3 balance sheet would change if the company had been able to account for Investments in Associated Companies on the cost basis. Assume only two account balances are affected.

4. Ignoring tax effects, calculate how NDCC's 19X3 and 19X2 net income would change if the company had been able to account for Investments in Associated Companies on the cost basis.

5. Prepare a journal entry dated May 19, 19X1 that would show the effects of the purchase of Emery Industries, Inc. on the consolidated balance sheet. As indicated the acquisition price amounted to $196 million. In reconstructing this entry, assume also that certain "other expenses" associated with the $196 million purchase were accrued directly by NDCC and, hence, not included in the $72.3 million cash payment. NDCC acquired certain of Emery's current assets and current liabilities in addition to net noncurrent assets and goodwill.

Based on an earlier case by Mark A. Wolfson.

NATIONAL DISTILLERS AND CHEMICAL CORPORATION AND SUBSIDIARIES
Consolidated Statement of Cash flow

Year ended December 31,	19X1
Cash provided by operating activities	
Net income	$ 106,814
Charges (credits) to income not requiring (providing) cash	
Depreciation and amortization	37,943
Deferred income taxes on income	9,463
Unremitted earnings--insurance companies	(15,828)
Unremitted earnings--associated companies	(10,625)
Other charges	3,827
Tax benefit attributable to partnership operations included in share of earnings of associated companies	4,064
Changes in operating current assets and liabilities	
Accounts and note receivable	(29,966)
Inventories	(72,743)
Prepaid expenses	(91)
Accounts payable	12,127
Federal excise taxes payable	(973)
Income taxes payable	(4,525)
Other accrued liabilities	20,992
Total changes in operating current assets and current liabilities	(75,179)
TOTAL FROM OPERATING ACTIVITIES	$ 60,479
Cash from investing activities	
Disposals of plant assets	2,633
Sale of investments and other long-term receivables	15,036
Additions to property, plant and equipment	(105,730)
Additions to investments in associated companies	(23,895)
Net noncurrent assets of company acquired	(87,790)
Goodwill arising from company acquired	(47,126)
Other assets	(1,026)
TOTAL FROM INVESTING ACTIVITIES	$ (247,898)
Cash from financing activities	
Issuance of common stock on conversion of debentures	648
Sales or issuance of common stock under stock option employee savings and dividend reinvestment plans	1,076
Additional long-term debt and capital lease obligations	114,543
Preference stock issued for company acquired	120,474
Dividends to stockholders	(50,484)
Reduction of long-term debt	(31,830)
Loans payable to banks	(3,026)
Conversion of subordinated debentures	(650)
Acquisition of preferred stocks	(4,292)
TOTAL FROM FINANCING ACTIVITIES	$ 146,459
NET INCREASE (DECREASE) IN CASH	$ (40,960)

NATIONAL DISTILLERS AND CHEMICAL CORPORATION AND SUBSIDIARIES

Notes to Consolidated Financial Statements
Dollar amounts in thousands, except per share data
Note 1—Business Combinations

On May 19, 19X1, the company acquired by merger Emery Industries, Inc. ("Emery"), a manufacturer of chemicals principally derived from natural fats and oils. In connection with the merger, the company issued 5,414,544 shares of $1.85 Preference Stock, redemption price $22.25 per share and paid $72,300 in cash. The total cost of the acquisition, excluding sundry expenses was approximately $196,000. The transaction has been accounted for as a purchase and the excess of the purchase cost over fair value of net assets acquired of $47,126 (Goodwill) is being amortized on the straight line basis over 40 years. The results of operations of Emery have been included in the Company's consolidated financial statements from the date of merger. The following summarizes unaudited proforma operating results for the year ended December 31, 19X1, as if the operations of the Company and Emery had been consolidated for the entire year.

Net sales	$ 1,942,454
Net income	$ 107,304
Net income per share	$ 3.12

Note 2—Investment in Associated Companies
Summary financial information for associated companies as a group is as follows:

	December 31	
Balance Sheet Data	19X3	19X2
Current assets	$ 286,394	$ 287,453
Property, plant and equipment	258,204	248,221
Other assets	89,835	60,515
	634,433	596,189
Current liabilities	$ 132,570	$ 106,963
Long-term debt	80,311	67,530
Other liabilities	60,770	61,430
Shareholders' equity	360,782	360,266
	634,433	596,189
National's share of shareholders' equity	$ 146,964	$ 146,028

At December 31, 19X3, the Company's share of the undistributed earnings of corporate associated companies was $30,909.

	Year ended December 31		
Income statement data	19X3	19X2	19X1
Revenues	$ 740,015	$ 619,228	$ 477,471
Net earnings	113,910	47,874	55,388
Distributions	74,262	55,781	36,709
National's share of earnings	39,381	25,744	26,075
National's share of distributions	34,910	24,901	15,450

14

Changing Prices and Foreign Currency

14.1 RUAPEHU SKI COMPANY

Constant dollar restatements

The Ruapehu Ski Company (a fictitious company) presents to its stockholders financial statements under historical cost and historical cost restated in units of constant purchasing power. The Company uses the consumer price index as the basis for the generalized purchasing power adjustments and restates all items into end-of-year dollars at the latest balance sheet date.

Use the information in the summarized balance sheets and statements of cash flow to answer the following questions. Carry all index calculations to three places after the decimal point.

1. The Company uses the consumer price index to restate its accounts in units of constant purchasing power. On April 30, 19X5, this index stood at 181.000. Use two separate calculations to estimate what the index would have been one year earlier on April 30, 19X4.

2. The Consolidated Statement of Cash Flow reports the General price level loss from holding noncurrent monetary assets and liabilities as $92,000 for fiscal year 19X5. Show how the Company would have calculated this amount using the relevant noncurrent accounts.

3. Estimate the consumer price index when Land held for investment was purchased (assumed bought as a single transaction only).

4. Calculate the end-of-year Retained earnings in units of constant purchasing power as of April 30, 19X4 that would have been reported in the annual financial statements for the fiscal year end April 30, 19X4.

5. The Company in its Consolidated Statement of Income reports its sales revenue as follows:

	April 30, 19X5	April 30, 19X4
Historical cost	$ 12,951,400	$ 10,353,700
Historical cost in April 30,19X5 constant dollars	C$ 13,197,500	C$ 11,954,100

Assume that prices rose at a constant (linear) function of time during the year, and show numerically—what any skier knows—that Ruapehu experienced more sales revenue in the second six months versus the first six months of the fiscal year.

RUAPEHU SKI COMPANY
Consolidated Balance Sheet
for the years ended April 30, 19X5 and 19X4

| | Historical cost | | Historical cost restated in units of constant purchasing power as of April 30, 19X5 | |
	19X5	19X4	19X5	19X4
Assets				
Cash	$ 1,080,900	$ 2,393,200	C$ 1,080,900	C$ 2,651,600
Other current assets	4,371,300	459,500	4,373,800	512,800
Total current assets	5,452,200	2,852,700	5,454,700	3,164,400
Land held for investment (at cost)	585,500	585,500	758,200	758,200
Fixed assets				
Ski lifts, buildings, and equipment	15,485,000	13,819,700	20,659,500	18,997,200
less accumulated depreciation	4,805,600	3,989,100	7,126,600	6,071,600
	10,679,400	9,830,600	13,532,900	12,925,600
Land	601,300	544,900	903,600	845,100
Notes receivable	993,500	1,143,800	993,500	1,267,300
Other assets (assume nonmonetary)	401,500	382,400	537,600	519,400
Total assets	$ 18,713,400	$ 15,339,900	C$ 22,180,500	C$ 19,480,000
Liabilities				
Current liabilities	2,699,500	1,370,000	2,699,500	1,517,900
Long-term debt less current maturities	146,000	183,100	146,000	202,900
Deferred income taxes (assume nonmonetary)	2,250,500	1,984,800	2,551,400	2,411,400
Total liabilities	$ 5,096,000	$ 3,537,900	C$ 5,396,900	C$ 4,132,200
Stockholders' equity				
Common stock of $1 par value; issued 1,159,454 shares in 19X5 and 1,158,205 shares in 19X4	1,159,500	1,158,200	1,913,000	1,911,700
Capital in excess of par value of common stock	3,282,900	3,285,700	4,155,700	4,158,600
Retained earnings	9,751,600	7,448,200	11,321,900	9,388,400
Less common stock in Treasury--at cost 86,396 shares in 19X5 and 7,000 shares in 19X4	(576,600)	(90,100)	(607,000)	(110,900)
Total stockholders' equity	$ 13,617,400	$ 11,802,000	C$ 16,783,600	C$ 15,347,800
Total liabilities and stockholders' equity	$ 18,713,400	$ 15,339,900	C$ 22,180,500	C$ 19,480,000

RUAPEHU SKI COMPANY
CONSOLIDATED STATEMENT OF CASH FLOW
for the years ended April 30, 19X5 and 19X4

	Historical cost		Historical cost restated in units of constant purchasing power as of April 30,	
	19X5	19X4	19X5	19X4
Sources of cash				
From operations				
Net earnings	$ 2,303,400	$ 1,713,000	C$ 1,933,500	C$ 1,612,400
Depreciation	997,900	865,600	1,289,800	1,160,800
General price level loss from holding noncurrent monetary assets and liabilities			92,000	98,500
Other sources of cash	286,000	1,349,900	276,500	1,665,700
Cash provided by operations	3,587,300	3,928,500	3,591,800	4,537,400
Proceeds from notes receivable	150,300	150,300	166,000	166,000
Proceeds from sale of common stock	7,539,200	8,192,500	7,404,800	9,274,300
Total sources of cash	$ 3,801,600	$ 4,113,700	C$ 3,739,000	C$ 4,669,400
Uses of cash				
Additions to fixed assets	1,927,200	2,848,400	2,000,400	3,289,100
Retirement of long-term debt	37,100	72,600	41,100	87,600
Other uses of cash	567,300	19,000	588,800	22,000
Net changes in working capital items other than change in cash	2,582,300	533,400	2,679,400	741,800
Total uses of cash	5,113,900	3,473,400	5,309,700	4,140,500
Net change in cash	$ (1,312,300)	$ 640,300	C$ (1,570,700)	C$ 528,900

14.2   EXXON CORPORATION

*Effects of restatement of historical cost
to current values*

The Exxon Corporation's principal business is energy, involving the exploration
for and production of crude oil and natural gas, manufacture of petroleum products,
and transportation and sale of crude oil, natural gas, and petroleum products.
Exxon's business also involves exploration for and mining and sale of coal and
uranium, and fabrication of nuclear fuel.

Study Exxon's 19X8–19X9 Consolidated Balance Sheet and Statement of
Income, and tables showing the effects of changing prices on Exxon's operations
for 19X9.

1. What were Exxon's realized holding gains (or realized cost savings) for
    19X9? In answering this question, compare the historical costs and the
    current (specific) costs columns only.

2. Estimate unrealized holding gains on inventories and property, plant, and
    equipment (valued using current [specific] prices) as of December 31,
    19X9. Approximately, how much of the unrealized gains at December 31,
    19X9 accrued (i.e., became realizable) in 19X9?

3. Calculate the ratio of income from continuing operations to total assets on
    the historical-cost and the current (specific) cost basis. From an outside
    investor's standpoint, which measure best gauges the company's rate of
    return on invested assets? Explain your answer in words.

EXXON CORPORATION
Consolidated Balance Sheet

	December 31	
	19X9	19X8
Assets		
Current assets		
Cash, including time deposits of $1,360,181,000 and $1,755,758,000	$ 2,515,964,000	$ 1,992,573,000
Marketable securities	1,991,644,000	2,763,375,000
Notes and accounts receivable, less estimated doubtful amounts of $95,774,000 and $12,293,000	9,011,237,000	6,725,741,000
Inventories		
Crude oil, products and merchandise	4,789,936,000	3,726,938,000
Materials and supplies	690,758,000	570,030,000
Prepaid taxes and expenses	1,478,809,000	590,094,000
Total current assets	20,478,348,000	16,368,751,000
Investments and advances	1,474,601,000	1,533,078,000
Property, plant and equipment, at cost, less accumulated depreciation and depletion of $12,748,577,000 and $14,307,410,000	26,292,952,000	22,805,824,000
Deferred charges and other assets	1,244,063,000	823,151,000
Total assets	49,489,964,000	41,530,804,000
Liabilities		
Current liabilities		
Notes and loans payable	1,867,924,000	1,400,735,000
Accounts payable and accrued liabilities	11,845,361,000	9,115,451,000
Income taxes payable	2,170,130,000	1,524,545,000
Total current liabilities	15,883,415,000	12,040,731,000
Long-term debt	4,258,018,000	3,749,241,000
Annuity and other reserves	1,413,881,000	1,099,722,000
Deferred income tax credits	4,385,082,000	3,436,848,000
Other deferred credits	104,925,000	95,264,000
Equity of minority shareholders in affiliated companies	892,692,000	880,400,000
Total liabilities	26,938,013,000	21,302,206,000
Shareholders' equity	22,551,951,000	20,228,598,000
Total liabilities and shareholders' equity	$ 49,489,964,000	$ 41,530,804,000

EXXON CORPORATION
Consolidated Statement of Income

	December 31	
	19X9	19X8
Revenue		
Sales and other operating revenue, including excise taxes	$ 83,555,471,000	$ 63,895,527,000
Interest, earnings from equity interests and other revenue	1,253,577,000	990,512,000
	84,809,048,000	64,886,039,000
Costs and other deductions		
Crude oil and product purchases	40,831,456,000	31,407,903,000
Operating expenses	8,481,740,000	6,394,777,000
Selling, general and administrative expenses	4,291,395,000	3,639,772,000
Depreciation and depletion	2,027,064,000	1,677,882,000
Exploration expenses, including dry holes	1,052,134,000	775,220,000
Income, excise and other taxes	23,091,713,000	17,516,326,000
Interest expense	493,989,000	424,740,000
Foreign exchange loss	102,957,000	186,271,000
Income applicable to minority interests	141,357,000	100,148,000
	80,513,805,000	62,123,039,000
Net Income	$ 4,295,243,000	$ 2,763,000,000
Per share	$ 9.74	$ 6.20

Income from continuing operations and other changes in shareholders' equity adjusted for changing prices

For the year ended December 31, 19X9	(millions of dollars) as reported	(millions of average 19X9 dollars) Adjusted for General inflation	(millions of average 19X9 dollars) Adjusted for Specific costs
Income from continuing operations			
Total revenue	$ 84,809	$ 84,809	$ 84,809
Costs and other deductions			
Crude oil and product purchases	40,831	40,831	40,831
Depreciation and depletion	4,027	3,270	3,932
Other	14,070	14,070	14,070
Interest expense	494	494	494
Income, excise and other taxes	23,092	23,092	23,092
Total costs and other deductions	$ 80,514	$ 81,757	$ 82,419
Income from continuing operations	$ 4,295	$ 3,052	$ 2,390
Gain from decline in the purchasing power of net amounts owed		998	998
Increase in current cost of inventories and property, plant and equipment during 19X9			9,333
Less effect of increase in general price level during 19X9			6,634
Excess of increase in specific prices over increase in the general price level			2,699
Net income	$ 4,295		
Adjusted net income		$ 4,050	
Net change in shareholders' equity from above	$ 4,295	$ 4,050	$ 6,087

Summarized balance sheet adjusted for changing prices

At December 31, 19X9	(millions of dollars) as reported	(millions of average 19X9 dollars) Adjusted for General inflation	(millions of average 19X9 dollars) Adjusted for Specific costs
Assets			
Inventories	$ 5,481	$ 7,585	$ 11,558
Property, plant and equipment	26,293	35,796	45,418
All other assets	17,716	16,892	16,892
Total assets	49,490	60,273	73,868
Total liabilities	26,938	25,599	25,599
Shareholders' equity	$ 22,552	$ 34,674	$ 48,269

14.3

CRANE COMPANY AND SUBSIDIARIES

Investments at cost vs. market value

Crane Company is a diversified manufacturer of products for basic industry. Principal products include steel, cement, fluid and pollution control equipment, building products, and aircraft and aerospace systems. Listed on the New York Stock Exchange (Ticker = CR).

Study the assets section of Crane's Consolidated Balance Sheet at December 31, 19X2 and a note to the financial statements explaining various "miscellaneous items" in the Statement of Income. Crane's "Net income before taxes," but after including $7,312,023 for miscellaneous items, totaled $62,723,486. Net purchases of investments during 19X2 amounted to $13,676,182. The original acquisition cost of net investments sold during the year was $1,638,289.

If Crane had used market values instead of cost in accounting for its "investments" and had included any unrealized market appreciation in the calculation of net income before taxes:

1. At what amount would investments have been reported as of 19X2 and 19X1?

2. Prepare a journal entry to convert Crane's balance sheet as of January 1, 19X2 from historical cost to market value for investments only.

3. Assume that the investments were sold in the market for cash on January 2, 19X2 (the New York Stock Exchange was closed on New Year's Day). Prepare journal entries to record the sale, assuming accounting on the basis of historical cost.

4. Given the assumed sale in part 3, state net income before taxes for 19X2 on a market-value basis.

5. Provide the entries necessary to maintain the investments account on a market-value basis throughout the year, including December 31, 19X2. Assume that the investment account as of January 1, 19X2 is already stated at market value. Distinguish between unrealized gains and realized gains, where the latter are credited to retained earnings.

CRANE COMPANY AND SUBSIDIARIES
Consolidated Balance Sheet

At December 31	19X2	19X1
ASSETS		
Current Assets		
Cash	$ 20,674,488	$ 31,367,545
Short-term investments, at lower of cost or market	93,286,903	70,535,634
Accounts receivable less allowances of $3,303,487		
($3,472,642 in 19X1)	178,755,201	175,112,126
Inventories, at lower of cost, principally last-in,		
first-out, or market LIFO reserves amounted to		
$88,914,390 ($83,372,559 in 19X1)		
Finished goods	86,812,759	84,660,137
Work in process	45,848,137	53,316,042
Raw materials and supplies	33,370,982	38,900,550
Prepaid expenses	4,029,373	3,996,853
Total Current Assets	$ 462,777,843	$ 457,888,887
Investments and other assets		
Investments (Market $142,580,000; $82,395,000 in 19X1)	57,849,696	45,811,803
Unamortized debt discount	6,163,187	8,240,982
Construction fund	2,088,840	4,293,119
Outlying lands	1,224,283	1,224,283
Other assets	3,995,831	6,057,722
	$ 71,321,837	$ 65,627,909
Property, plant and equipment, at cost		
Land	32,725,441	34,799,160
Buildings	200,439,399	208,387,435
Machinery and equipment	845,912,255	856,244,060
	1,079,077,095	1,099,430,655
Less accumulated depreciation	609,059,683	580,693,139
	$ 470,017,412	$ 518,737,516
TOTAL ASSETS	$ 1,004,117,092	$ 1,042,254,312

Miscellaneous—Net

(In thousands)	19X2	19X1	19X0
Gain on sale of investments	$ 5,015	$ 2,547	$ 8,079
Disposal of capital assets	2,690	(1,379)	969
Termination of certain operations	(1,084)	(1,427)	(5,243)
Gain (loss) on repurchase of debentures	984	(178)	(168)
Minority interest	(1,076)	(1,733)	(701)
Foreign exchange adjustments	931	485	(659)
Other	(148)	(328)	(74)
	$ 7,312	$ (2,013)	$ 2,203

14.4 THE ROUSE COMPANY

Current-value-basis financial statements

The Rouse Company and Subsidiaries develops, owns, and manages shopping places, office projects, and mixed use commercial properties. The company's 100 projects—in operation or development—comprise almost 46 million feet of space across the United States and Canada. The company is also the developer of the new city of Columbia, Maryland, comprising more than 70,000 residents and 2,000 businesses. Listed on the NASDAQ exchange (Ticker = ROUS).

Study Rouse's 19Y7–19Y8 Balance Sheets on a cost basis and current value basis and Notes 1a–1c to the 19Y8 financial statements.

1. Provide a journal entry, dated December 31, 19Y8, that would convert the 19Y8 historical balance sheet to a current value basis. Assume that the company made the decision to convert from historical cost to current value accounting on December 31, 19Y8.

   Provide a similar journal entry, dated December 31, 19Y7, that would convert the 19Y7 historical balance sheet to a current value basis. Assume that the company made the decision to convert from historical cost to current value accounting on December 31, 19Y7.

2. Reconcile the change in the revaluation equity account from 19Y7 to 19Y8 to changes in the differences between the current value and historical cost amounts of the various assets and liabilities. Comment specifically on the reason for the change in the Deferred Income Taxes account.

3. How do market interest or investment rates affect the various components of the company's Revaluation Equity account?

4. The 19Y8 annual report states: "Management believes that the current values of the Company's assets and liabilities are the most realistic indicators of the company's financial strength and future profitability." Use the data below to calculate the compound annual growth rate of stockholders' equity per share for 19Y3–19Y8 on a cost and current value basis and comment on the appropriateness of management's views.

Per share of common stock*	19Y8	19Y7	19Y6	19Y5	19Y4	19Y3
Shareholders' equity						
Historical cost basis	$1.41	$1.46	$1.71	$1.75	$1.90	$1.33
Current value basis	30.65	27.13	24.04	20.08	15.92	13.38
Market price, year end	24.00	19.00	20.92	17.50	11.33	10.59

*Data from multi-year comparison of selected annual data.

THE ROUSE COMPANY
Consolidated Cost Basis and Current Value Balance Sheets
December 31, 19Y8 and 19Y7

(in thousands)	19Y8 Current value basis	19Y8 Cost basis	19Y7 Current value basis	19Y7 Cost basis
Assets				
Operating properties				
Current value	$ 2,955,440		$ 2,425,863	
Property and deferred costs of projects		$ 1,732,791		$ 1,379,840
less accumulated depreciation and amortization		(204,924)		(169,721)
TOTAL OPERATING PROPERTIES	2,955,440	1,527,867	2,425,863	1,210,119
Development operations				
Construction and development in progress	131,216	122,311	124,263	117,119
Pre-construction costs, net	6,223	6,223	1,777	1,777
Land held for development and sale	163,088	80,010	154,428	74,827
Other property	29,851	20,867	30,376	21,693
Other assets	62,668	62,668	64,106	64,106
Accounts and notes receivable	69,564	69,564	54,384	54,384
Investments in marketable securities	73,625	73,625	50,122	50,122
Cash and cash equivalents	117,074	117,074	146,885	146,885
Total	$ 3,608,749	$ 2,080,209	$ 3,052,204	$ 1,741,032
Liabilities				
Debt				
Property debt not carrying a parent company guarantee of payment	928,470	928,470	815,880	815,880
Parent company debt and debt carrying a parent company guarantee of payment	739,698	739,698	536,082	536,347
TOTAL DEBT	1,668,168	1,668,168	1,351,962	1,352,227
Accounts payable and accrued expenses	131,236	131,236	130,525	130,525
Obligations under capital leases	97,922	97,922	85,089	85,513
Deferred income taxes	194,166	90,309	169,495	78,184
Redeemable cumulative preferred stock	25,000	25,000	25,000	25,000
Common stock and other shareholders' equity				
Common stock of 1¢ par value	478	478	477	477
Additional paid-in capital	75,547	75,547	71,895	71,895
Retained earnings (deficit)	(8,048)	(8,048)	(1,091)	(1,091)
Revaluation equity	1,424,683		1,220,550	0
less Receivables for common stock sold to officers	(403)	(403)	(1,698)	(1,698)
TOTAL SHAREHOLDERS' EQUITY	1,492,257	67,574	1,290,133	69,583
Total	$ 3,608,749	$ 2,080,209	$ 3,052,204	$ 1,741,032

THE ROUSE COMPANY
Notes to the Consolidated Financial Statements

1. Current value basis financial statements

a. *Current value reporting*

The Company's operating properties, land held for development and sale and certain other assets have appreciated in value and, accordingly, their current values exceed their cost basis net book values determined in conformity with generally accepted accounting principles. Management believes that the current value basis financial statements more realistically reflect the underlying financial strength of the Company.

The current values of the operating properties, including interests in retail centers managed under contract, and certain other assets represent management's estimates of the value of these assets primarily as investments which are held for the long-term benefit of operating cash flows. The current values of land held for development and sale represent management's estimates of the value of these assets under long-term development and sales programs. These values do not necessarily represent the liquidation value of these assets. Consequently, current value shareholders' equity does not represent the liquidation value of the Company or the market value of its net assets taken as a whole.

Shareholders' equity on a current value basis was $1,492,257,000 or $30.65 per share at December 31, 19Y8 and $1,290,133,000 or $27.13 per share at December 31, 19Y7. The per share calculations reflect the assumed conversion of the convertible subordinated debentures.

b. *Bases of valuation*

Operating properties and managed retail centers—The current value of the Company's operating properties has been defined as the value of each property's equity interest (i.e., the present value of its forecasted net cash flow after deducting principal and interest payments on the debt specifically related to the property) plus the outstanding balance of related debt. The current value of the Company's interests in retail centers managed under contract has been defined as the lower of the present value of incentive fees which will be earned based on forecasts of net cash flow of the respective retail centers or payments which will be received in the event the management contracts are terminated. The forecasts of net cash flow are based on an evaluation of the history and future of each property and are supported by market studies; analyses of tenant lease terms and projected sales performance; and estimates of revenues and operating expenses over projection periods ranging from five to eleven years. The present values of forecasted net cash flows are determined using internal rates of return which vary by project and between years as investor yield requirements change.

The resulting values recognize the considerable differences between properties in terms of quality, age, outlook and risk as well as the prevailing yield requirements of investors for income-producing properties.

Development operations—Properties under development are carried at the same values as in the cost basis financial statements except for certain parcels of land which are being actively developed. Management believes that other properties under construction have values in excess of stated costs, but has taken the conservative position of not recognizing any value increment until these properties are completed and operating.

Land held for development and sale—The current value of land held for development and sale is based on long-term development and sales programs for each parcel of land. These programs set forth the proposed pace and cost of all improvements necessary to bring the land to saleable condition, the pace and price of all land sales and the costs to administer the land programs and sell the land.

Debt—Long-term mortgage debt relating to the operating properties is carried at the same amount as in the cost basis balance sheet. Since the value of the Company's equity interest in each property is based on net cash flow after mortgage principal and interest payments, any difference between the current value and cost basis of long-term mortgage debt is reflected in the value of the operating property. The current values of certain other debt and certain of the obligations under capital leases have been computed using estimated market interest rates for similar obligations.

Deferred income taxes—The deferred income taxes on a current value basis is an estimate of the present value of income tax payments which may be made based on projections of taxable income through 2046. The projections of taxable income include projects presently under development and future, unnamed development projects and reflect all allowable deductions permitted under the Internal Revenue Code. The inclusion of future, unnamed projects in the projections reduced the estimated present value of potential tax payments by approximately $16,619,000 at December 31, 19Y8 and $13,319,000 at December 31, 19Y7. The discount rates used to compute the present value of income taxes are based on the internal rates of return used to compute the current values of assets, adjusted to reflect the Company's assessment of the greater uncertainty with respect to the ultimate timing and amounts of income tax payments.

Other assets and liabilities—Substantially all other assets and liabilities are carried in the current value basis balance sheet at the lower of cost or net realizable value—the same stated value as in the cost basis balance sheet.

The application of the foregoing methods for estimating current value, including the potential income tax payments, represents the best judgment of management based upon its evaluation of the current and future economy and anticipated investor rates of return at the time such estimates were made. Judgments regarding these factors are not subject to precise quantification or verification and may change from time to time as economic and market factors, and management's evaluation of them, change.

The current value basis financial statements have been and will continue to be an integral part of the Company's annual report to shareholders, but consistent with previous practice, current value information will not be presented as part of the Company's quarterly reports to shareholders. The extensive market research, financial analysis and testing of results required to produce reliable current value information make it impractical to report this information on an interim basis.

c. *Revaluation equity*

The aggregate difference between the current value basis and cost basis of the Company's assets and liabilities is reported as revaluation equity in the shareholders' equity section of the consolidated current value basis balance sheets. The components of revaluation equity at December 31, 19Y8 and 19Y7 are as follows (in thousands):

	19Y8	19Y7
Value of interests in operating properties	$ 1,733,242	$ 1,529,776
Value of land held for development and sale	137,154	136,138
Value of land in development operations	7,500	6,862
Total equity value	1,877,896	1,672,776
Debt related to equity interests	1,252,632	917,687
Total asset value	3,130,528	2,590,463
Depreciated cost of operating properties and costs of land held for development and sale and land in development operations	(1,610,972)	(1,287,974)
Present value of potential income taxes related to revaluation equity, net of cost basis deferred income taxes	(103,857)	(91,311)
Other	8,984	9,372
Total revaluation equity	$ 1,424,683	$ 1,220,550

14.5 WITCO CHEMICAL CORPORATION

Reserve recognition accounting, present value calculations

The Witco Chemical Corporation produces a wide range of special-purpose chemical and petroleum products as well as engineered materials and parts for industrial and consumer use. Witco reported 1981 Income before Federal and Foreign Income Taxes of $68.4 million, including operating income from oil and gas activities of $9.2 million.

The accompanying supplemental financial data relating to oil and gas activities is reported in compliance with disclosure rules established by the Securities and Exchange Commission, called reserve recognition accounting (RRA).

1. Assume that future net revenues from proved developed and proved undeveloped oil and gas reserves will continue for 20 years only, and that the net revenues for the years 1985–2001 (i.e., the 17 years following 1984) are expected to be constant.[1] What is the constant annual net revenue stream to be generated in each of years 1985, 1986, etc.? (Note: The present value of proved reserves as of December 31, 1981, was $76,520,000, assuming a 10 percent discount rate.)

2. Assume that a subsidiary of Witco called Witco Oil and Gas Exploration Company has assets of cash $10,000,000 and oil and gas properties with an end-of-1980 present value of $85,419,000. The subsidiary has no liabilities, contributed capital of $20,000,000, with the remainder of equity retained in the business as undistributed earnings.

   a. Prepare a journal entry that would establish a beginning-of-1981 balance sheet for Witco Oil and Gas.

   b. Based on Witco's Summary of Oil and Gas Producing Activities, prepare a 1981 Statement of Income and end-of-1981 Balance Sheet for Witco Oil and Gas in accordance with reserve recognition accounting. Assume that all transactions with outside parties are for cash, except a federal taxes refund that the company receives on January 2, 1982.

---

[1] In actuality, the estimated future net revenues are not expected to be constant over periods 4–20. This means that the sum of the *constant* annual net revenue stream derived in part 1 will not equal the $112,732,000 value assigned to the 1985-plus future net revenues.

(Note: Additional development expenses of $4,282,000 are assumed paid in cash.)

3. Explain in words why the present value of proved oil and gas reserves decreased by $8,899,000 in 1981 when, in fact, the company discovered, extended, or added to it oil and gas quantities in 1981 by 4,336,000 barrels and 1,134 cubic feet, respectively.

WITCO CHEMICAL CORPORATION
Oil and Gas Producing Information

Valuation of Proved Reserves: The present value and summary of oil and gas producing activities have been prepared in accordance with the methodology prescribed by the Securities and Exchange Commission (SEC) called Reserve Recognition Accounting (RRA). Under RRA, an asset is recognized and earnings are recorded when oil and gas reserves are proved through exploration and development activities. Proved oil and gas reserves are the estimated quantities of crude oil and natural gas which geological and engineering data demonstrate with reasonable certainty to be recoverable in future years from known reservoirs under existing economic and operating conditions.

The RRA valuation of proved reserves is determined as follows:

1. Estimates are made of quantities of proved reserves and the future periods during which they are expected to be produced based on year end economic conditions;

2. The estimated future production of proved reserves is priced on the basis of year end prices;

3. The resulting future gross revenue streams are reduced by estimated future costs to develop and to produce the proved reserves, based on year end cost estimates;

4. The resulting future net revenue streams are reduced to present value amounts by applying a 10 percent discount factor.

As acknowledged by the SEC, this valuation procedure does not necessarily yield the best estimate of the fair market value of a company's oil and gas properties. An estimate of fair market value should also take into account, among other factors, a discount factor that reflects current economic conditions, the likelihood of future recoveries of oil and gas in excess of proved reserves and anticipated future prices of oil and gas along with related development and production costs.

WITCO CHEMICAL CORPORATION

Summary of Changes in Present Value of Estimated Future Net Revenues from Proved Oil and Gas Reserves

(Thousands of dollars)	1981	1980	1979
Additions and revisions			
Revisions to reserves proved in prior years	$ (32,337)	$ 9,951	$ 104,726
Revisions to reserves due to Windfall Profit Tax	26,559	(40,112)	—
Purchase of reserves in place (at acquisition cost)	—	—	353
Revisions to reserves purchased	—	—	1,758
Extensions, discoveries and other additions	4,886	1,765	2,674
Estimated future development costs incurred during the year	6.075	5.833	5.326
	5,183	(22,563)	114,837
Decreases for sales of oil and gas and value of transfers, net of lifting costs	(14,082)	(14,867)	(11,529)
Net increase (decrease)	(8,899)	(37,430)	103,308
Balance at beginning of year	85,419	122,849	19,541
Balance at end of year	$ 76,520	$ 85,419	$ 122,849

Summary of Oil and Gas Producing Activities Prepared on the Basis of Reserve Recognition Accounting

(Thousands of dollars)	1981	1980	1979
Additions and revisions to proved reserves			
Revisions to reserves proved in prior years			
Increase (decrease) in prices	$ (7,459)	$ 3,571	$ 114,332
Interest factor—accretion of discount	8,542	12,285	1,954
Other	(33,420)	(5,905)	(11,560)
Total revisions to reserves proved in prior years	(32,337)	9,951	104,726
Revisions due to Windfall Profit Tax	26,559	(40,112)	—
Extensions, discoveries and other additions	4,886	1,765	2,674
Revisions to reserves purchased	—	—	1,758
Total additions and revisions to proved reserves	(892)	(28,396)	109,158
Development costs in excess of amounts previously estimated	4,282	1,251	438
Results of oil and gas producing activities on the basis of reserve recognition accounting before federal income taxes	(5,174)	(29,647)	108,720
Provision (benefit) for federal income taxes	(1,372)	(13,111)	51,149
Results of oil and gas producing activities on the basis of reserve recognition accounting	$ (3,802)	$ (16,536)	$ 57,571
Operating income from oil and gas producing activities before federal income taxes based upon historical costs	$ 9,150	$ 12,032	$ 9,010

Analysis of RRA Presentation: Results of oil and gas producing activities on the basis of reserve recognition accounting are arrived at by (i) additions to proved reserves from new field discoveries and extensions and revisions to the RRA valuation of reserves proved in prior years, and (ii) costs incurred in development activities.

Included in the revisions of reserves proved in prior years are the changes in valuation resulting from the use of the year end price. During the year 1981, the market value of crude oil declined affecting the RRA valuation by $7,459,000 while in previous years the year end market prices increased, thereby contributing $3,571,000 and $114,332,000 in 1980 and 1979, respectively.

Interest factor—accretion of discount, results from applying a discounted cash flow technique in the RRA valuation of proved reserves. The resulting increase is due to the production schedule of proved reserves being moved up one year on the discount table.

Also included in revisions to reserves proved in prior years—other are revisions to reserves estimates, changes in cost and changes in timing of production which all individually and collectively affect the RRA valuation. In 1981, downward revisions to previous years' reserves estimates and increases in costs are the primary factors contributing to the change in this caption.

The favorable impact of Windfall Profit Tax is due to amendments to the 1980 Windfall Profit Tax Act as prescribed by the Economic Recovery Tax Act of 1981, which restored $26,559,000 of the 1980 reduction.

The caption extensions, discoveries and other additions represent proved reserves added through exploration and development activities. The increase in the current period is reflective of an expanded scope of exploration activity on previously unproven properties.

Development costs in excess of amounts previously estimated reflects the actual costs incurred during the year adjusted for development costs estimated in prior years.

The RRA provision for income taxes is based on the year end tax rates taking into account differences in the timing of recognizing RRA and taxable income and giving effect to investment tax credits. The effective tax rate as a percent of the results of oil and gas producing activities on the basis of RRA before federal income taxes was 27 percent, 44 percent, and 47 percent for the years 1981, 1980, and 1979, respectively.

Other Considerations: The Company cautions against projecting future RRA results on the basis of individual past years. RRA seeks to reflect events relating to developments projected to occur, whereas under generally accepted accounting principles, the impact of such events is reported over many future years. A number of years may elapse between incurring costs and knowing the economic results of the expenditures. New information about reservoir characteristics may significantly change previous estimates of proved reserves and their valuation. For these and other reasons, a year is too short a period to evaluate the results of a development program. An analysis of the RRA information should not, therefore, give undue emphasis to the results of any particular year; rather, the RRA information should help explain and demonstrate the impact of major factors affecting the Company over a number of years.

As discussed above, the RRA valuation of proved reserves will be revised in the future on the basis of new information as it becomes available, as estimates of proved reserves are imprecise. The Company's production and its exploration and development programs will require the continued revisions of reserve estimates. Further, future RRA valuations of the Company's proved reserves will reflect prices and related costs in effects in the future.

RRA estimated future net revenues and operating income from oil and gas producing activities have been reduced to reflect the Windfall Profit Tax. In calculating the amounts of such reductions the Company has applied the provisions applicable to independent producers, under which as a result of the 1981 amendment, (i) the tax rate until 1983 for most of the Company's production is 30% rather than 60% of the windfall profit amount on the first 1,000 barrels per day of production and (ii) such production beginning in 1983 is exempt. The Company believes it has good grounds for its position that it is an independent producer, but the factors controlling the determination are complex and no definitive interpretation has been promulgated by the Internal Revenue Service. The Company is currently involved in a proceeding seeking judicial affirmation of its status as an independent producer for 1975, and the outcome of that litigation is expected to affect its status for future years. Until the criteria for such status are established, estimates of future net revenues are subject to this additional uncertainty. The Company is hopeful that the issue will be resolved during calendar 1982 and believes that an adverse determination of its independent producer status would not have a material adverse effect on earnings for such year. However, such an adverse determination could, unless the Company subsequently qualifies as an independent producer, have a significant effect on RRA estimated future net revenues and operating income if the Windfall Profit Tax remains in effect without amendment and if the amount of the estimated windfall profit for future periods remains substantial.

Since December 31, 1981 the market value of crude oil has declined further. The impact of these price declines would have an adverse affect on RRA unless offset by future price increases. At present, management cannot assess the impact of the future market conditions on the price of crude oil.

The Company will review and adjust oil and gas reserves to reflect current conditions. The Company is not aware of any other event either favorable or unfavorable that occurred since December 31, 1981, that would cause a significant change in the Company's proved reserves.

All of these uncertainties should be considered in reviewing the RRA data.

WITCO CHEMICAL CORPORATION
Estimated Future Net Revenues from Proved Oil and Gas Reserves

(Thousands of dollars)	Proved Developed and Undeveloped	Proved Developed
Year ended December 31		
1982*	$ 8,544	$ 13,079
1983	14,261	13,928
1984	13,950	11,390
Remainder	112,732	50,876
Total	$ 149,487	$ 89,273
Present Value of Estimated Future Net Revenues From Proved Oil and Gas Reserves at December 31		
1979	$ 122,849	$ 71,459
1980	85,419	58,643
1981	76,520	59,093

*1982 estimated future net revenues from proved developed oil and gas reserves are greater than the estimated future net revenues from proved developed and undeveloped oil and gas reserves because a significant amount of development costs have been projected.

14.6 DUNBAR SLOANE & EUROPEAN ART LIMITED

Effects of currency rate changes

Dunbar Sloane is a New Zealand investment company, whose main activity is the acquisition of European art for the purposes of gain and eventual resale. Its major assets—cash deposits and art—(and liabilities) are held in the United Kingdom and denominated in pounds sterling (£s).

The company translates its foreign currency financial statements according to the current rate method for independent overseas entities, wherein all overseas assets and liabilities are converted to New Zealand dollars (the reporting currency) at the rate of exchange ruling at the end-of-period balance sheet date. Exchange gains and losses arising from the translation of foreign currency financial statements are reported as Currency Translation Reserves. Other exchange gains and losses are included in the income statement. Revenues and expenses are translated at the rate at which the transactions took place, assumed to be the average rate for the year in the absence of other information.

1. Consider the following simplified situation of a U.K. company that starts operations at the beginning of year 1. Assume the company makes net cash earnings of zero for year 1. No new investment/financing transactions are conducted. However, during the year, the company's art portfolio increases in value by one sixth (i.e.,16.667 percent). The company's accountant credits the increase to a revaluation reserve account.

U.K. Company: Balance Sheets (£s)

	Beginning of year 1	End of year 1
Cash deposits	5,000	5,000
Art investments	10,000	11,667
Total assets	£ 15,000	£ 16,667
Current liabilities	2,500	2,500
Long-term liabilities	7,500	7,500
Common stock	5,000	5,000
Retained earnings	-	-
Revaluation reserve	-	1,667
Common equity	£ 5,000	£ 6,667

Exchange rates:

Beginning of year:	$2.00 = £1.00
Midyear:	$1.75 = £1.00
End of year:	$1.50 = £1.00

Translate the beginning- and end-of-year balance sheets into New Zealand dollars using the current rate method and the exchange rates given above. Comment on the relation between the Foreign Currency Reserve and translated Revaluation Reserve accounts. What if the unrealized appreciation on art had been credited to the income statement instead of the Revaluation Reserve account?

2. Refer to the excerpts from the 1988 financial statements of Dunbar Sloane and comment on the following.

  a. Explain the company's treatment of Unrealized Revaluation of Art Investments in the income statement and statement of shareholders' equity. Under what circumstances, if any, would this treatment comply with generally accepted accounting principles for public companies in the United States?

  b. Relative to the currencies in which Dunbar denominates its net assets, did the New Zealand dollar strengthen or weaken during the year, and what effect would that have on the reported New Zealand values of the overseas net assets?

  c. Given your answer in b, comment on the fairness and representativeness of the income statement item Unrealized Revaluation of Art Investments.

DUNBAR SLOANE & EUROPEAN ART LIMITED
Statement of Income for Year Ended

	February 28	
	1988	1987
INVESTMENT INCOME	$ 889,390	$ 795,319
EXPENSES		
Audit fees	8,172	5,000
Amortization of issue costs	273,893	114,338
Depreciation	509	298
Directors' fees	72,000	24,000
Foreign currency translation	78,481	4,505
Other expenses	124,052	128,481
Realized equity investment losses	1,293,004	-
Unrealized writedown of equity investments	218,695	-
Total expenses	2,068,806	276,622
Net Earnings (loss) for the year before income tax	(1,179,416)	518,697
Income tax	-	269,986
NET EARNINGS (LOSS) AFTER INCOME TAX	(1,179,416)	248,711
Unrealized revaluation of art investments	1,633,854	-
NET INCOME AFTER UNREALIZED GAINS	$ 454,438	$ 248,711
Net income for year including unrealized gains	454,438	248,711
Transfer to revaluation reserve	(1,633,854)	-
Income (deficit) available for appropriation	(1,179,416)	248,711
RETAINED EARNINGS AT MARCH 1, 1987	248,711	-
RETAINED EARNINGS AT FEBRUARY 28, 1988	$ (930,705)	$ (248,711)

Shareholders' equity

	February 28	
	1988	1987
15,000,007 $1 common shares outstanding	$ 15,000,007	$ 15,000,007
Retained earnings (deficit)	(930,705)	248,711
Revaluation reserve	1,633,854	-
Currency translation reserve	(2,680,038)	(866,947)
Total shareholders' equity	$ 13,023,118	$ 14,381,771

14.7 XEROX CORPORATION

Foreign currency translation adjustments, voluntary accounting change

Xerox Corporation manufactures and markets information products and systems with about 44 percent of its revenue outside the United States. Xerox's principal industry segment is reprographics, consisting of the development, manufacture, and marketing of xerographic copiers and duplicators, and electronic printing systems. Xerox also provides related information systems services. Listed on the New York Stock Exchange (Ticker = XRX).

Study the Consolidated Balance Sheets for 1980–1981 and 1979–1980, Consolidated Statement of Retained Earnings for 1979–1981, and notes to 1981 financial statements on Accounting Changes and Foreign Currency Translation.

1. Prepare a table that compares the 1980 Balance Sheet in the 1980 statements with the 1980 Balance Sheet in the 1981 statements. The comparative 1980 figures in the 1981 statements have been restated for accounting changes. An example is provided to demonstrate the format of the table (in millions of dollars).

Account Title	1980 Restated	1980 Original	Effect on Stockholders' Equity
Inventories	$ 1,090.2	$ 1,086.4	$ 3.8 increase

2. Xerox's 1977, 1978, 1979, and 1980 net income numbers before accounting changes for foreign currency and vacation pay were $415, $484, $563, and $619 million, respectively.

   a. Plot Xerox's 1977–81 net income assuming the accounting changes for foreign currency and vacation pay had not been made in 1981.

   b. Plot Xerox's 1977–81 net income after the accounting changes. Net income for 1977 and 1978 after such changes was $432 million and $497 million. Comment on Xerox's retrospective recognition of the accounting changes.

   c. Suppose an investor wanted a measure of net income absent the effects of currency rate changes and exchange gains or losses. Compute Xerox's 1979–81 income without foreign currency gains or losses.

Reconcile the data on accounting changes in the Consolidated Statement of Retained Earnings with the numbers provided in the Note on Accounting changes.

Suggest a most likely cause of the drop in cumulative translation adjustments from $98.8 million (credit) in 1980 to $150.1 million (debit) in 1981?

XEROX CORPORATION
Consolidated Balance Sheets

ASSETS

Dollars in millions	December 31 1981	1980
Current Assets		
Cash	$ 45.2	$ 86.8
Bank time deposits, interest bearing	234.0	228.8
Marketable securities, at the lower of cost or market	148.0	207.3
Trade receivables (less allowance for doubtful receivables:		
1981--$56.5; 1980--$59.1)	1,245.3	1,163.8
Receivable from Xerox Credit Corporation	178.2	196.3
Accrued revenues	403.3	376.8
Inventories, at the lower of average cost or market	1,131.9	1,090.2
Other current assets	230.2	210.0
Total current assets	3,616.1	3,560.0
Trade Receivables Due After One Year	245.5	199.4
Rental Equipment and Related Inventories		
At cost (less accumulated depreciation: 1981--$2,715.4;		
1980--$2,878.6)	1,905.1	1,966.8
Land, Buildings and Equipment		
At cost (less accumulated depreciation: 1981--$1,126.7;		
1980--$1,049.6)	1,438.7	1,410.4
Investments, at equity	319.6	226.6
Other assets	149.4	150.6
	4,058.3	3,953.8
TOTAL ASSETS	$ 7,674.4	$ 7,513.8
LIABILITIES AND SHAREHOLDERS' EQUITY		
Current Liabilities		
Notes payable	$ 224.2	$ 208.4
Current portion of long-term debt	96.3	80.0
Accounts payable	340.2	315.8
Salaries, profit sharing and other accruals	909.9	907.3
Income taxes	346.5	425.4
Other current liabilities	163.7	147.8
Total current liabilities	2,080.8	2,084.7
Long-Term Debt	869.5	898.3
Other Noncurrent Liabilities	145.0	133.0
Deferred Income Taxes	247.0	142.7
Deferred Investment Tax Credits	108.9	85.6
Outside Shareholders' Interests in Equity of Subsidiaries	495.6	539.5
	1,866.0	1,799.1
Shareholders' Equity		
Common stock, $1 par value		
Authorized 100,000,000 shares	84.3	84.3
Class B stock, $1 par value		
Authorized 600,000 shares	0.2	0.2
Additional paid-in capital	306.0	304.9
Retained earnings	3,500.1	3,155.4
Cumulative translation adjustments	(150.1)	98.8
Total	3,740.5	3,643.6
Deduct Class B stock receivables and deferrals	(12.9)	(13.6)
Total shareholders' equity	3,727.6	3,630.0
TOTAL LIABILITIES AND SHAREHOLDERS' EQUITY	$ 7,674.4	$ 7,513.8

XEROX CORPORATION
Consolidated Balance Sheets

ASSETS	December 31	
Dollars in millions	1980	1979
Current Assets		
Cash	$ 86.8	$ 42.2
Bank time deposits, interest bearing	228.8	267.7
Marketable securities, at the lower of cost or market	207.3	447.7
Trade receivables (less allowance for doubtful receivables:		
1980—$59.1; 1979—$60.1)	1,163.8	1,120.4
Receivable from Xerox Credit Corporation	196.3	-
Accrued revenues	376.8	259.3
Inventories, at the lower of average cost or market	1,086.4	785.8
Other current assets	168.9	180.5
Total current assets	3,515.1	3,103.6
Trade Receivables Due After One Year	199.4	274.2
Rental Equipment and Related Inventories		
At cost (less accumulated depreciation: 1980—$2,770.1; 1979—$2,678.0)	1,922.3	1,736.4
Land, Buildings and Equipment		
At cost (less accumulated depreciation: 1980—$1,033.4; 1979—$880.3)	1,369.4	1,222.3
Investments, at equity		
Fuji Xerox Co., Ltd.	114.8	105.7
Xerox Credit Corporation	79.2	-
Total investments	194.0	105.7
Other Assets	149.0	111.4
	3,834.1	3,450.0
TOTAL ASSETS	$ 7,349.2	$ 6,553.6
LIABILITIES & SHAREHOLDERS' EQUITY		
Current Liabilities		
Notes payable	208.4	96.3
Current portion of long-term debt	80.0	40.2
Accounts payable	315.8	325.1
Salaries, profit sharing and other accruals	791.5	689.5
Income taxes	440.5	426.0
Other current liabilities	147.8	102.2
Total current liabilities	1,984.0	1,679.3
Long-Term Debt	898.3	913.0
Other Noncurrent Liabilities	133.0	127.9
Deferred Income Taxes	123.8	110.4
Deferred Investment Tax Credits	85.6	70.1
Outside Shareholders' Interests in Equity of Subsidiaries	499.8	431.5
	1,740.5	1,652.9
Shareholders' Equity		
Common stock, $1 par value		
Authorized 100,000,000 shares	84.3	83.9
Class B stock, $1 par value		
Authorized 600,000 shares	0.2	0.2
Additional paid-in capital	304.9	286.8
Retained earnings	3,248.9	2,866.2
Total	3,638.3	3,237.1
Deduct Class B stock receivables and deferrals	(13.6)	(15.7)
Total shareholders' equity	3,624.7	3,221.4
TOTAL LIABILITIES AND SHAREHOLDERS' EQUITY	$ 7,349.2	$ 6,553.6

XEROX CORPORATION
Consolidated Statement of Retained Earnings

Dollars in millions, except per share data	Year Ended December 31		
	1981	1980	1979
Retained Earnings			
Balance at beginning of year, as previously reported	$ 3,248.9	$ 2,866.2	$ 2,501.3
Add (deduct) adjustments for the cumulative effect on prior years of retroactively applying the new methods of accounting for			
Foreign currency translation	(35.4)	11.1	51.6
Vacation pay benefits	(58.1)	(50.3)	(42.7)
Balance at beginning for year, as adjusted	3,155.4	2,827.0	2,510.2
Net income	598.2	564.9	515.0
Total	3,753.6	3,391.9	3,025.2
Deduct cash dividends declared			
On common and Class B stocks (Per share: 1981—$3.00; 1980—$2.80; 1979—$2.40)	(253.5)	(236.5)	(195.5)
On capital stock of pooled company prior to acquisition	--	--	(2.7)
Total cash dividends	(253.5)	(236.5)	(198.2)
Balance at end of year	$ 3,500.1	$ 3,155.4	$ 2,827.0

Notes to Consolidated Financial Statements
Accounting Changes

Foreign Currency Translation

In December 1981, the Financial Accounting Standards Board (FASB) issued Statement No. 52, Foreign Currency Translation, which revised the existing accounting and reporting requirements for translation of foreign currency transactions and foreign currency financial statements. The Company has elected the early application of the Statement encouraged by the FASB. As permitted by the Statement, the financial statements for the four years prior to 1981 have been restated. The effects of this change in accounting on net income and net income per common share were (in millions, except per share data):

Increase (decrease)	Net Income	Per Share
1981	$ 26.2	$ .31
1980	(46.5)	(.55)
1979	(40.5)	(.48)

Vacation Pay

Effective January 1, 1981, the Company adopted Statement No. 43 of the FASB whereby the costs of employees' vacation pay benefits are accrued as they are earned. Financial statements for the four years prior to 1981 have been restated as required by the Statement, resulting in a decrease in retained earnings as of January 1, 1979 of $42.7 million, net of $40.6 million of income taxes. The effects of this change in accounting on net income and net income per common share were (in millions, except per share data):

Increase (decrease)	Net Income	Per Share
1981	$ (7.6)	$ (.09)
1980	(7.8)	(.09)
1979	(7.6)	(.09)

XEROX CORPORATION
Foreign Currency Translation

An analysis of the changes in cumulative translation adjustments for each of the years in the three year period ended December 31, 1981 follows:

Dollars in millions	1981	1980	1979
Cumulative translation adjustments at beginning of year	$ 98.8	$ 76.5	$ 119.3
Translation adjustments and intercompany foreign currency transactions	(376.7)	35.5	(64.7)
Outside shareholders' interests	127.8	(13.2)	21.9
Cumulative translation adjustments at end of year	$ (150.1)	$ 98.8	$ 76.5

The consolidated statements of income include net aggregate exchange losses of $64.5 million, $16.7 million and $4.5 million in 1981, 1980 and 1979, respectively.

14.8 INTERNATIONAL BUSINESS MACHINES CORPORATION

Foreign currency translation

The International Business Machines Corporation (IBM) operates in the fields of information-handling systems, equipment, and services. The company's products include data processing machines and systems, telecommunication systems and products, information distributors, office systems, typewriters, copiers, educational and testing materials, and related services and supplies. Listed on the New York Stock Exchange (Ticker = IBM).

Study IBM's 1980–1982 Consolidated Statement of Earnings and Notes to Consolidated Financial Statements for 1982, "Accounting Change—Foreign Currency Translation" and "Non-U.S. Operations."

1. During 1980-1982, the dollar generally strengthened against the major currencies in which IBM conducted most of its business.

   For the years 1980–1982, calculate (a) the percentage of gross income from sales, rentals, and services derived from non-U.S. operations to total gross income and (b) the percentage of net earnings derived from non-U.S. operations to total net earnings. (c) In broad terms (e.g., increase, decrease, no change), how would those ratios have been affected if the dollar had *weakened* against the major currencies during the same period?

2. Prepare a chart showing 1980–1982 earnings per share computed on the basis of (a) FASB Statement No. 52, adopted in the fourth quarter 1982, and (b) FASB Statement No. 8, the accounting standard in use by IBM prior to that date.

3. Calculate the percentage change in earnings from non-U.S. operations had IBM not adopted Statement 52 in late 1982.

4. Companies could have adopted Statement 52 at any time during the 1981–1983 transition period. Comment on why IBM might have been motivated to adopt Statement 52 as of fourth quarter 1982. Explain the statement "adopted ... in the fourth quarter of 1982, *effective January 1, 1982*." [emphasis added]

5. Discuss the stock price reaction to IBM's preliminary announcement of increased 1982 earnings, as reported in the excerpt from the *Wall Street Journal*, January 25, 1983, and the extent to which such price behavior is consistent with the efficient market hypothesis. Comment also on the role

of the financial analyst in ensuring that adequate information is available for assessing securities' values.

INTERNATIONAL BUSINESS MACHINES CORPORATION AND SUBSIDIARY COMPANIES
Consolidated Statement of Earnings
for the year ended December 31:

(Dollars in millions except per share amounts)	1982	1981*	1980*
Gross Income:			
Sales	$ 16,815	$ 12,901	$ 10,919
Rentals	11,121	10,839	10,869
Services	6,428	5,330	4,425
	$ 34,364	$ 29,070	$ 26,213
Cost of sales	6,682	5,162	4,238
Cost of rentals	3,959	4,041	3,841
Cost of services	3,047	2,534	2,187
Selling, general and administrative expenses	9,578	8,583	8,094
Research, development and engineering expenses	3,042	2,451	2,287
Interest expense	454	407	273
	26,762	23,178	20,920
	7,602	5,892	5,293
Other income, principally interest	328	368	430
Earnings before income taxes	7,930	6,260	5,723
Provision for U.S. Federal and non-U.S. income taxes	3,521	2,650	2,326
Net Earnings	$ 4,409	$ 3,610	$ 3,397
Per share	$ 7.39	$ 6.14	$ 5.82

Average number of shares outstanding:
1982–596,688,501
1981–587,803,373
1980–583,516,764

* Restated. See Accounting Change–Foreign Currency Translation note.

INTERNATIONAL BUSINESS MACHINES CORPORATION AND SUBSIDIARY COMPANIES

Accounting Change–Foreign Currency Translation

The company adopted Statement of Financial Accounting Standards (SFAS) No. 52, "Foreign Currency Translation," in the fourth quarter of 1982, effective January 1, 1982. The consolidated financial statements for the years 1981 and 1980 have been restated to give effect to this change in accounting principle.

Non-U.S. subsidiaries which operate in a local currency environment account for approximately 85 percent of the company's non-U.S. gross income. In applying SFAS No. 52 to financial statements of these subsidiaries, assets and liabilities are translated to U.S. dollars at year-end exchange rates. Income and expense items are translated at average rates of exchange prevailing during the year.

Translation adjustments are accumulated in a separate component of stockholders' equity.

The remaining 15 percent of the company's non-U.S. gross income is derived from subsidiaries and branches which operate in U.S. dollars or whose economic environment is highly inflationary. In accordance with SFAS No. 52, inventories and plant, rental machines and other property, applicable to these operations, are remeasured in U.S. dollars at approximate rates prevailing when acquired. Inventories charged to cost of sales and depreciation are remeasured at historical rates. Gains and losses which result from remeasurement are included in earnings.

The effects of this accounting change on net earnings and earnings per share are an increase of $449 million and $.75 in 1982, an increase of $302 million and $.51 in 1981 and a decrease of $165 million and $.28 in 1980.

Aggregate transaction gains (losses) included in earnings are $(7) million in 1982, $78 million in 1981 and $(18) million in 1980.

Non-U.S. Operations (Dollars in millions)	1982	1981	1980
At end of year:			
Net assets employed			
Current assets	$ 6,299	$ 5,436	$ 5,531
Current liabilities	4,240	4,108	3,914
Working capital	2,059	1,328	1,617
Plant, rental machines and other property, net	6,740	7,152	7,006
Deferred charges and other assets	887	890	931
	9,686	9,370	9,554
Reserves for employees' indemnities and retirement plans	1,198	1,184	1,443
Long-term debt	480	496	437
	1,678	1,680	1,880
Net assets employed	$ 8,008	$ 7,690	$ 7,674
Number of employees	150,444	149,794	146,973
For the year:			
Gross income from sales, rentals and services	$ 15,336	$ 13,982	$ 13,787
Earnings before income taxes	3,226	2,664	2,772
Provision for U.S. Federal and non-U.S. income taxes	1,577	1,123	1,035
Net earnings	1,649	1,541	1,737
Investment in plant, rental machines and other property	2,682	3,274	3,367

For the years 1982 and 1981, non-U.S. financial results were severely impacted by the strength of the U.S. dollar relative to the currencies of many countries around the world. The Management Discussion on page 29 refers to this effect in greater detail. The graphs on the following page further illustrate the decline in value, in relation to the dollar, of the five major foreign currencies in which IBM conducts most of its non-U.S. business.

Undistributed earnings of non-U.S. subsidiaries included in consolidated retained earnings amounted to $7,538 million at December 31, 1982, $6,565 million at December 31, 1981, and $5,943 million at December 31, 1980. These earnings are indefinitely reinvested in non-U.S. operations. Accordingly, no provision has been made for taxes that might be payable upon remittance of such earnings.

Excerpt from *Wall Street Journal*, January 25, 1983.

IBM's Second Set of 1982 Earnings Statistics Brings a Sigh of Relief From Puzzled Analysts

Even a computer couldn't help Wall Street securities analysts untangle International Business Machines' fourth quarter and 1982 earnings announcement late last week. Friday, the stock sagged 3-1/4 in the confusion...

Wall Street was dismayed to find that a sizable chunk of the increase [earnings] didn't come from the company's growth but from an accounting change in the way IBM reports its overseas operations. IBM rushed a second set of figures to analysts yesterday, and a collective sigh of relief gusted through the analyst community...

Alex D. Stein, a *Dataquest* analyst, says he was surprised by the market's reaction to IBM's original earnings report. "The market's been very emotional, but I was surprised that people paid as much attention to it as they did."

15

Accounting Analysis

15.1 RELIANCE ELECTRIC COMPANY

Ratio analysis, cash flow projection, calculation
of present value of assets and stockholders' equity

This case uses ratio analysis to address certain valuation issues related to the late-1979 merger between the Reliance Electric Company and Exxon Corporation. Specifically, Reliance's 1978 financial statements are analyzed in order to derive accounting data relevant to an independent valuation of Reliance's common stock.

Although the first news of a possible merger came on May 18, 1979, it was not until May 25, 1979, that Exxon (through a subsidiary called Enco Corporation) announced its intention to make a cash tender offer of $72.00 per share for Reliance's common stock and $202.72 per share for the Series A preferred stock. The closing common stock prices for Reliance were $34.50 and $48.25 on May 17, 1979 and May 24, 1979, respectively. By November 2, 1979, the price had risen to $69.50 per share. Exxon's reason for seeking to acquire Reliance was that it needed manufacturing and marketing expertise to fully develop and exploit a new alternating current synthesizer that would supposedly revolutionize the industry for electric motors, producing—among other things—massive energy savings.

Study Reliance's 1977–1978 Consolidated Balance Sheets and the Five-Year Financial Summary from 1974 to 1978 and calculate:

1. a. Percentage growth in Earnings Applicable to Common Stock for 1976–1977 and 1977–1978.

    b. Dividend payout ratio for 1977 and 1978 (based on primary earnings per share).

    c. Percentage growth in Net Sales for 1976–1977 and 1977–1978.

    d. Ratio of Earnings before Income Taxes plus Interest Expense to Net Sales for the years 1977 and 1978.

    e. Ratio of Actual Taxes Paid to Earnings before Income Taxes (assume that Actual Taxes Paid equals Income Tax Expense less Change in Deferred Income Tax Liability) for 1978 only.

    f. Ratio of 1976 (1977) Capital Expenditures, net of Depreciation, to Change in Sales for 1977 (1978), respectively (two ratios).

    g. Ratio of Change in Working Capital (Current Assets less Current Liabilities) to Change in Sales for 1977 and 1978.

h. Ratio of Common Stock Price (high) to Fully Diluted Earnings per Share for 1977 and 1978.

2. Use the information derived in part 1 to compute the cash flow for periods $t = 1,2,...,10$ according to the following formula (period $1 = 1979$):

$$C_t = S_t - (1 + g)(p)(1 - T) - (S_t - S_{t-1})(f + w), \text{ where:}$$

C_t = cash flow for period t

S_{t-1} = net sales for period $(t-1)$

g = ratio (c), based on 1978 data

p = ratio (d), based on 1978 data

T = ratio (e), based on 1978 data

f = ratio (f), based on 1978 data

w = ratio (g), based on 1978 data

3. a. Compute the present value of cash flows $C_1, C_2,...,C_{10}$ discounted at an assumed rate of 12 percent. Assume that the net cash flows are received at the end of each year.

   b. Assume that Year 10 operating earnings after taxes [i.e., $OE_{10} = S_9 (1 + g)(p)(1 - T)$] will continue indefinitely at a constant amount. Compute the present value of operating earnings $OE_{11},...,OE_{\infty}$ assuming a discount rate of 12 percent. (Note: $OE_{10} = OE_{11}$.)

4. Combine the present values in part 3a and 3b and, with appropriate subtractions for debt (use book value) and preferred stock (use October 31, 1978 book value of $55 million), calculate the present value of one share of the outstanding common stock of the Reliance Company.[1]

5. Use the information derived in part 1 above to compute dividends per share (D_t) for period $t = 1,2,...,5$ plus a terminal per share price at the end of period 5 (TP_5), where

D_t = $E_t \times$ (dividend payout = ratio [b] for 1978, assume constant).

E_t = earnings applicable to common for period t divided by the number of common shares outstanding at year-end (assume constant at 15,401,000 shares).

E_t = $E_{t-1} \times$ (earnings growth = ratio [a] for 1978, assume constant).

TP_5 = $E_5 \times$ (terminal price-earnings ratio = ratio [h] for 1978, assume constant).

---

[1] The steps taken in parts 2, 3, and 4 are in essence an application of the discounted-cash-flow equity valuation model. See, for example, A. Rappaport, "Strategic Analysis for More Profitable Acquisitions," *Harvard Business Review,* July–August 1979, pp. 99-110.

6. Compute the present value of the sum of dividends per share, D_t, for $t = 1,\dots,5$ plus terminal stock price (TP_5), assuming a discount rate of 14 percent.[2]

7. What discount rate makes the present value of future dividends plus terminal stock price equal to (a) $34.50 and (b) $72.00?

---

[2] The steps taken in parts 5, 6, and 7 are in essence an application of a dividend/earnings equity valuation model. See, for example, D. F. Hawkins and W. J. Campbell, *Equity Valuation: Models, Analysis, and Implications* (New York: Financial Executives Research Foundation, 1978), Chap. 3.

RELIANCE ELECTRIC COMPANY
Consolidated Balance Sheets

Thousands of dollars	1978	1977
ASSETS		
Currents Assets		
Cash	$ 10,405	$ 10,123
Short-term investments	30,044	43,570
Trade accounts receivable	175,437	144,608
Inventories	189,065	159,629
Deferred taxes	19,714	13,907
Total current assets	424,665	371,837
Investments and Other Assets		
Affiliated companies	3,503	2,938
Costs of businesses over net assets acquired	7,572	8,157
Deposits and deferred items	15,177	14,832
	26,252	25,927
Property, Plant, and Equipment		
Land	8,383	7,450
Buildings	82,892	76,575
Machinery and equipment	213,071	187,264
	304,346	271,289
Less allowances for depreciation	142,015	127,406
	162,331	143,883
TOTAL ASSETS	$ 613,248	$ 541,647
LIABILITIES AND STOCKHOLDERS' EQUITY		
Current Liabilities		
Notes payable	$ 4,084	$ 2,304
Trade accounts payable	49,751	45,417
Compensation and employee benefits	38,122	29,149
Other liabilities and accrued items	47,477	37,208
Customer advances	14,593	12,120
Income taxes	13,626	21,121
Current maturities of long-term debt	1,009	1,431
Total current liabilities	168,662	148,750
Long-term Debt	99,395	94,910
Other Long-term Liabilities	7,971	6,945
Deferred Income Taxes	13,167	9,637
Stockholders' Equity	324,053	281,405
TOTAL LIABILITIES AND STOCKHOLDERS' EQUITY	$ 613,248	$ 541,647

RELIANCE ELECTRIC COMPANY
Five-Year Financial Summary

Dollars in thousands, where applicable	Year Ended October 31				
	1978	1977	1976	1975	1974
Statements of Consolidated Earnings*					
Net sales	$ 966,264	$ 829,139	$ 712,007	$ 680,384	$ 624,930
Costs and expenses:					
Cost of products sold	657,681	564,254	485,477	478,449	447,661
Selling, administrative and general expenses	158,040	134,437	118,079	112,483	100,223
Depreciation	19,548	16,698	14,031	12,107	9,898
Interest expense	8,577	8,124	8,772	9,082	7,987
	843,846	723,513	626,359	612,121	565,769
Earnings before income taxes:	122,418	105,626	85,648	68,263	59,161
Income taxes	57,770	52,110	41,893	31,910	27,420
Net earnings	64,648	53,516	43,755	36,353	31,741
Dividend requirements on Serial Preferred Stock	(1,081)	(1,861)	(3,359)	(4,527)	(4,631)
Net earnings applicable to common stock	$ 63,567	$ 51,655	$ 40,396	$ 31,826	$ 27,110
Net earnings per common share:					
Primary	4.18	3.63	3.26	2.87	2.55
Fully diluted	3.96	3.32	2.72	2.32	2.07
Cash dividends per common share	$1.40	$1.15	$1.03	$0.88	$0.80

*Years prior to 1977 restated for pooling of interests.

Financial Position—historical					
Current Assets	$ 424,665	$ 371,837	$ 311,163	$ 288,401	$ 269,496
Current Liabilities	168,662	148,750	124,420	110,669	141,980
Working Capital	256,003	223,087	186,743	177,732	127,516
Current Ratio	2.52	2.50	2.50	2.61	1.90
Long-term Debt	99,395	94,910	92,304	92,341	52,988
Stockholders' Equity	324,052	281,405	222,037	192,501	168,177
Debt to Total Capital	23.5%	25.2%	29.4%	32.4%	24.0%
Property, Plant & Equipment—Net	162,331	143,883	119,861	107,811	93,544
TOTAL ASSETS	$ 613,248	$ 541,647	$ 454,473	$ 409,435	$ 375,702

Per Share Common Stock Data—historical					
Primary Earnings	$ 4.18	$ 3.63	$ 3.60	$ 3.20	$ 2.67
Fully Diluted Earnings	3.96	3.32	2.92	2.48	2.1
Dividends Paid	1.4	1.15	1.025	0.875	0.8
Dividends to Fully Diluted Earnings	35.4%	34.6%	35.1%	35.3%	38.1%
Stockholders' Equity	20.91	19.04	17.87	18.54	16.67
Stock Price (Range) (High-Low)	$41-275/8	$351/2-291/4	$35-18	$185/8-101/4	$231/8-91/4

Other Items—historical					
Incoming Orders	$ 1,048,000	$ 869,000	$ 671,000	$ 566,000	$ 721,000
Order Backlog	$ 292,000	$ 221,000	$ 214,000	$ 222,000	$ 315,000
Product Development and Engineering	$ 36,541	$ 30,290	$ 26,532	$ 24,446	$ 21,706
Capital Expenditures	$ 33,552	$ 33,434	$ 24,269	$ 23,155	$ 23,726
Number of Employees—Worldwide	21,717	20,416	19,454	17,585	20,069
Number of Stockholders	14,035	14,401	14,607	16,785	15,639
Number of Common Shares Outstanding at Year-end (thousands)	15,401	14,556	12,044	9,582	9,177

15.2 GANNETT CO., INC.

*Derive proforma financial statements based on
ratio analysis*

Gannett Co. is a nationwide, diversified news and information company that
operates newspapers, television and radio stations and outdoor advertising,
research, marketing, printing, news, and broadcast program production facilities.
The company is the largest newspaper group in the United States, with 90 daily
papers, including *USA Today*. Listed on the New York Stock Exchange (Ticker =
GCI).

Use the following ratios and other (simplifying) assumptions, based on
Gannett's 19X2 financial statements, to project the 19X3 income statement and
end-of-19X3 balance sheet. Gannett predicts that sales and net income for 19X3
will be 10 percent higher than for 19X2. Other ratios (and shares outstanding) are
assumed to remain unchanged during the next fiscal year.

Gross profit margin percentage	44.00%
Net income after income taxes to sales	10.00%
Selling expenses to sales	17.00%
Accounts receivable turnover	8.00
Inventory turnover	25.00
Quick asset ratio	1.00
Current ratio	1.25
Cash to quick assets	3.00%
Marketable securities to quick assets	3.00%
Accounts receivable to quick assets	94.00%
Sales to total assets (asset turnover)	1.00
Total assets to intangible assets	2.00
Plant assets (at cost) to accumulated depreciation on plant assets	3.00
Accounts receivable to accounts payable	2.00
Working capital to stockholders' equity	8.00%
Long-term loans to stockholders' equity	100.00%
Income tax rate	35.00%
Net income after taxes	$319,395.00
Earnings per share	$1.97
Par value of common stock (per share)	$1.00
Excess over par value of common stock (per share)	$0.175
Interest rate on long-term loans	5.00%
Dividend payout	100.00%

Based on materials provided by George Foster.

Other information:

During the year 19X3, assume that the average values of inventory and accounts receivable approximate the values expected as of the end of the year. In addition to those mentioned or implied by the ratios or assumptions above, use the following accounts: other current assets, other current liabilities, other long-term liabilities (non-interest bearing), retained earnings, other expenses. It is not necessary to reconstruct the 19X2 balance sheet.

15.3 SAFETY-KLEEN CORPORATION

Time series analysis and earnings growth rates

The Safety-Kleen Corporation provides cleaning services for parts and components in the vehicular and industrial markets. In addition, the company has operations that include auto repair outlets, restaurants, dry cleaners, and industrial plants. Listed on the New York Stock Exchange (Ticker = SK).

Recently in an issue of the *Wall Street Journal* the company proclaimed the following in a full-page advertisement:

> *"We are pleased to report that Safety-Kleen has achieved net earnings growth in excess of 20% for the sixteenth consecutive year."*

Use the History of Growth shown on the next page and the following footnote from the 19X6 financial report to answer the following questions:

Footnote 1: In 19X5, the company changed its method of accounting for investment tax credits from the deferral to the flow-through method. The effect of the change was to increase earnings before cumulative effect of change in accounting principle by $673,000 or $.02 per share for the fiscal year ended December 28, 19X5. The cumulative prior years' effect of the change increased net earnings by $3,706,000 or $.11 per share. If the flow through method of accounting for the investment credit had been used in prior years, 19X4 net earnings would have been $440,000 or $.01 per share higher than as reported.

---

1. Calculate the annual growth rate in Earnings *after* extraordinary items (19X0) and the cumulative effect of an accounting change (19X5) for each year, 19X1 through 19X6. After considering those adjustments, did management achieve its stated earnings objective? Calculate, also, the average, annual compound growth rate in Earnings for the 19X0–19X6 period. (Management reported 19X5 earnings of $27,185,000 in their 19X5 History of Growth.)

   To calculate the average, annual compound growth rate, use the formula:
   $X_N = X_0 (1+g)^N$, where X_0 = base-year earnings, X_N = earnings N years from the end of the base year, and g = average, annual compound growth rate.

Calculate the annual growth rate in Sales and Earnings per share as reported in the History of Growth schedule and the average, annual compound growth rate for both series for the 19X0–19X6 period. Use the formula given in (1) for the compound growth calculation. Which growth rate (sales, earnings, or earnings per share) is more useful for investors?

The table below lists Safety-Kleen's stock prices at the end of each year, adjusted for stock splits and stock dividends:

12/31/19X0	$ 5.037
12/31/19X1	5.679
12/31/19X2	8.259
12/30/19X3	10.074
12/31/19X4	11.722
12/31/19X5	17.167
12/31/19X6	22.250

Comment on the trend in the ratio of price to earnings per share and price change to earnings per share change for the 19X0–19X6 period. Do those trends generally reflect the 20 percent growth rate of earnings heralded by management?

SAFETY-KLEEN CORPORATION
HISTORY OF GROWTH
(amounts, except per share amounts, expressed in thousands)

	Sales revenues	Earnings (loss) before extraordinary items and cumulative effect of change in accounting principle	
		Amount	Earnings per share
19X0	$ 115,648	$ 7,906	$ 0.26
19X1	134,887	10,002*	0.33
19X2	149,244	13,024	0.43
19X3	162,771	15,759	0.51
19X4	185,630	19,428	0.62
19X5	221,080	23,479†	0.73
19X6	255,356	28,254	0.86

*19X1 earnings excludes $975,000 ($.03 per share) for U.S income tax benefits resulting from the sale of the company's West German subsidiary.

†19X1 earnings excludes $3,706,000 ($.11 per share) for the cumulative effect of change in accounting for tax credits.

15.4 DISCOUNT, INC.

Time series analysis of quarterly earnings

Discount, Inc. sells general merchandise and apparel throughout the world primarily in the high-volume, low-markup segment of the market place. Discount, Inc.'s quarterly net income (loss) per share numbers for years 19X4–19X7 are reported below:

	quarter 1	quarter 2	quarter 3	quarter 4
19X4	$ (.18)	$.09	$ .45	$ 2.27
19X5	.01	.50	.75	2.56
19X6	.10	.62	.82	2.91
19X7	.17	.84	1.20	3.20

Discount, Inc.'s end of quarter common stock price and the S&P 400 industrials stock price index are also given for years 19X6 and 19X7.

Year	price	quarter 1	quarter 2	quarter 3	quarter 4
19X6	Discount	$ 30.63	$ 37.75	$ 35.75	$ 41.00
19X6	S&P 400	180.14	174.73	187.41	186.36
19X7	Discount	$ 43.25	$ 49.50	$ 51.00	$ 58.00
19X7	S&P 400	201.67	211.92	203.67	234.56

Use the preceding information to answer the following questions:

1. Predict Discount, Inc.'s *19X8* earnings per share (all quarters) under the assumption that the fourth difference of the quarterly earnings series follows a random walk, that is, $x_t - x_{t-4} = x_{t-1} - x_{t-5} + e_t$, where the error term e_t is assumed independently and identically distributed with zero expected value. Thus, the forecast of x_{t+1} at time t, say, $F(x_{t+1}) = x_t - x_{t-4} + x_{t-3}$.

2. Calculate the unexpected change in quarterly earnings per share for quarters 19X6-q2 to 19X7-q4 assuming that investors predict future quarters' earnings per share on the basis of a random walk in the fourth difference of the series--the same assumed process as in (1).

3. For quarters 19X6-q2 to 19X7-q4, calculate the amount of (abnormal) price change in common stock from one quarter to the next that is *not* explained by the change in the market index. In other words, assume that on the

average Discount, Inc.'s price changes match the market movements on a one-for-one basis.

Using the data calculated in (2) and (3), prepare a graph of the relationship between abnormal price change (y axis) and unexpected change in earnings (x axis). Comment briefly on how responsive Discount, Inc.'s stock price is to unexpected changes in *reported* quarterly earnings. If you have a computer available, calculate the regression line of the relation between y and x.

16

Review of Corporate Financial Reporting: Navistar International

16.0 NAVISTAR INTERNATIONAL CORPORATION

Review of corporate financial reporting

Navistar International Corporation conducts its operations under four groups: trucks, parts, engine and foundry, and financial services. Navistar is the only leading truck manufacturer in North America with a leading presence in medium and heavy trucks. Until 1985, Navistar was known as International Harvester Company. Listed on the New York Stock Exchange (Ticker = NAV).

The Company's financial statements, including Notes 1–23, accompany this case. The Statement of Shareowners' equity has not been provided. Each set of questions relates to a particular area of accounting and reporting, though no attempt has been made to cover every area covered elsewhere in the casebook. While each set can be treated independently of the other sets of questions, it is best initially to read and generally review the entire set of financial statements prior to addressing any single group of questions.

Finally, an appendix provides Navistar's weekly stock prices, the Standard & Poor's weekly 400 industrial stock price index, and dates of announcement of quarterly earnings during the January 1, 1988 to March 31, 1989 period. No specific assignment is developed regarding these data, but they may be helpful as a backdrop for the cases that follow. In addition, a simplified analysis of the association between Navistar's stock prices (and trading volume) and announcements of quarterly earnings could be discussed.

16.1 STATEMENT OF CASH FLOW

A common method of preparing a statement of cash flow is to generate memorandum journal entries that would account for all changes in the balance sheet. Those balance sheet changes either reflect cash inflows and outflows directly or are the basis for other adjustments so that the balance sheet changes adequately reflect the cash flows that have occurred. This is often called the indirect method of preparation of the statement of cash flow.

1. Use the Navistar's financial statements and Notes to provide memorandum journal entries that would derive the following items that appear in the Statement of Cash Flow and at the same time account partially for certain changes in the 1988 and 1987 balance sheets. Such journal entries can involve two or more accounts but should only use account names that appear in the Statements of Financial Position. In terms of the Statement of Cash Flow, identify whether the amount refers to cash flow from

operations, investment programs, and financing activities. Numbers are in millions of dollars.

a. Depreciation and amortization, $48.7
b. Equity in earnings of nonconsolidated subsidiaries, net of dividends received, $4.4
c. Gain on pension settlement, $33.7
d. Tenneco stock valuation adjustment, $15
e. Provision for losses on receivables and investment in dealerships (assume long-term receivables), $7.5
f. Special dividend from finance subsidiaries, $90
g. Special pension funding, $90
h. Capital expenditures (assume property purchases), $126.5
i. Principal payments under long-term lease obligations, $14.9
j. Cash dividends on preferred stock, $28.8

2. In preparing a statement of cash flow, significant transactions can occur that affect changes in balance sheet accounts but which do not directly involve an inflow or outflow of cash. Use Note 17 and other information in the financial statements to derive the memorandum journal entries that would account for the change in balance sheet amounts but would exclude the following transactions that occurred in fiscal 1988 from the Statement of Cash Flow.

a. At October 31, 1988, a current receivable from an affiliate of $143 million was reflected in the Statement of Financial Condition. The transfer of funds will occur in the first quarter of 1989. See Note 9.
b. A special payment of $220 million was made on December 1, 1988 to the U.S. hourly pension plan which was reflected as a prepaid and other pension asset and an accrued liability in the Statement of Financial Condition as of October 31, 1988. See Notes 3 and 14.
c. In the third quarter of 1988, the Tenneco Participating Preferred Stock received in 1985 was sold to Tenneco Inc. In exchange for the shares, the Company received a promissory note in the principal amount of $105 million which was settled in December 1988 prior to maturity. See Note 9.
d. Capital lease obligations of $3 million were incurred as a result of lease agreements for capital assets in 1988.
e. During 1988, 333,995 shares of Series D Preferred Stock, with carrying value $8 million, were converted into Common Stock.
f. The tax benefits from net operating loss carryforwards recognized in 1988 net income of $65 million were reclassified as Common stock and warrants. See Note 5.

16.2 INCOME TAXES AND TAX BENEFITS

The Company adopted FASB Statement No. 96, *Accounting for Income Taxes,* in the fourth quarter of fiscal 1987. Statement 96 provides that the manner of reporting tax benefits should be determined by the source of the income in the current year. The 1987 financial statements reflected no cumulative effect of this change since prior periods were restated to reflect the change as if applied in those prior periods.

Use the information in Notes 1 and 5 to answer the following questions.

1. a. Provide a journal entry that would record 1988 taxes on income of $10.2 million (rounded to $10 million in the Note). Use appropriate balance sheet accounts to record current taxes, deferred taxes, and tax benefits.

   b. After consideration of tax benefits, how much did the company pay (or accrue as payable) for income taxes in 1988?

2. a. Identify the amount as of October 31, 1988 of domestic and foreign operating loss carryforwards available to reduce future *taxable* income.

   b. Explain why such amounts are different from the domestic and foreign operating loss carryforwards available to reduce future *financial* income.

3. Estimate the minimum net present value as of October 31, 1988 of the domestic and foreign net operating loss carryforwards assuming a 7.5 percent discount factor applied at the end of each NOL expiration period (namely, the years 1998, 2000, 2002, and "indefinite" assume equals 2004). Use a 30 percent tax rate in the calculations. Calculate the effect that this net present value amount would have on shareowners' equity if fully recognized in the 1988 financial statements.

16.3 CAPITAL AND OPERATING LEASES

Use the information in Note 13 and the assumptions that follow to analyze Navistar's capital and operating lease position. Assume an interest (discount) rate of 7.5 percent; ignore sublease rentals in your calculations; and assume that the *capital* lease obligation will be fully amortized at the end of 20 years; that the *operating* lease obligation will be fully amortized at the end of 15 years; that the minimum lease payments are made annually on October 31; and that all capital and operating lease payments made after 1993 (the sixth year) are of equal amounts.

1. With regard to the capital lease obligations, prove that the present value of the minimum lease payments equals $39 million (rounded to the nearest million).

2. With regard to the operating lease obligations, calculate as of October 31, 1988 the present value of the minimum lease payments and the amount representing imputed interest.

3. Provide a journal entry that would record the 1989 operating lease *payment* (assumed made at the end of that year) on the basis that the company accounted for all operating leases as capital leases.

4. Using the balances as of October 31, 1988, calculate Navistar's ratio of total liabilities to total assets. Calculate the impact on that ratio of capitalizing *all* lease obligations on the company's October 31, 1988 balance.

16.4 DEFINED BENEFIT PENSION PLANS

Use the information in Note 3, Retirement Benefits and the following additional assumptions to analyze Navistar's accounting treatment of defined benefit pension plans under FASB Statement No. 87, *Employers' Accounting for Pensions,* which the Company adopted on October 31, 1987. Numbers are in millions of dollars.

1. Show the journal entry in Navistar's books to recognize 1988 net pension expense of $83 million.

2. Identify the amounts of projected benefit obligation as of 11/1/1987 and 10/31/1988 and prepare a table that shows all the adjustments to the various off-balance sheet, unrecognized items and reconciles to the prepaid account. Note: Fill in only those cells in which there is a "x." The other amounts cannot be calculated or are not relevant based on the information given.

	11/1/1987 balance	Pension Expense	Pension Funding	Plan Settlement	Amendment and other	10/31/1988 balance
Plan assets		x	x			x
less projected benefit obligation		x				x
Excess (deficiency)	x	x	x	x	x	x
Unrecognized net losses (gains)	x	x			x	x
Unrecognized plan amendments	x				x	x
Unrecognized net obligation at 11/1/1987 adoption	x	x			x	x
Prepaid (accrued) pension cost	x	x	x	x	x	x

Assumptions regarding defined benefit pension plans:

a. Debit balance as of November 1, 1987 in the prepaid/accrued pension account, $19.

b. Pension funding during the year ended October 31, 1988, $220 million special payment and $90 million dividend.

c. Zero balances in the unrecognized net losses and unrecognized plan amendment accounts as of November 1, 1987.

d. Combine both the "Assets Exceed Accumulated Benefits" and "Accumulated Benefits Exceed Assets, Proforma" plans when deriving the appropriate amounts to enter into the reconciliation.

e. The unrecognized plan amendment amount of $58 ($53+$5) million occurred on October 31, 1988. Specific effects on plan assets and plan liabilities unknown.

f. The after-tax settlement gain of $24 million was debited to the prepaid pension asset account. Specific effects on plan assets and plan liabilities unknown.

16.5 RECAPITALIZATION AND RELATED ENTRIES

In 1986 and 1987, Navistar effected several financial transactions to implement a recapitalization of the company. On December 9, 1986, the company issued 128.3 million shares of common stock; during the first quarter of 1987 funds were used to redeem four high-coupon debt issues; effective January 14, 1987 certain preferred stock was reclassified; and on October 31, 1987, the company reclassified its deficit in retained earnings to capital in excess of par value. Note that the reclassification of tax benefits is also analyzed in Case 16.1 on the statement of cash flow.

Using the Statements of Financial Position and the information in Note 2, prepare journal entries that would record the four groups of transactions that occurred in 1986 and 1987. Use account titles given in the Statements of Financial Position where possible, otherwise use appropriately descriptive titles as suggested by Note 2. The book value of the Series E preferred stock at the time of the conversion was $176.1 million. Assume conversions were on the book value basis. The par values of both the Series C and G preferred stocks were $50 per share.

16.6 EARNINGS PER SHARE

Note 7 explains the computation of primary income (loss) per common share giving the numerator (net income applicable to common stock) and the denominator (average common stock and dilutive common equivalent shares). Use the information in this note to answer the following questions:

1. Explain the difference between Net Income, $244 million, as shown in the 1988 Statement of Income and Net income (loss) applicable to common stock, $215.2 million, as shown in Note 7.

2. Calculate approximately when (during which month in fiscal 1988) the Series D junior preferred stock converted into common stock. According to Note 20, during the year, 333,995 Series D shares converted to common shares.

3. Explain in general terms (it is not possible to make precise calculations based on the information in the Notes) the addition of 9.1 million common stock equivalents for option and warrants and the 7.7 million reduction due to common stock assumed to be repurchased.

16.7 ACCOUNTING FOR NONCONSOLIDATED SUBSIDIARIES

This case reconstructs the entries in the account for nonconsolidated subsidiaries and estimates the impact on leverage ratios of a full consolidation.

1. Use the information in Note 11 to identify which companies Navistar includes in their 1988 statement of financial position as nonconsolidated subsidiaries.

2. Use the information in Notes 5 and 11 to reconcile the change in the account Equity in nonconsolidated subsidiaries. Assume that the tax benefits of net operating losses relating to net income from nonconsolidated subsidiaries amounted to $4.7 million in 1988. Wherever possible, use numbers from the Statements of Financial Position (which have not been rounded to the nearest million).

3. Calculate the effect on the Navistar's ratio of total liabilities to total assets at October 31, 1988 and 1987 as if all nonconsolidated subsidiaries were consolidated rather than having been accounted for on the equity basis.

16.8 DERIVE PROFORMA FINANCIAL STATEMENTS USING RATIOS

These questions use ratios based on the actual financial data from Navistar's 1988 statements to derive proforma financial statements. The statements are derived by starting with the net income number and using that as the basis for the estimate of sales, expenses, assets, and so forth. The only ratio not based on the 1988 data is the dividend payout, which is assumed to be 100 percent.

1. Use Navistar's 1988 Statement of Financial Position and Statement of Income to calculate and thus verify the following ratio calculations (rounded to four significant digits). Dollars are in millions unless stated otherwise.

Gross margin percentage	0.1245
Net income after taxes to sales	0.0598
Marketing and administrative expenses to sales	0.0554
Accounts receivable turnover (based on ending balance)	10.8545
Inventory turnover (based on ending balance)	11.3122
Quick assets ratio	0.8335
Current ratio	1.1365
Cash (Note 8) to quick assets	0.0096
Short-term investments (Note 8) to quick assets	0.5898
Accounts receivable to quick assets	0.4006

Sales to total assets (based on ending balance)	1.6177	
Total assets to investments and long-term receivables	6.8875	
Total assets to prepaid pension assets and other (long-term)	6.9406	
Plant assets at cost to accumulated depreciation	2.1002	
Accounts receivable to accounts payable	0.6670	
Working capital to shareowners' equity	0.1775	
Long-term debt to shareowners' equity	0.2061	
Income tax rate	0.0401	
Net income after taxes	$ 244.00	given
Earnings per share	$ 0.84	given
Preference dividend	$ 28.80	given
Preferred stock	$ 258.30	given
Par value of common stock per share	$1.00	given
Excess of par value over common stock per share	0.8498*	
Interest rate on long-term debt (for interest expense)	0.0667	
Dividend payout	100%	given

*Based on weighted average shares outstanding

2. Construct a proforma income statement and balance sheet for Navistar for the following year, 1989, using the ratios and assumptions given above with the additions that (1) Navistar expects next year's earnings and sales to grow by 15 percent and (2) asset turnover (ratio of sales to total assets) is expected to increase from the present level of 1.6177 to 1.80. In constructing the proforma statements, use the accounts and statement format as shown in the statements that follow.

NAVISTAR INTERNATIONAL CORPORATION
PROFORMA STATEMENT OF INCOME
FOR THE YEAR ENDED OCTOBER 31, 1989

(Numbers in thousands)

Net sales
Less cost of sales
Gross profit
Less expenses
    Marketing and administrative expenses
    Other expenses
    Total operating expenses
Net operating income before interest and taxes
    Interest on long-term debt
Net income before taxes
    Income tax expense
Net income after taxes
Less Preference dividend
Net income available for common

PROFORMA BALANCE SHEET AS OF OCTOBER 31, 1989

(Numbers in thousands)

ASSETS
Cash
Short-term investments
Accounts receivable
Quick assets
Inventory
Other current assets
    Current assets

Plant, at cost
Less accumulated depreciation on plant
Plant assets, net of accumulated depreciation
Investments and long-term receivables
Prepaid pension assets and other noncurrent assets

TOTAL ASSETS

LIABILITIES AND SHAREOWNERS' EQUITY
Accounts payable
Other current liabilities
    Current liabilities

Long-term debt
Other long-term liabilities
    Total liabilities

SHAREOWNERS' EQUITY
Preference shares
Common stock at par value $1 per share
Common stock in excess of par
Retained earnings and other
    Total shareowners' equity

TOTAL EQUITIES

Weekly stock prices and volume and the S&P 400 industrial stock index from Navistar International Corporation: January 1, 1988 to March 31, 1989.

Date	Number of shares traded	Closing stock price	S&P 400 index
1/1/88	5,591,000	4.25	285.86
1/8/88	5,752,500	4.25	280.91
1/15/88	4,850,000	4.125	290.58
1/22/88	2,563,400	4	282.44
1/29/88	3,670,800	4	293.7
2/5/88	2,452,600	3.875	286.47
2/12/88	4,604,600	4.25	296.07
2/19/88	8,635,000	4.875	301.48
2/26/88	14,282,000	5.5	302.63
3/4/88	7,938,000	5.625	308.98
3/11/88	6,522,000	5.625	307.39
3/18/88	5,834,000	5.875	314.64
3/25/88	14,662,000	6.625	299.53
4/1/88	5,870,000	6.5	300.39
4/8/88	5,402,100	6.75	313.6
4/15/88	6,802,000	6.375	302.68
4/22/88	4,276,000	6	302.92
4/29/88	2,969,700	6.25	304.48
5/6/88	5,284,000	6.5	300.01
5/13/88	3,341,700	6.125	298.23
5/20/88	3,564,700	6.125	293.42
5/27/88	2,083,000	5.875	292.55
6/3/88	8,167,000	6.875	307.58
6/10/88	11,574,000	7	313.62
6/17/88	5,163,000	6.625	312.8
6/24/88	2,986,600	6.625	316.18
7/1/88	3,470,600	6.625	313.75
7/8/88	2,965,700	6.625	312.28
7/15/88	4,010,300	6.25	314.38
7/22/88	2,888,100	6.125	304.36
7/29/88	2,418,600	6.375	313.98
8/5/88	1,796,200	6.125	312.21
8/12/88	5,369,000	5.875	301.94
8/19/88	5,296,600	5.5	298.44
8/26/88	4,102,000	5.125	298.01
9/2/88	3,641,800	5.25	303.35
9/9/88	3,006,800	5.375	305.97
9/16/88	5,542,000	5	310.81
9/23/88	3,810,600	5.25	309.4
9/30/88	3,899,400	5.375	311.67

Date	Number of shares traded	Closing stock price	S&P 400 index
10/7/88	2,699,500	5.625	319.17
10/14/88	2,987,900	5.375	316.7
10/21/88	3,926,800	5.625	326.84
10/28/88	3,524,000	5.375	320.67
11/4/88	3,317,900	5.25	318.09
11/11/88	3,111,800	5	308.11
11/18/88	4,456,800	5.125	306.36
11/25/88	1,702,600	5	307.64
12/2/88	2,115,900	5.125	313.16
12/9/88	4,060,400	5	319.06
12/16/88	3,530,500	5	318.7
12/23/88	4,073,700	4.875	321.28
12/30/88	5,643,000	5.375	321.26
1/6/89	3,121,300	5.5	324.93
1/13/89	3,707,300	5.25	328.81
1/20/89	3,677,100	5.25	331.41
1/27/89	7,940,000	5.75	339.55
2/3/89	6,358,000	6.375	343.84
2/10/89	10,929,000	6.375	337.26
2/17/89	6,666,000	5.875	342.66
2/24/89	6,233,000	6	331.33
3/3/89	3,588,100	6	336.35
3/10/89	5,243,000	6.25	338.17
3/17/89	4,581,700	5.875	337.78
3/24/89	1,885,700	5.875	332.79
3/31/89	1,903,400	6	339.42

Announcement dates for quarterly earnings: Source: *The Wall Street Journal Index*, 1988, 1989.

February 18, 1988:	Net income for January 31 quarter, $44,900,000.
May 19, 1988:	Net income for April 30 quarter, $70,000,000
August 18, 1988:	Net income for July 31 quarter, $46,800,000
December 6, 1988:	Net income for October 31 quarter, $82,300,000
February 17, 1989:	Net income for January 31 quarter, $37,400,000

NAVISTAR INTERNATIONAL CORPORATION
STATEMENTS OF CONSOLIDATED INCOME

For the Years Ended October 31	1988	1987	1986	Note Reference
	(Millions of dollars, except per share data)			
Sales	$ 4,080.2	$ 3,529.7	$ 3,356.5	
Cost of sales	3,572.4	3,054.2	2,942.0	
Gross margin	507.8	475.5	414.5	
Expenses:				
Engineering expense	81.1	75.5	67.0	
Marketing and administrative expenses	225.9	214.1	213.1	
Provision for losses on receivables	8.3	7.7	11.9	
Financing charges on sold receivables	68.3	58.9	56.6	
Interest expense	11.9	40.9	102.4	
Tenneco stock valuation adjustment	15.0	-	65.9	Note 9
Gain on pension settlement	(33.7)	-	-	Note 3
Other (income) expense, net	(55.3)	(5.2)	(20.5)	
Total expenses	321.5	391.9	496.4	
Income (loss) before income taxes:				
Consolidated companies	186.3	83.6	(81.9)	
Nonconsolidated companies	82.7	68.3	88.1	Note 11
Income before income taxes	269.0	151.9	6.2	
Taxes on income	10.2	5.6	4.5	Note 5
Income from continuing operations	258.8	146.3	1.7	
Loss on discontinued operations	(14.8)	-	-	Note 6
Income before extraordinary item	244.0	146.3	1.7	
Extraordinary item-loss on debt extinguishment	-	(112.9)	-	Note 2
Net income	$ 244.0	$ 33.4	$ 1.7	
Net income (loss) applicable to common stock	$ 215.2	$ 6.9	$ (12.2)	Note 7
Income (loss) per common share:				Note 7
Continuing operations	$ .89	$ .50	$ (.14)	
Discontinued operations	(.05)	-	-	
Before extraordinary item	.84	.50	(.14)	
Extraordinary item-loss on debt extinguishment	-	(.47)	-	
Net income (loss) per common share	$ .84	$ .03	$ (.14)	
Average number of common and dilutive common equivalent shares Outstanding (millions)	257.4	239.0	89.1	Note 7

NAVISTAR INTERNATIONAL CORPORATION
STATEMENTS OF CONSOLIDATED FINANCIAL CONDITION

October 31	1988	1987	Note Reference
	(Millions of dollars)		
ASSETS			
Current assets			
Cash and short-term investments	$ 562.4	$ 383.9	Note 8
Receivables, net	375.9	114.2	Note 9
Inventories	315.8	265.9	Note 10
Other assets	25.4	21.2	
Total current assets	1,279.5	785.2	
Investments and long-term receivables			Note 11
Equity in nonconsolidated companies	313.8	435.4	
Participating preferred stock of Tenneco Inc.	-	120.0	Note 9
Long-term receivables and other investments, at cost	52.4	64.8	
Total investments and long-term receivables	366.2	620.2	
Property, net of accumulated depreciation and amortization	460.8	397.0	Note 12
Prepaid and other pension assets	363.4	18.5	Note 3
Other non-current assets	52.3	81.3	
Total assets	$ 2,522.2	$ 1,902.2	
LIABILITIES AND SHAREOWNERS' EQUITY			
Current liabilities			
Notes payable and current maturities of long-term debt	$ 15.5	$ 15.2	
Accounts payable	563.6	481.7	
Accrued liabilities	546.7	339.1	
Total current liabilities	1,125.8	836.0	Note 14
Non-current liabilities			
Long-term debt	178.4	191.0	Note 15
Other liabilities	352.2	232.0	Note 16
Total non-current liabilities	530.6	423.0	
Shareowners' equity			Note 2,
Series G convertible preferred stock (liquidation preference $240 million)	240.0	240.0	20 & 21
Series D convertible junior preference stock (liquidation preference $18 million)	18.3	26.7	
Common stock (252.9 and 251.8 million shares issued) and warrants	473.9	400.1	
Retained earnings—balance accumulated after the reclassification of deficit accumulated as of October 31, 1987 of $1,968 million	150.2	-	
Accumulated foreign currency translation adjustments	(4.4)	(11.4)	
Common stock held in treasury, at cost	(12.2)	(12.2)	
Total shareowners' equity	865.8	643.2	
Total liabilities and shareowners' equity	$ 2,522.2	$ 1,902.2	

NAVISTAR INTERNATIONAL CORPORATION
STATEMENTS OF CONSOLIDATED CASH FLOW

For the Years Ended October 31	1988	1987	1986	Note Reference
	(Millions of dollars)			
Cash flow from operations:				
Net income	$ 244.0	$ 33.4	$ 1.7	
Adjustments to reconcile net income to cash provided by operations:				
Depreciation and amortization	48.7	41.1	40.4	
Equity in earnings of nonconsolidated companies, net of dividends received	4.4	(35.3)	(51.2)	
Gain on Canadian pension settlement	(33.7)	-	-	Note 3
Tenneco stock valuation adjustment	15.0	-	65.9	Note 9
Provision for losses on receivables and investment in dealerships	7.5	19.1	19.6	
Loss on debt extinguishment	-	112.9	-	Note 2
Other	23.7	33.2	2.5	
Change in current assets and liabilities:				
(Increase) decrease in accounts and notes receivables	(13.3)	(13.4)	11.0	
(Increase) decrease in inventories	(46.9)	29.5	40.3	
(Increase) decrease in prepaids and other current assets	(18.7)	13.6	.3	
Increase in accounts payable and accrued expenses	103.5	110.4	6.4	
Cash provided by operations	334.2	344.5	136.9	
Cash flow from investment programs:				
Special dividends from finance subsidiaries	90.0	27.0	367.0	Note 3
Proceeds from sale of Navistar Financial Corporation Canada	-	116.6	-	
Special pension funding	(90.0)	-	(350.0)	Note 3
Capital expenditures	(126.5)	(110.4)	(69.9)	
Restructuring outlays, net of other investment programs	15.8	6.2	(58.8)	
Cash provided by (used in) investment programs	(110.7)	39.4	(111.7)	
Cash flow from financing activities:				
Repayment of debt	-	(639.7)	(350.7)	Note 2
Principal payments under capital lease obligations, other debt instruments and notes	(14.9)	(27.9)	(55.2)	
Issuance of senior and subordinated debenture	-	-	275.0	
Cash dividends paid on preferred stock	(28.8)	(22.3)	-	
Proceeds from issuance of common stock	-	468.6	.2	
Cash used in financing activities	(43.7)	(221.3)	(130.7)	
Effect of exchange rate changes on cash	(1.3)	3.6	-	
Cash and short-term investments:				
Increase (decrease) during the year	178.5	166.2	(105.5)	Note 17
At beginning of the year	383.9	217.7	323.2	
Cash and short-term investments at end of the year	$ 562.4	$ 383.9	$ 217.7	

NOTES TO CONSOLIDATED FINANCIAL STATEMENTS

FOR THE THREE YEARS ENDED OCTOBER 1988

---

1. SUMMARY OF ACCOUNTING POLICIES

Basis of Consolidation

The consolidated financial statements include the accounts of Navistar International Corporation, a holding company, and its subsidiaries except for wholly-owned finance and insurance subsidiaries which are included on the equity basis. Investments in dealerships are carried at the lower of cost or realizable value. As used hereafter, "Company" refers to Navistar International Corporation and its subsidiaries and "Parent Company" refers to Navistar International Corporation alone. "Transportation" refers to Navistar International Transportation Corp., a wholly-owned subsidiary of the Parent Company which operates in one principal industry segment—manufacture of medium and heavy trucks, diesel engines and service parts.

Cash and Short-term Investments

The Company considers all its short-term investments to be highly liquid. All short-term investments are considered cash equivalents for purposes of disclosure in the Statements of Consolidated Financial Condition and Statements of Consolidated Cash Flow.

Income Taxes

The tax effect of each item in the Statements of Consolidated Income is recognized in the current period regardless of when the related tax is paid. Taxes on amounts which affect financial and taxable income in different periods are reported as deferred income taxes. Deferred taxes are provided only on items which will result in a next tax liability in future years. Taxes on income in the Statements of Consolidated Income include the benefit of tax loss carryforwards.

Investment tax credit carryforwards will be recognized as a reduction of income tax expense in the year they reduce the Company's tax liability.

Inventory Valuation

Inventory is valued at the lower of average cost or market.

Property

Significant expenditures for replacement of equipment, tooling and pattern equipment, and major rebuilding of machine tools, are capitalized.

Depreciation and amortization are generally computed on the straight-line basis; gains and losses on property disposals are included in other income.

Research and Development

Expenses for research and development activities related to new product development and major improvements to existing products and processes are expensed as incurred. These expenses were $80 million, $79 million and $62 million in 1988, 1987 and 1986, respectively. Engineering expense, as shown on the Statements of Consolidated Income, includes certain research and development expenses and routine on-going efforts to improve existing products and processes.

Retirement Benefits

Effective November 1, 1987, the Company adopted for all pension plans Statement of Financial Accounting Standards No. 87, "Employers' Accounting for Pensions" ("SFAS 87"), and No. 88, "Employers' Accounting for Settlements and Curtailments of Defined Benefit Pension Plans and for Termination Benefits." The provisions of SFAS 87 were adopted prospectively and, accordingly, previous years' results have not been restated. See Note 3.

In addition to pension benefits, health care and life insurance benefits are provided for employees who retire from operations in the United States and Canada. The cost of retiree health care is recognized when claims are paid and the cost of life insurance benefits is recognized when the premiums are paid.

Statements of Consolidated Cash Flow

Statement of Financial Accounting Standards No. 95, "Statement of Cash Flows," was adopted for fiscal 1988, and prior years were restated to conform with the current year presentation. Supplemental information required by this Statement is presented in Note 17.

Reclassifications

Certain 1987 and 1986 amounts have been reclassified to conform with the presentation used in the 1988 financial statements.

2. RECAPITALIZATION

On December 9, 1986, the shareowners approved the proposals necessary to implement a recapitalization. As part of the recapitalization, the Company issued 128.3 million shares of Common Stock as follows:

- 104.5 million shares were sold in a public offering resulting in proceeds of $470 million.

- 22 million shares, valued at $105 million, were contributed to the U.S. pension plans serving as payment of regular annual contributions that would otherwise have been made in 1987 and also reducing the unfunded pension liability for one of the pension plans.

- 1.8 million shares were sold in a secondary public offering by holders of the Company's Series E Preferred Stock who had converted such stock into Common Stock; the Company realized no proceeds on this transaction.

During the first quarter of 1987, funds of $621 million, comprised of the $470 million proceeds from the Common Stock offering and $151 million from internal sources, were used to redeem four high coupon public debt issues with a total carrying value of $508 million. The redemption resulted in a $113 million extraordinary loss.

Effective January 14, 1987, 3 million shares of series C Preferred Stock and the accumulated dividends on this stock of $90 million were reclassified as 4.8 million shares of Series G Preferred Stock.

Effective October 31, 1987, the Company reclassified its deficit in retained earnings of $1,968 million to capital in excess of par value, thereby reducing the amounts reported as Common Stock and Warrants. The reclassification did not change total shareowners' equity and had no effect on the carrying value of assets or liabilities of the Company. As a result of the deficit reclassification, tax benefits arising from the utilization of net operating loss carryforwards subsequent to October 31, 1987 are reclassified from Retained Earnings to Common Stock and Warrants.

3. RETIREMENT BENEFITS

The Company and its domestic and Canadian subsidiaries have pension plans covering substantially all of their employees. Generally, the plans are non-contributory and benefits are related to an employee's length of service and compensation rate.

The Company's policy is to fund the minimum requirements under the Employee Retirement Income Security Act of 1974 ("ERISA") and make additional payments as funds are available to achieve full funding of the accumulated benefit obligation. The Company's pension plans vary in the extent to which they are funded, but for plan years which ended during the current fiscal year, all funding obligations have been fulfilled. Plan assets are primarily invested in dedicated portfolios of long-term fixed income securities.

Pension costs for these plans and related disclosures as of October 31, 1988 are determined under provisions of SFAS 87, adopted on November 1, 1987. The change in accounting policy and changes from increased benefits incorporated into negotiated contracts increased pension expense by $29 million for 1988, or $.11 per share, to $83 million. Pension costs charged to income for 1987 and 1986, which have not been restated, were $54 million and $68 million, respectively.

Net pension cost for 1988 includes the following cost components:

Millions of dollars

Service cost for benefits earned during the period		$ 16
Interest cost on projected benefit obligation		210
Return on plan assets-actual	(230)	
-deferred	58	
-recognized		(172)
Net amortization of deferred costs		29
Net pension cost		$ 83

The unrecognized net transition obligation at November 1, 1987, is amortized on a straight-line basis over 15 years. Plan amendments resulting from negotiated contracts are amortized on a straight-line basis over the length of the agreement. Other amendments are generally amortized over the average remaining service life of active employees.

During fiscal 1988 and 1987, the Company made special payments to its U.S. pension plans in excess of the minimum required by ERISA. A contribution of 22 million shares of Navistar Common Stock valued at $105 million was made in December 1986. A $90 million payment was made during the first quarter of 1988 from funds made available by a $90 million dividend from Navistar Financial Corporation. These special payments increased prepaid and other pension assets, reduced unfunded pension liabilities and significantly reduced annual pension expense. The Company, on December 1, 1988, made a special $220 million payment to the U.S. hourly pension plan. This contribution was reflected in the Statement of Consolidated Financial Condition at October 31, 1988 as a pension asset and an accrued liability. On a proforma basis at October 31, 1988, including the special $220 million contribution, the relationship of plan assets at fair value to the actuarial present value of the Company's hourly and total vested pension liability is as follows:

Millions of dollars	Hourly Plan	Total All Plans
Plan assets at fair value	$ 1,216	$ 2,031
Actuarial present value of the vested benefit obligation	1,153	1,992
Plan assets in excess of vested benefit obligation	$ 63	$ 39

During January 1988, the Company settled a large portion of the projected benefit obligation of the two major pension plans of its Canadian operating subsidiary through the purchase of non-participating annuities. In connection with this settlement, the Company recorded a pre-tax settlement gain of $34 million or $24 million net of income taxes.

The actual and proforma funded status of the Company's plans as of October 31, 1988 and the amounts recognized in the Statement of Consolidated Financial Condition are as follows. The proforma amounts assume the $220 million was contributed on October 31, 1988.

Millions of dollars	Assets Exceed Accumulated Benefits-Actual	Accumulated Benefits Exceed Assets Actual	Proforma
Actuarial present value of:			
Vested benefits	$ (24)	$ (1,968)	$ (1,968)
Non-vested benefits	(1)	(158)	(158)
Accumulated benefit obligation	(25)	(2,126)	(2,126)
Effect of projected future compensation levels	(2)	(32)	(32)
Total projected benefit obligation	(27)	(2,158)	(2,158)
Plan assets at fair value	60	1,751	1,971
Excess or (deficiency) of plan assets over projected benefit obligation	33	(407)	(187)
Unrecognized net losses	7	17	17
Unrecognized plan amendments	5	53	53
Unrecognized net obligation at date of SFAS 87 adoption	(6)	394	394
Net pre-paid pension asset	$ 39	$ 57	$ 277

The projected benefit obligation was determined using a weighted average discount rate of 10.0% and a projected rate of compensation increase of 5.5%. The assumed weighted average long-term rate of return on plan assets was 10.4% for 1988.

The Company also has a non-qualified, unfunded pension program which is excluded from the unfunded obligation shown above. This plan provides officers and certain other employees with defined pension benefits in excess of qualified plan limits imposed by federal tax law. The liability for this pension program is estimated to be $42 million at October 31, 1988.

For 1988, costs for retiree health care and life insurance benefits for operations in the United States and Canada totalled $108 million as compared with $100 million and $91 million for 1987 and 1986, respectively.

4. FOREIGN OPERATIONS

Sales by the consolidated Canadian subsidiary accounted for 11.2% of total sales in 1988, 11.1% in 1987 and 9.4% in 1986.

Net income of consolidated foreign subsidiaries and equity in income of nonconsolidated foreign companies totalled $70 million in 1988, $44 million in 1987 and $33 million in 1986.

Net assets of foreign operations at October 31 consist of the following:

Millions of dollars	Canada	Europe	Caribbean	Caribbean
1988				
Working capital	$ (2)	$ 17	$ 82	$ 97
Non-current assets	64	3	2	69
Non-current liabilities	(14)	(11)	(65)	(90)
Net assets	$ 48	$ 9	$ 19	$ 76
1987				
Net assets	$ 143	$ 9	$ 52	$ 204

Net assets in Europe consist primarily of an insurance subsidiary in the United Kingdom. Caribbean assets represent the Company's investment in nonconsolidated finance and insurance subsidiaries.

5. INCOME TAXES

The domestic and foreign components of income (loss) before income taxes consist of the following:

Millions of dollars	1988	1987	1986
Domestic	$ 186	$ 107	$ (30)
Foreign	83	45	36
Total income before income taxes	$ 269	$ 152	$ 6

Taxes on income are comprised of the following:

Millions of dollars	1988	1987	1986
Tax (benefits) expenses provided before the effects of net operating losses:			
Consolidated companies	$ 62	$ 44	$ (35)
Nonconsolidated companies	24	30	43
Tax benefits of net operating losses	(65)	(68)	(4)
Tax benefits from settlement of prior years' income tax audits	(11)	-	-
Total taxes on income	$ 10	$ 6	$ 4

Taxes on income are analyzed by category as follows:

Millions of dollars	1988	1987	1986
Current:			
Federal	$ 59	$ 48	$ -
Foreign	8	17	7
State and local	5	9	1
Total current	72	74	8
Deferred taxes	14	-	-
Tax benefits of net operating losses	(65)	(68)	(4)
Tax benefits from settlement of prior years' income tax audits	(11)	-	-
Total taxes on income	$ 10	$ 6	$ 4

The relationship of the tax benefits' expenses to the pre-tax income in 1988, 1987 and 1986 differs from the U.S. statutory rate primarily because of the benefits of net operating loss ("NOL") carryforwards in the U.S. and foreign countries. Consequently, an analysis of deferred taxes and variance from the statutory rate is not provided.

Undistributed earnings of foreign companies were $52 million at October 31, 1988. No taxes have been provided on $37 million of these undistributed earnings considered to be permanently reinvested. Substantially all tax expense associated with the receipt of such undistributed earnings would be offset by the utilization of NOL carryforwards.

At October 31, 1988, the Company's continuing operations had an estimated $1,202 million of domestic and $7 million of foreign NOL carryforwards available to reduce future taxable income. For financial reporting purposes, the Company had a NOL carryforward of $1,726 million available to reduce financial income at October 31, 1988. Substantially all of the $517 million difference between the tax and financial loss carryforwards will expire by the year 2005. The $517 million, which arises primarily as a result of differences in the recognition of expense items for financial and tax purposes, will reduce taxable income when the expenses are actually paid. The Company has domestic investment tax credit ("ITC") carryforwards of approximately $41 million at October 31, 1988, which are available to reduce future U.S. federal income tax liabilities. The tax carryforwards will expire as detailed below (in millions):

Year of Expiration	Domestic and Foreign NOL	ITC
1992–1996	$ -	$ 31
1997–1998	692	8
1999–2000	363	2
2001–2002	147	-
Indefinite	7	-
Total	$ 1,209	$ 41

6. DISCONTINUED OPERATIONS

In February 1988, Transportation settled all claims by or on behalf of the class of former Wisconsin Steel employees in the litigation commonly referred to as the Lympkin Case. A provision for this settlement of $15 million was recorded in the first quarter of 1988 as a loss of discontinued operations. On September 2, 1988, the settlement was paid to the former Wisconsin Steel employees. See Note 19.

7. INCOME (LOSS) PER COMMON SHARE

For computation of earnings per share, income (loss) applicable to common stock is determined as follows:

Millions of dollars	1988	1987	1986
Income of continuing operations	$ 258.8	$ 146.3	$ 1.7
Preferred dividend requirements	(28.8)	(26.5)	(17.3)
Amortization of difference between redemption value and carrying value of Series E preferred stock	-	-	3.4
Income (loss) of continuing operations applicable to common stock	230.0	119.8	(12.2)
Loss on discontinued operations	(14.8)	-	-
Extraordinary loss	-	(112.9)	-
Common stock	$ 215.2	$ 6.9	$ (12.2)

Average common and dilutive common equivalent shares outstanding are derived as follows:

Millions of shares	1988	1987	1986
Common Stock outstanding or unconditionally issuable	253.2	219.1	89.1
Common Stock equivalents of:			
Series D preference stock	2.8	16.9	-
Options and warrants	9.1	12.4	-
Common Stock assumed to be repurchased with proceeds received upon exercise of options and warrants	(7.7)	(9.4)	-
Total average common and dilutive common equivalent shares	257.4	239.0	89.1

Common stock equivalents were not dilutive during 1986.

Income (loss) per common share is as follows:

	1988	1987	1986
Continuing operations	$ .89	$ .50	$ (.14)
Discontinued operations	(.05)	-	-
Before extraordinary item	.84	.50	(.14)
Extraordinary loss	-	(.47)	-
Net income (loss) per common share	$ .84	$ .03	$ (.14)

Income (loss per common share assuming full dilution) is not presented because the Series G Preferred Stock for 1988 and 1987 and the series C Preferred Stock for 1986 did not have a dilutive effect for the years presented.

8. CASH AND SHORT-TERM INVESTMENTS

Cash and short-term investments (stated at cost, which approximates market value) are as follows:

Millions of dollars	1988	1987
Cash	$ 9	$ 12
Navistar Financial Corporation Commercial paper	25	100
Nonaffiliated companies:		
Commercial paper	227	176
Other short-term investments	301	96
Total cash and short-term investments	$ 562	$ 384

Other short-term investments consist primarily of time and certificates of deposits, bankers' acceptances, U.S. Treasury securities, and loan participation notes.

9. RECEIVABLES

Major classifications of receivables at October 31 are as follows:

Millions of dollars	1988	1987
Accounts and notes receivables:		
Customers	$ 122	$ 98
Tenneco Inc.	105	-
Nonconsolidated subsidiaries and affiliated companies	157	24
Total accounts and notes receivables	384	122
Allowance for losses-customers	(8)	(8)
Receivables, net	$ 376	$ 114

Navistar Financial Corporation purchases nearly all notes receivable and some accounts receivable arising from operations in the United States. The Canadian operation sells certain receivables to a nonaffiliated finance company.

In the third quarter of 1988, the Company sold to Tenneco Inc. the Tenneco Participating Preferred Stock received in 1985 as partial consideration for the sale of its agricultural equipment business. In exchange for the shares, the Company received a promissory note in the principal amount of $105 million. The note, with accrued interest, was settled in December 1988 prior to maturity. There was no gain or loss on the transaction because the Company previously had reduced the carrying value of the investment from $120 million to $105 million in the second quarter of 1988 to reflect the current valuation of the expected proceeds.

During the fourth quarter of 1988, the Company ceased to insure certain general and product liability exposures of Transportation through its insurance subsidiary. The Company has released the affiliate from further liability in exchange for $116 million. This decision reduced the amount of equity required in the subsidiary and a dividend of $27 million to reduce the capital structure was declared in the fourth quarter of 1988. As of October 31, 1988, both amounts are included as a receivable from nonconsolidated subsidiaries and affiliated companies.

10. INVENTORIES

Inventories at October 31 are summarized as follows:

Millions of dollars	1988	1987
Finished products	$ 149	$ 120
Work in process	47	36
Raw materials and supplies	120	110
Total	$ 316	$ 266

11. INVESTMENTS AND LONG-TERM RECEIVABLES

Nonconsolidated Companies

Equity in Nonconsolidated Companies consists of the Company's investment in its wholly-owned finance and insurance subsidiaries.

Dividends from nonconsolidated subsidiaries for the years ended October 31 are as follows:

Millions of dollars	1988	1987	1986
Cash	$ 158	$ 36	$ 359
Non-cash	-	-	27
Declared and not paid	27	-	-
Total	$ 185	$ 36	$ 386

The $27 million dividend in 1988 represents a receivable from a foreign insurance subsidiary as a result of a reduction in its capital structure at October 31, 1988. See Note 9. In 1986, non-cash dividends of $13 million were remitted by Navistar Financial Corporation in the form of a debt cancellation and $14 million was remitted by the Company's foreign finance and insurance subsidiaries as dividends of stock of various subsidiaries.

Navistar Financial Corporation

Operating results of Navistar Financial Corporation, the Company's wholly-owned non-consolidated U.S. finance subsidiary, for the years ended October 31 are summarized as follows:

Millions of dollars	1988	1987	1986
Revenues	$ 217	$ 213	$ 221
Expenses:			
Cost of borrowing	110	105	121
Marketing and administrative	20	24	23
Provision for losses on receivables	3	2	3
Insurance claims and underwriting losses	32	28	14
Other expense	1	2	-
Total	166	161	161
Income before income taxes	51	52	60
Taxes on income	(19)	(23)	(29)
Net income	$ 32	$ 29	$ 31

In accordance with financing agreements between Transportation and Navistar Financial Corporation relating to financing of wholesale notes, wholesale accounts, and retail accounts, the subsidiary receives interest income from Transportation at an agreed upon interest rate applied to the average outstanding balances less interest amounts paid by dealers on wholesale notes and wholesale accounts. Revenues collected from Transportation and included above for wholesale notes, wholesale accounts, and retail accounts were $38 million in 1988, $37 million in 1987 and $45 million in 1986.

The financial condition of Navistar Financial Corporation at October 31 is as follows:

Millions of dollars	1988	1987
Assets:		
Cash and marketable securities	$ 112	$ 83
Receivables, net	1,567	1,478
Amounts due from sale of receivables	45	63
Repossessions	7	6
Other assets	31	33
Total assets	$ 1,762	$ 1,663
Liabilities:		
Commercial paper:		
Transportation	$ 25	$ 100
Others	997	648
Accounts payable	55	51
Other liabilities	90	86
Long-term debt	306	400
Total liabilities	1,473	1,285
Shareowners' Equity:		
Capital stock	171	171
Retained earnings	118	207
Total shareowners' equity	289	378
Total liabilities and shareowners' equity	$ 1,762	$ 1,663

oreign Finance and Insurance Subsidiaries

In December 1986, Navistar Financial Corporation Canada, a Canadian nance subsidiary, was sold for approximately its book value of $98 million.

Operating results of the Company's wholly-owned nonconsolidated foreign nance and insurance subsidiaries are summarized as follows:

Millions of dollars	1988	1987	1986
Revenues from:			
Affiliates	$ 4	$ 31	$ 40
Outsiders	29	19	73
Total	$ 33	$ 50	$ 113
Income before income taxes	$ 32	$ 16	$ 28
Taxes on income	(5)	(7)	(14)
Net income	$ 27	$ 9	$ 14

The financial condition of these subsidiaries at October 31 is summarized as follows:

Millions of dollars	1988	1987
Assets	$ 251	$ 289
Liabilities	$ 226	$ 232
Shareowners' equity	25	57
Total liabilities and shareowners' equity	$ 251	$ 289

Long-Term Receivables and Other Investments

These amounts primarily represent investments in the capital stock of and long-term loans to truck dealerships in the United States and Canada and are valued at cost which approximates realizable value.

12. PROPERTY

At October 31, property includes the following:

Millions of dollars	1988	1987
Land	$ 5	$ 4
Buildings, machinery, equipment, tooling and patterns as cost:		
Manufacturing	743	677
Distribution	67	67
Other	65	47
Sub-Total	875	791
Total Property	880	795
Less accumulated depreciation and amortization	(419)	(398)
Property, net	$ 461	$ 397

Buildings, machinery, and equipment include $63 million and $64 million at October 31, 1988 and 1987, respectively, representing gross amounts of property under capitalized lease obligations.

13. LEASES

The Company has long-term noncancelable leases for use of various facilities. Lease terms are generally for 5 to 25 years and in many cases provide for renewal options. The Company is generally obligated for the cost of property taxes, insurance and maintenance.

At October 31, 1988, future minimum lease payments required under capital and noncancelable operating leases having lease terms in excess of one year are as follows:

Millions of dollars	Capital Leases	Operating Leases
1989	$ 10	$ 24
1990	9	22
1991	6	18
1992	6	17
1993	3	9
Thereafter	25	39
Total minimum payments	59	$ 129
Less imputed interest	(20)	
Present value of minimum lease payments	$ 39	
Minimum sublease rentals		$ 68

The amount of total rent expense for all operating leases was $35 million in 1988, $29 million in 1987 and $34 million in 1986. Contingent rentals were not material. Income received from sublease rentals was $6 million in 1988 and $7 million in both 1987 and 1986.

14. CURRENT LIABILITIES

Major classifications of current liabilities at October 31 are as follows:

Millions of dollars	1988	1987
Notes payable and current maturities of long-term debt	$ 15	$ 15
Accounts payable:		
Trade	546	469
Affiliated companies	3	3
Other	15	10
Total accounts payable	564	482
Accrued liabilities:		
Pension, health and welfare	261	56
Product liability and warranty	83	73
Payrolls and commissions	97	76
Taxes	36	55
Interest	4	6
Other	66	73
Total accrued liabilities	547	339
Total current liabilities	$ 1,126	$ 836

The accrued pension and health and welfare balance at October 31, 1988 includes a $220 million liability for special funding paid on December 1, 1988 to the U.S. hourly pension plan. See Note 3.

The Company has a total of $95 million available through lines of credit or letters of credit for the purpose of providing working capital and financing foreign purchases. At October 31, 1988, $38 million of letters of credit had been issued. Commitment fees on the unused portion of these range up to 1/2% per annum.

15. LONG-TERM DEBT

Long-term debt, all issued by Transportation, at October 31, excluding amounts maturing within one year, is summarized as follows:

Millions of dollars	1988	1987
4.80% Subordinated Debentures, due 1991	$ 2	$ 7
8 5/8% Sinking Fund Debentures, due 1985	41	44
6 1/4% Sinking Fund Debentures, due 1998	14	14
9% Sinking Fund Debentures, due 2004	84	84
Capitalized leases	33	38
Other	4	4
Total long-term debt	$ 178	$ 191

Maturities

The aggregate annual maturities and sinking fund requirements for long-term borrowings are as follows for the years ended October 31: 1990, $15 million; 1991, $11 million; 1992, $9 million; 1993, $11 million; and 1994, $17 million.

16. OTHER LIABILITIES

Major classifications of other liabilities at October 31 are as follows:

Millions of dollars	1988	1987
Product liability	$ 167	$ 42
Restructuring costs	53	68
Other	132	122
Total other liabilities	$ 352	$ 232

Approximately $106 million of the product liability balance at October 31, 1988 represents the liability for certain general and product liability exposures which were assumed by the Company in the release of an affiliated company from further liability. See Note 9.

Restructuring costs primarily represent certain insurance and product liability costs to be paid over an extended period on the disposal of the agricultural equipment business which was sold on January 31, 1985.

17. SUPPLEMENTAL DISCLOSURES TO STATEMENTS OF CASH FLOW

Interest and taxes have been classified as an operating cash outflow in the Statements of Consolidated Cash Flow. The amounts actually paid, shown below, differ from the amounts reflected in the Statements of Consolidated Income because of accruals and the timing difference between income recognition and actual payment. Since certain taxes paid on investment and financing cash flows could be considered non-operating and interest paid could be considered the result of financing decisions, the following table of total interest and taxes paid has been provided:

Millions of dollars	1988	1987	1986
Cash paid for:			
Interest	$ 20	$ 63	$ 98
Income taxes	7	--	--

The following provides information about investing and financing activities of the Company that affect assets or liabilities but do not result in cash flow for the three years ended October 31, 1988 and, therefore, are excluded from the Statements of Consolidated Cash Flow.

- At October 31, 1988, a current receivable from an affiliate of $143 million was reflected in the Statement of Financial Condition. The transfer of funds will occur in the first quarter of 1989. See Note 9.

- A special payment of $220 million was made on December 1, 1988 to the U.S. hourly pension plan which was reflected as a prepaid and other pension asset and an accrued liability in the Statement of Financial Condition as of October 31, 1988. See Notes 3 and 14.

- In the third quarter of 1988, the Tenneco Participating Preferred Stock received in 1985 was sold to Tenneco Inc. In exchange for the shares, the Company received a promissory note in the principal amount of $105 million which was settled in December 1988 prior to maturity. See Note 9.

- Capital lease obligations of $3 million, $9 million and $19 million were incurred as a result of lease agreements for capital assets in 1988, 1987 and 1986, respectively.

- During 1988, 1987 and 1986, the following shares of Series E Preferred Stock (See Note 20) and Series D and A Preference Stocks were converted into Common Stock:

Millions of dollars	1988		1987		1986	
	Shares	Amount	Shares	Amount	Shares	Amount
Series E Preferred	-	$ -	160,960	$ 176	419,863	$ 532
Series D Preference	333,995	8	54,360	1	242,861	6
Series A Preference	-	-	-	-	669,923	18

- In December 1986, a contribution of 22 million shares of Common Stock ($105 million) was made to the pension plans. See Notes 2 and 3.

- During 1987, 3 million shares of Series C Preferred Stock ($150 million) and the accumulated dividend on this stock ($90 million) were reclassified as 4.8 million shares of Series G Preferred Stock. See Note 2.

- During 1986, Navistar Financial Corporation remitted dividends to Transportation in the form of debt cancellation in the amount of $13 million.

- In 1986, 4 million Series C Warrants ($11 million) were issued to Navistar Financial Corporation which increased the Company's equity in this subsidiary.

- In 1986, the principal amount of $25 million of the Company's 14 1/2% Senior Sinking Fund Debentures was contributed to the pension plans.

18. COMMITMENTS, CONTINGENT LIABILITIES AND RESTRICTIONS ON ASSETS

At October 31, 1988, commitments for capital expenditures in progress were approximately $117 million.

Transportation was contingently liable at October 31, 1988 for approximately $17 million for guarantees of debt and for bid and performance bonds. As of October 31, 1988, nonconsolidated subsidiaries were contingently liable for claims in the amount of $5 million.

At October 31, 1988, $41 million of cash and marketable securities classified as Other Non-Current Assets were restricted as to use under various agreements.

Certain of Transportation's subsidiaries are restricted by debt covenant agreements from distributing their equity to Transportation in the form of dividends, loans or advances. Consolidated subsidiaries' equity in the amount of $20 million and nonconsolidated subsidiaries' equity in the amount of $238 million were subject to such restrictions as of October 31, 1988.

Transportation is obligated under agreements with private lenders of Navistar Financial Corporation to maintain the subsidiary's income before interest expense and income taxes at not less than 125% of its total interest expense. Amounts paid by Transportation under these agreements have no effect on the consolidated results of the Company. No income maintenance payments were required in 1988, 1987 or 1986.

19. LEGAL PROCEEDINGS

The following legal matters concern the Wisconsin Steel Division, which was sold by Transportation to EDC Holding Company ("EDC") on July 31, 1977.

The Lumpkin Case. On December 1, 1981, a class action suit was filed against Transportation in the United States District Court for the Northern District of Illinois on behalf of approximately 3,500 former employees of the Wisconsin Steel Division alleging that Transportation had breached its duty to pay certain employment benefits. The total amount sought was approximately $82 million. The amended complaint also alleged claims under the Racketeer Influenced and Corrupt Organizations Act ("RICO") which, if successful, could have resulted in the trebling of all or any portion of the damages awarded. This case was settled in February 1988 for approximately $14.8 million.

EDC Bankruptcy Case. On March 31, 1980, EDC filed Chapter 11 bankruptcy petitions in the Bankruptcy Court for the Northern District of Illinois. After Transportation filed a claim on October 31, 1980 in the bankruptcy proceeding seeking $146 million owed to it by EDC, EDC objected and filed counterclaims against Transportation. The counterclaims sought to set aside Transportation's mortgages, liens and security interest; to require Transportation to return to EDC the value of certain iron and coal mining properties; to charge Transportation for all claims against EDC; and to enter a monetary judgment against Transportation based on purchases of iron ore pellets by Transportation prior to the bankruptcy.

EDC amended its counterclaims on March 30, 1982 to add Transportation's directors as of July 31, 1977 as defendants and to allege fraud by Transportation and by the directors in connection with the Wisconsin Steel Division sale. EDC later filed amended counterclaims which alleged that Transportation violated the RICO Act in connection with that sale. The total amount sought by the counterclaims was approximately $330 million. All or any portion of any damages awarded could have been trebled if the RICO claim was upheld.

This case was consolidated for trial with the Pension Plan Cases discussed below:

Pension Plan Cases. On December 18, 1981, a declaratory judgment action was filed against Transportation and other defendants in the United States District Court for the Northern District of Illinois by the Pension Benefit Guaranty Corporation ("PBGC"). The action requested that the Wisconsin Steel Works non-Contributory Pension Plan be judged terminated as of May 16, 1980 and sought to hold Transportation responsible for some or all of the pension benefits for which the PBGC would otherwise be responsible. On November 10, 1982, the PBGC filed a second action requesting that the Retirement Plan for Certain Salaried Employees of WSC Corp., Chicago West Pullman & Southern Railroad, and Benham Coal, Inc., be judged terminated as of May 16, 1980, and sought to hold Transportation responsible for some or all of the pension benefits for which the PBGC would otherwise be responsible.

This case and the EDC Bankruptcy Case were tried in the spring and summer of 1988, and a ruling was handed down November 16, 1988.

In the EDC Bankruptcy Case, the judge rejected assertions that Transportation engaged in any form of concealment, fraud or overreaching in the 1977 sale of its Wisconsin Steel operations. Accordingly, the judge rejected all counterclaims against Transportation by EDC except that the judge has not yet decided whether Transportation must return to EDC the value of certain iron and coal mining properties.

In the Pension Plan Cases, the judge ruled that Transportation had not engaged in any form of concealment, fraud or overreaching. He also rejected the PBGC's claim that Transportation is responsible for pension obligations incurred after the sale. However, the judge announced a special legal standard that imposed the obligation on Transportation only for the pension liabilities prior to the sale in July 1977. The judge also stated that he recognized that the proper legal standard for determining liability for pension obligations is a matter of dispute that will ultimately have to be resolved through the appellate process.

The amount sought by the PBGC for both pre- and post-sale pension obligations was previously estimated by the PBGC to be approximately $65 million plus accrued interest from May 16, 1980 to the date of payment. Since the judge held that Transportation would be obligated only for the pension liabilities vested prior to sale in July 1977, the amount of the award will have to be determined in subsequent proceedings. While the amount is not yet determined, the PBGC has stated that the amount would be less than the amount previously estimated by the PBGC.

Because the amount of the potential liability in the Pension Plan Cases has not been determined and since Transportation has been advised by its outside counsel that it has strong legal arguments in an appeal of the Pension Plan Cases, no material provision for the liability has been made in the financial statements.

Transportation has adequate resources to be able to satisfy any final judgment in the Pension Plan Cases without interfering with its ongoing operations.

The judge will enter final judgments in such cases after he has ruled on the amount of the award in the Pension Plan Cases and the remaining counterclaim in the EDC Bankruptcy Case. The appeal period for the cases will begin to run when final judgments are entered.

20. PREFERRED AND PREFERENCE STOCKS

Information pertaining to preferred and preference stocks outstanding is summarized as follows:

	Series G, $6.00 Cumulative Preferred	Series D Convertible Junior Preference Stock
Number authorized	4,800,000	3,000,000
Number issued	4,799,979	3,000,000
Number outstanding at October 31		
1988	4,799,979	733,620
1987	4,799,979	1,067,615
Dividend rate	$6.00 per share, payable quarterly	120% of the cash dividends on Common Stock as declared on a common equivalent basis
Optional redemption price	$ 51.15 per share plus accrued dividends, decreasing annually to $ 50 after 1990	$25 per share plus accrued dividends
Conversion rate per share into Common Stock (subject to adjustment in certain circumstances)	1 1/3 shares	3 1/8 shares
Ranking as to dividends and upon liquidation	Senior to all other equity securities	Senior to Common; junior to Series G
Liquidation preference	$50 per share plus accrued dividends if involuntary, or the optional redemption price plus accrued dividends if voluntary	$25 per share plus accrued dividends

In the first quarter of 1987, 17,957.21 shares of Series E Preferred Stock were converted into Common Stock and simultaneously sold to the public in a secondary offering. A similar conversion and simultaneous sale of 419,863.4 shares occurred in 1986.

The remaining 143,002.82 shares of Series E Redeemable Preferred Stock were converted into 14,300,282 shares of Common Stock in accordance with an agreement between the holders of Series E and the Company. The conversion was recorded in the Statement of Consolidated Financial Position as of October 31, 1987. The Common Stock was issued to the former holders of Series E at the closing on November 10, 1987.

At a special meeting of shareowners held on December 9, 1986, a par value of $1 per share on all classes of preferred and preference stocks and Common Stock was established and the reclassification of 3 million shares of Series C Preferred Stock into 4.8 million shares of Series G Preferred Stock was approved.

Dividends may be paid out of surplus, as defined, under Delaware corporation law. At October 31, 1988, the Company had such defined surplus of $607 million.

21. COMMON STOCK AND WARRANTS

Common Stock

At October 31, 1988 and 1987, respectively, there were 252,931,530 and 251,774,285 shares of Common Stock issued. Common Stock held in treasury amounted to 405,016 shares at a cost of $12 million as of October 31, 1988 and 1987. Included in the shares of Common Stock issued are 116,901 shares of Restricted Stock, which have been issued in accordance with the provisions of the former 1984 Stock Option and Long-Term Incentive Plans.

At a special meeting on December 9, 1986, the shareowners approved the establishment of a par value of $1 per share on all shares of Common Stock and approved an increase in authorized Common Stock from 200 to 325 million shares.

Dividends may be paid out of surplus, as defined, under Delaware corporation law. At October 31, 1988, the Company had such defined surplus of $607 million.

Warrants

Information regarding warrants is summarized as follows:

	Series A	Series B	Series C
Number authorized	11,200,000	8,000,000	4,000,000
Number issued	10,846,480	7,972,440	4,000,000
Number outstanding at October 31			
1988	10,833,890	7,972,440	4,000,000
1987	10,833,990	7,972,440	4,000,000
Number exercised during			
1988	100	-	-
1987	5,800	-	-
Cash exercise price (subject to adjustment in certain events)	$5	$9	$7
Alternate to cash in payment of exercise price	None	None	Navistar Financial 11.95% Subordinated Debentures at face value plus accrued interest
Expiration date	December 15, 1993	December 31, 1990	December 4, 1992

Repurchase

On October 20, 1988, the Company's Board of Directors approved the repurchase of up to 22 million shares of Common Stock and Common Stock equivalents including warrants and Series D Preference Stock over the next five years. This program is designed to reduce the number of shares outstanding to 250 million and maintain that approximate level. As part of the program, on November 15, 1988, the Company announced an odd-lot repurchase program designed to reduce the number of shareowners who own fewer than 100 shares. Absent the repurchase program, the actual number of shares of Common Stock outstanding would be expected to increase as a result of the exercise of outstanding warrants and options, conversion rights of Series D Preference Stock and the issuance of shares under various employee performance plans.

22. STOCK OPTION PLANS

In March 1988, shareowners approved the 1988 Performance Incentive Plan ("1988 Plan") which amended and combined into one integrated plan the previously approved Annual Incentive Plan, the Long-Term Incentive Plan and the 1984 Stock Option Plan. The 1988 Plan provides for the granting of shares and stock options to key employees based on performance targets as determined by the Committee on Organization of the Board of Directors ("Committee"). Under the 1988 Plan, 10 million shares of Common Stock are authorized for use to satisfy all stock option awards. Shares to be used under the 1988 Plan will be either shares authorized, but previously unissued, or shares reacquired by the Company. See Note 21.

The 1988 Plan includes the granting of three types of stock option awards-deferred award options, non-qualified options and incentive options. Deferred award options, which enable a participant to defer all or a portion of an annual incentive award, are exercisable at the greater of $1.00 per share or 10% of the market value per share and are exercisable thirty days after the date of grant for a period of ten years and two days from the date of grant. Non-qualified and incentive options, which may be granted by the Committee in amounts and at times as it may determine, have a term of not more than ten years and one day of ten years, respectively, and are exercisable at a price equal to the fair market value of the stock on date of grant. Generally, these options are not exercisable during the first year. There were 9,840,000, 3,311,844 and 3,751,844 shares available for grant and 1,562,890, 1,249,295 and 1,383,340 options exercisable at October 31, 1988, 1987 and 1986, respectively. Payment for the exercise of any of the options may be made by delivering, at fair market value, shares of Common Stock already owned by the option-holder.

The Committee's authority to grant stock appreciation rights under the 1984 Stock Option Plan was eliminated in the 1988 Plan. Holders of previously granted stock options with stock appreciation rights are entitled to receive cash or cash and shares of Common Stock equal in value to the difference between the option price and the current market value of the Common Stock at the date the option is surrendered. During 1987, 155,000 stock appreciation rights were granted. No stock appreciation rights were granted during 1988 and 1986. Stock appreciation rights outstanding at October 31, 1988, 1987, and 1986 were 484,755, 499,215 and 361,485, respectively.

The following table summarizes changes in Common Stock under option for the year ended October 31, 1988:

	Number of Shares	Option Price Per Share		
Outstanding options at beginning of year	1,688,795	$ 3.94	to	$ 40.58
Options-granted	1,169,000	4.37	to	6.75
Options-exercised	(1,750)			3.94
Options-terminated	(124,155)	3.94	to	36.81
Outstanding options at end of year	2,731,890	3.94	to	40.58
Options becoming exercisable during the year	444,500			

23. QUARTERLY FINANCIAL INFORMATION (UNAUDITED)

Millions of dollars, except per share data	1st Quarter		2nd Quarter		3rd Quarter		4th Quarter	
	1988	1987	1988	1987	1988	1987	1988	1987
Sales	$ 923	$ 806	$ 1,054	$ 932	$ 976	$ 791	$ 1,127	$ 1,001
Gross margin	$ 112	$ 100	$ 140	$ 133	$ 122	$ 110	$ 134	$ 133
Income (loss):								
Continuing operations	$ 60	$ 14	$ 70	$ 47	$ 47	$ 31	$ 82	$ 54
Discontinued operations	(15)	-	-	-	-	-	-	-
Extraordinary loss	-	(113)	-	-	-	-	-	-
Net income (loss)	$ 45	$ (99)	$ 70	$ 47	$ 47	$ 31	$ 82	$ 54
Income (loss) per share:								
Continuing operations	$ .21	$ .05	$ .24	$ .15	$ .15	$ .09	$ .29	$ .18
Discontinued operations	(.06)	-	-	-	-	-	-	-
Extraordinary loss	-	(.58)	-	-	-	-	-	-
Net income (loss)	$ .15	$ (.53)	$ .24	$ .15	$ .15	$ .09	$ .29	$ .18

During the first quarter of 1988, the Company recorded a provision for discontinued operations pursuant to the settlement of the class action suit by former employees of Wisconsin Steel. See Note 6.

In the first quarter of 1988, the Company's Canadian operating subsidiary settled the projected benefit obligation for all retirees covered by the two major Canadian pension plans through the purchase of non-participating annuities. See Note 3.

During the fourth quarter of 1988, a settlement was made on prior years' income tax audits. See Note 5.

During the first quarter of 1987, the Company recorded the redemption of four high coupon public debt issues. See Note 2.

Fourth quarter 1987 results reflect an $11 million reduction in the carrying value of selected dealer operations.

APPENDIX A   CHECK FIGURES

These check figures are intended to assist students in developing answers to the cases in a time-efficient manner. Rather than give detailed solutions and notes, which are available in an instructor's solutions manual, the check figures should help students get a start on each case and examine whether the approach taken is appropriate. However, they should not be viewed as a substitute for a firm understanding of the issues and may not agree with answers based on alternative interpretations and assumptions about the data.

1. FUNDAMENTALS

1.1 Assets = $6,700; liabilities = $5,472; stockholders' equity = $1,228; revenues = $9,305; expenses = $8,705; gains = $524; losses = $0; net income = $1,124.

1.2 A. $2,499; B. $597; C. $167; D. $496.

1.3 A. $6,954; B. $9,101; C. $2,708.

1.4 a. $387.2; b. $338.9; c. $623.6; d. $42.7.

1.5 a. Cash and cash-related items, $179; b. short-term investments, $4; c. accounts and notes receivable, net, $659; d. inventories, $482; e. prepaid expenses, $115; f. properties, plants, and equipment, net, $1,173; g. investments, at cost, $26; h. other assets, $265.

1.6 Cash, $778; total assets, $110,192; stockholders' equity, $9,494.

1.7 J.P.'s net income 72,000 bbls; Ronnie's net income 96,000 bbls.

2. CASH FLOW

2.1 2. Net working capital provided by operating activities, $295,516; reduction of minority interest due to increased ownership, assuming no other changes during 19X3, $38,844; retained earnings, December 31, 19X3, $940,989.

2.2 Total cash from/applied to operating activities, $1,006.3; financing activities, $140.2; investment activities, $1,150.9.

2.3 5. Reduction in short-and long-term debt = $1,449.4; 6. cash dividends paid = $204.2; 7. investments purchased for cash = $131.3; 8. book value of intangibles sold = $192.7; 9. treasury stock purchases = $777.6.

3. RECEIVABLES

3.1 2. Provision for loan losses, $645. Amount assumed to include additional credit losses associated with loans sold or swapped to third parties.

| 3.2 | 1. Actual sales returns and allowances, $36,478; accounts written off, $21,795; cash paid, $1,819,500. |
| 3.3 | 2. Percentage of receivables unbilled, 19.80; |

3. Growth rate model.

	Regression-based	Direct
Growth from Q1 to Q9	22.55%	22.73%
Growth from Q1 to Q10	21.97%	24.19%
Growth from Q1 to Q11	21.75%	24.16%

3.4 Pretax profit to Lincoln: $11.1 (stated in question); Net cash out from Lincoln = $3.5-$19.6-$4.4 = $ (20.5);
Other assets and liabilities:
Note receivable from E.C. Garcia: $19.6 (original loan)
Note receivable from E.C. Garcia: $10.5 (Westcon loan assumed)
Unused commitment to Garcia: $10.4 ($30.0 - $19.6).

4. INVENTORY

4.1 Earnings would have been lower under FIFO by $5,290,000.

4.2 2. Journal entry:

DR:	Retained earnings (after tax effect)	$5.8	
DR:	Federal taxes benefit (tax effect)	4.9	
CR:	Inventories (write down inventories to LIFO)		$10.7

4.3 Journal entry:

DR:	Loss on decline in inventories (+E)	$300	
CR:	Inventory reserve (CA) or inventories (-A)		$300

3. Restated 19X3 pretax income, $57 million.

4.4 3. Restated 19X4 Net Income on a FIFO basis, $170,782,000.

4.5 3b. Data for 19X2 and 19X1, respectively.

Earnings before taxes higher by	$ (55,678,912)	$ 86,743,955
Tax expense	(22,271,565)	34,697,582
Earnings after taxes	(33,407,347)	52,046,373
6a. Loss on Disposal (on FIFO basis)		(28,631,000)

5 OTHER CURRENT ASSETS

5.1 3. Estimated net profit on completed contract basis, $19,128,867.

5.2 4. Footnote on contracts in process and inventories states that $74 million of tooling and $349 million of production costs included in such balance sheet amounts at December 31, 19X8. Thus, $423 million of costs and production expenditures have been deferred to future periods when the future costs are expected to be lower due to learning, cost efficiencies, and economies of scale.

6. PROPERTY, PLANT, AND EQUIPMENT

6.1 Accumulated depreciation on assets sold = cost $1,800,000 less net book value $1,056,783 = $743,217.

6.2 3. Book value of disposals, $7,863,554; add pretax gain on disposals, $4,472,135; Sales price of disposals, $12,335,689.

6.3 3. General Motors reported a 79.57 and 20.56 % increase in operating income and net income, respectively, in fiscal 19X2 relative to 19X1.

Without the accounting change, earnings and income would have declined by almost 7 %.

6.4 1. Journal entries for 19X9 and 19X8, respectively.

DR:	Interest Costs	$ 79,422		$ 67,179
CR:	Cash		$ 79,422	$ 67,179

6.5 A: Net after-tax loss, December 31, 19X2, $117.908; B: Net after-tax loss, December 31, 19X3, $34.113; C: Net after-tax loss, December 31, 19X4, $20.527.

7. INTANGIBLES

7.1 1. Historical cost of plant assets disposed, $35,347.
5. Assuming Other assets sold at book value, plant assets sold = $13,268 - $181 = $13,087. Book value of plant assets sold, $13,142. Thus, gain (loss) of plant assets sold = $13,142 - $13,087 = $(55).

7.2 3. Journal entry:

DR:	Television Program Rights	$14,880,000	
CR:	Taxes Payable		$5,952,000
CR:	Retained Earnings		8,928,000

7.3 1. Journal entry:

DR:	Production Acquisition Costs	$340,017	
DR:	Amortization Expense	60,003	
DR:	Other Assets ($58,445 - $33,742)	24,703	
CR:	Accumulated Amortization		$60,003
CR:	Cash or Accounts Payable		364,720

7.4 2. Journal entry:

DR:	Cash (or receivable)	$212	
DR:	Customer advances (deferred revenue)	90	
CR:	Sales revenue		$302

7.5 2. TriStar inventories, 1974, including R&D, $735,100; TriStar inventories, 1974 restated, $185,300; amount of writedown, $549,800.
Journal entry:

DR:	TriStar initial planning, etc.	$549,800	
CR:	TriStar inventories		$549,800

7.6 Possible journal entry ignoring any tax effects of the transactions.

DR:	Unrecoverable TriStar Costs	$280.2	
CR:	TriStar Initial Planning, etc.		$280.2

1980 profit would thus be recast as a $27.6 – $280.2 = 252.6 million loss. 1980 assets would be reduced by $280.2 million.

8. DEBT

8.1 2 and 3. Present value of the debt, $280,075. Answer assumes present value of interest and principal amounts, with interest based on *carrying value* of loan and principal amounts but with assumed final payment of principal on December 31, 19X7.

8.2 Present value of payments discounted at 12%, $123,613.73. Amount is lower than the book value of the debt because the discount rate (12%) is higher than weighted average interest rate.

8.3   Journal entries, December 1979:
DR: Accrued liability for tire recall, etc. $46.9
CR: Credit from tire recall and related costs $46.9
DR: Accrued liability for tire recall etc.   123.9
CR: Cash (assumed) or inventory of tires   123.9

8.4   Charges to income, pretax and after tax, respectively:
1984   Extraordinary charge $32.0 $18.0
1985   Litigation expenses   185.0   138.8
1987   Litigation expenses   85.0   53.0
Total expenses to end of 1987   302.0   209.8

8.5   2. Monthly amortization = $111,000÷12 = $9,250; total amount of amortization, $9,250 x 108 months (the stated term of the new debentures) = $999,000 = discount on the new debentures issued prior to March 31, 19X1, $931,000, plus the additional discount on the April 15, 19X1 debentures, $68,000.

8.6   Part A: a Journal entry:
DR: Bonds payable $2,000,000
CR: Bond discount $76,800
CR: Deferred bond issue expenses   10,125
CR: Common stock at $10 par value   100,000
CR: Common stock in excess of par   1,813,075
Part B: b Journal entry:
DR: Bonds payable $10,000,000
CR: Discount on bonds payable $107,475
CR: Cash to purchase Treasury Bonds   8,828,205
CR: Extraordinary gain on extinguishment of debt   1,064,320

9.   INCOME TAXES

9.1   1a. Deferral method; b. flow-through method; c. currently receivable $6,347,000 - currently payable $5,862,000, implies a refund due of $485,000.

9.2   1a. Journal entry:
DR: Provision for restructuring $790.3
CR: Other current liabilities $343.8
CR: Other noncurrent liabilities   140.5
CR: Inventories, fixed assets, goodwill, etc.   306.0

9.3   Potlatch's reported earnings declined from $71,011 to $48,751 in 1980 and increased in 1981 by 18.6% to $57,804. Without the tax credit gain, after-tax earnings would have fallen from 1980 by 20.6 % to $38,704.

9.4   1. Journal entry:
DR: Cash or Accounts Receivable $60,000
CR: Deferred Income Taxes $28,906
CR: Other Income   31,094

9.5   N = 6.56 years = the number of periods so that an annuity of $299,124 per period has a present value of $1,043,334 (purchase price $1,410,613 - investment in tax leases $367,279).

9.6   2a. Maximum recognizable tax benefit (deferral) = Provision for possible credit losses x tax rate. 1988: $452 = $1,330 x 34 %.
3. Recognizable tax effects of 1987 loan loss provision, $ (1,119). Amount derived so as to reconcile to the December 31, 1988 balance. Based on a

40% statutory tax rate, amount consistent with a credit loss deduction for federal tax purposes for 1987 and future years of $2,797.5 ($1,119÷40%).

10.   LEASES

10.1   1. Combined journal entry:

DR:	Interest expense	$178	
DR:	Amortization of leased property	97	
DR:	Obligation under capital leases (plug)	76	
CR:	Accumulated amortization on leased assets		$97
CR:	Cash (or accounts payable)		254

10.2   Periods 1-5 payments=$9,141; with present val. at t=0 $7,114.00
Present val. of 6-20 payments at t=0   9,521.08
Present val. of 6-20 payments at t=beg. of period 6   15,333.80

10.3   3a. Weighted avg. int. rate, 11.57407% ($195,684.20 ÷ $1,690,712); 3b. present value of long-term debt, $1,849,916.51; 3c. present value of long-term debt, $ 2,023,046.61.

11.   EMPLOYEE BENEFITS

11.1   2. N = 25.89 years, F = $8,611.07; 4. At 8%, present value = $8,611.07 $(1.08)^{-25.89} = $1,174.07$. Thus, change in net income after taxes would be ($1,904.9-$1,174.07) x 65% = $730.83 x 65% = $475.04.

11.2   Reconciliation at 12/31/19X2:

Accumulated benefit obligation	$1,435
Projected benefit obligation	2,150
Plan assets at fair value	1,475
Funded status	(675)
Unrecognized prior service cost	432
Unrecognized net obligation at transition	243
Accrued/prepaid	0

11.3   1. Journal entry for 19X2:

DR:	Pension expense	$7	
DR:	Prepaid pension cost	55	
CR:	Cash		$62

11.4   2. Journal entry:

DR:	Noncurrent plant rationalization	$89	
CR:	Employee (health care and ins.) benefits		$89

Reclassification of obligations previously recorded in conjunction with idlings or shutdowns of facilities.

DR:	Cumulative effect of acctg. change	$2,263	
DR:	Deferred tax liability	11	
CR:	Employee (health care and ins.) benefits		$2,274

Cumulative effect of accounting change as of January 1, 19X2, net of tax benefit recorded by the company as a reduction in liability for deferred taxes.

11.5   3. Service cost $31.97; interest cost, $(149.09); unrecognized net gain amortization, $(1.19); prior service cost amortization, $0.09; unrecognized net asset amortization, $(7.73); forecasted 19X3 periodic domestic pension expense, $(15.55).

12. SHAREHOLDERS' EQUITY

12.1 2. Journal entry:

DR:	Property, plant and equipment	$51,951	
DR:	Net current assets	52,297	
DR:	Goodwill	14,619	
DR:	Other (net)	738	
CR:	Long-term liabilities assumed		$19,184
CR:	Cash (from Note on Business Combinations)		98,000
CR:	Cash (assumed)		2,421

12.2 2. Primary eps.= $707,000 ÷ (1,999,500 + 71,000) = $0.34.

12.3 3. Journal entry:

DR:	Cash	$947,328,855	
CR:	Treasury stock		746,184,820
CR:	Additional paid-in capital		201,144,035

Assumed reissued at market price $69.50 and treasury stock originally on cost method. Numbers do not match decrease in cost per the statement of stockholders' equity of $189.2+$557.8=$747.0 due to rounding in average cost per share.

12.4 1b. 19X2: $37.2-(2.6 mill x preferred dividend rate)÷26,462,074=$ 1.41; 19X3: $48.3-(1.1 mill x preferred dividend rate)÷34,648,994=$ 1.39.

12.5 4. Reported earnings per share from continuing operations for 19X3, 19X2, and 19X1 = $5.97, $8.37, $5.37, respectively.

13. BUSINESS COMBINATIONS

13.1 3. (5 months ÷ 240) x $91,303,000 = $1,902,146.

13.2 Net earnings (Cost method) for 19X2, $ 7,827.

13.3 1d. Net Income (Equity method), $135,753, less National's Share of Equity, 19X2, $25,744, plus National's Share of Distribution, 19X2, $24,901 = Net Income (Cost method), $134,910.

14. CHANGING PRICES AND FOREIGN CURRENCY

14.1

1. Cash	1.1079726 = $2,651,600 ÷ $2,393,200
Notes receivable	1.1079734 = $1,267,300 ÷ $1,143,800
Current liabilities	1.1079562 = $1,517,900 ÷ $1,370,000
Long-term debt	1.1081376 = $202,900 ÷ $183,100

4. Retained earnings in April 30, 19X4 dollars = $9,388,400 ÷ 1.108 = C$8,473,285

14.2 2. 19X9 Unrealized holding gains = $25,202 ($56,976 - $31,774).

14.3 4. Net income before taxes using market values, $110,870,593.

14.4 4.

	H.C.equity	C.C. equity	Mkt. price
Growth rate	-1.48%	18.44%	18.09%

14.5 1. Present value of the 1985-2001 annuity at the beginning of 1985 = $46,485.9 ÷ 0.75131 = $61,873.1. In 1985, the 17 year, 10 % annuity factor is 8.0216. Therefore, the constant annual net revenue stream over the 17 years would be $61,873.1 ÷ 8.0216 = $7,713.3.

14.6 Dunbar has chosen to report the art appreciation in the income statement, and to report income numbers before and after $1,633,854 unrealized appreciation on art investments. This enables Dunbar to report a bottom-line net profit for the year of $454,438, an increase of 82.7% over the previous year's.

14.7 2a and b. After accounting changes and retroactive restatement of the 4 years prior to 1981, Xerox's growth in earnings is consistently positive. If it were not for the accounting changes, earnings would have declined from 1980 to 1981.

14.8 Under Statement 52, the trend is uniformly positive, with a 20.36 percentage in earnings per share from 1981 to 1982. However, the trend under Statement 8 shows a dip from 1980 to 1981 and a smaller earnings per share increase (17.94%) from 1981 to 1982.

15. ACCOUNTING ANALYSIS

15.1 4. Net present value of future cash flows, $1,196,249, less assumed long-term debt (book value), $99,395, less preference shares (book value), $55,000 = present value of net cash flow available to stockholders, $1,041,854. Number of shareholders at end of 1978, 15,401; hence, net present value of one share of common stock based on future cash flows, $67.65.

15.2 Shareholders' equity: Common stock at par value $1 per share, $162,129; Common stock in excess of par, $28,373; Retained earnings, $1,269,498; Stockholders' equity, $1,460,000; Total equities, $3,513,345; Net income available for common, $351,335.

15.3 1. Annual growth rates:

Year	As reported in 19X6	Adjusted
19X1	0.2651	0.3884
19X2	0.3021	0.1865
19X3	0.2100	0.2100

15.4 1. 1986-q1 = $0.46; q2 = $1.13; q3 = $1.49; q4 = $3.49; total for 1986 = $6.57.

16. REVIEW: NAVISTAR INTERNATIONAL

16.1 1.a. Journal entry:

DR:	Cash flow from operations	$48.7	
CR:	Property, net of accum. depr. and amort.		$48.7

2.a. Journal entry:

DR:	Other liabilities	$143.0	
CR:	Receivables, net		$143.0

16.2 3. Present value of net operating losses — $505.83
Present value of NOL benefits at 30% assumed rate — 151.75
Shareowners' equity without present value of tax benefits — 865.80
Shareowners' equity incl. present value of tax benefits — 1,017.55
% increase in 1988 ending shareowners' equity — 17.53

16.3 4. Capital leases (incl. in reported liabilities and assets) — $ 38.75
Present value of operating leases — 93.50
Reported total liabilities — 1,656.40
Reported total assets — 2,522.20
% of debt to assets *without* operating leases capitalized — 66
% of debt to assets *with* operating leases capitalized — 67

16.4   1. Journal entry:

DR:	Pension expense	$83	
CR:	Prepaid (accrued) pension costs		$83

16.5   b. Journal entry: First quarter of 1987

DR:	Long-term debt (debentures)	$508	
DR:	Loss on redemption of debt	113*	
CR:	Cash (from common stock offering)		$470
CR:	Cash (from internal sources)		151

       * =$112.9 per the income statement.

16.6   2. Common stock equivalent of average Series D pref. stock, $2.8;
Month (M) when conversion took place = (3.125 x 1,067,615 x 12÷12) -
(3.125 x 333,995 x M ÷ 12) = $2.8; Hence, M = approximately 6 months.

16.7   2. Journal entry:

DR:	Taxes on income ($19 plus $5)	$24.0	
DR:	Cash dividends paid	158.0	
DR:	Dividends declared but not paid	27.0	
CR:	Equity in nonconsolidated companies		$121.6
CR:	Equity in nonconsol. subsidiaries		82.7
CR:	Tax benefit of frgn. net oper. losses (assumed allocation)		4.7

16.8   2. Account balances: Cash, $10.3; Current assets, $1,471.4; Plant, at
cost, $727.9; Accumulated depreciation on plant, $346.6; Plant assets, net
of accumulated depreciation, $381.3; Total assets, $2,606.8.

All cases attributed to and written by Paul A. Griffin, unless otherwise stated.